PICTON

A Novel by Jasper Wolf

"Horror is like a serpent; always shedding its skin, always changing. And it will always come back. It can't be hidden away like the guilty secrets we try to keep in our subconscious."

Dario Argento

For more information on Jasper's latest releases, or to become a subscriber and receive chapter excerpts, signed editions and pre-release specials, go to: www.jasperwolfauthor.com

Or follow Jasper on Facebook:
http://www.facebook.com/JasperWolf99

Foreword

Dear Reader,

Before you go any further I must warn you that *Picton* is the third book in the Jake Miller series and to fully appreciate this book, you need to have read *Hunted* and *The Waiting Room*.

Picton has been by far my scariest, and most enjoyable adventure; I'll not say why here as it may spoil the story before you. However, I spent many late nights writing and looking over my shoulder at the slightest sound.

I'll say this is my first and hopefully not my last adventure into the crime/horror genre, and I hope you enjoy reading it as much as I did writing it.

On a personal note, as I write the foreword I am a week away from being placed on the heart transplant list, so this could very well be my last book. I would like to leave my readers one piece of advice I unfortunately learnt way too late. Do what you love; life is too short, so follow your dreams no matter how far away or unattainable they may seem.

I'll be posting updates on my health when my operation occurs.

If you want to follow everything Jasper Wolf, follow my Facebook page or Twitter and if you want to join my mailing list please sign up at

www.jasperwolfauthor.com

Chapter 1

Picton Town NSW December 1916

Two nights before, Anne had played with black magic – powers beyond her control. Ruth and Stanley had told her it would be fun to talk to the spirits, summon the dead. How wrong they were.

They all sat in a circle on Stanley's lounge room floor. In the middle of them all was his handmade wooden Ouija board. On it were all the letters of the alphabet. 'Yes' was carved on the right and 'No' on the left. Stanley had crafted a pointed cursor, a simple triangle with a hole cut into the middle to allow the letter to be seen.

All three of them placed their hands over the cursor, and all three of them let the cursor take control. At first there was nothing, no movement, only stillness, and the candle flame remained steady.

Then Anne felt a cold breeze blow past her, as if someone had opened a window. The candle almost lost its battle to stay alight. After a flicker, it kept aglow.

Anne could smell sulphur. It was strong.

"What's that smell?" she asked.

"Shh, something's here," Stanley said.

"Stop trying to scare us." Ruth sounded cranky.

Before Stanley could reply, their hands flew across the board. Everyone screamed, including Stanley.

"Are you dead?" Stanley asked the air around him.

Their hands once again flew across the board and landed on 'Yes'.

Stanley asked a second question. "What's your name?"

The cursor moved to the letter S.

"You're doing that!" Anne yelled at Stanley.

"I am not."

Anne withdrew her hand from the cursor.

Ruth followed her example.

"Take your hand off it then, Stanley," Ruth requested.

"If I do, it will stop working," he replied.

"Yes, because you're doing it," Anne said.

He removed his hand and shuffled his bum backwards away from the board.

The cursor stayed resting on the S.

"See, it was you," Anne said.

The cursor sat like the chiselled lifeless piece of wood it was.

Ruth joined in bagging Stanley. "You're a mean prankster, Stanley Roberts."

"But, it wasn't me. Seriously, I didn't do it."

As Stanley began his second round of pleading, the cursor flew to its second letter. C.

All three gasped and screamed. Anne almost jumped into Stanley's lap and Ruth wasn't far behind her.

The cursor paused and then moved again to its third letter, A, and then the fourth, T. The cursor kept moving.

With each movement the girls screamed, and sometimes Stanley screamed too.

Ruth held Stanley's hand so tightly her knuckles were turning white.

The cursor came to a stop.

"Scat. What does that mean?" Ruth asked the others.

"I don't know," Stanley replied, his voice shaking.

The cursor answered. It flew to the letter D, paused, and then moved on to the letter E and then A, followed by T and finally H.

The three of them slid themselves further away from the board. Death had been spelt out to them.

They were terrified.

Stanley reached in to collect the board and end the game. It had gone too far. As he reached for the board, he was violently thrown back by an invisible force that he could not resist. Within an instant, Stanley found himself on the other side of the room. The board itself levitated and began to spin in a clockwise direction. The cursor hovered just above it, eerily still.

Without warning, the board and cursor flew in opposite directions, as if someone had aimed the cursor at Ruth, and the board at Anne.

Anne managed to duck the fast-flying board. Ruth struggled to see the smaller cursor in the dimmed room, and it clocked her on the temple as it flew at her.

The cut wasn't severe, but it was no graze either. Anne raced to Ruth as she hit the floor, tearing up her yellow and white polka-dot summer dress to provide gauze for Ruth's head. Her mum would be furious if she knew she'd ripped her new summer dress on purpose. Her mother had bought it for her at the start of the school term. It was light and perfect for her to teach in, especially in the December heat. At twenty-one, she was still her mum's little girl.

She padded the torn fabric on Ruth's temple.

"Apply pressure," Ruth instructed. She would know; she was a nurse after all.

"You'll be okay," Anne said.

The board and the cursor had both come to rest in different areas of the room as if a spoilt child having a temper tantrum had thrown them. Seconds later, in a final act of defiance, the spirit blew the candle out.

The girls screamed as the room descended into complete darkness.

*

Anne shook the memories of the séance and continued her walk to Stanley's home, just under four kilometres from the school, on the outskirts of the township. Anne had left the school and headed down the dirt track out of town. She would need to walk about a kilometre before cutting through the Redbank Range Tunnel. The last train wasn't expected until 5.20 and she should make the tunnel with plenty of time to cut through it before the train arrived.

The town was expanding rapidly. A second railway line was being added and was due for completion within six months. No more having to time crossings through the tunnel. Trains would be re-routed, and the tunnel would become obsolete.

Stanley should be on his way home from working on the line. His job was to lay the sleepers. Twenty-five men from Picton had gained jobs on the railway with years of work, soon to come to an end.

The summer dust swept up against the bottom of her dress as she headed south out of town. While the séance had given her a fright, it was nothing compared to the horrifying encounter of the night before.

Chapter 2

Melbourne 2016

Jake had spent the last eleven months beside Brodie's bed and had seen no improvement. Brodie was in a coma. Lying in the paddock as long as he had without a pulse had starved his brain of oxygen for too long.

Early on, the doctors had suggested his parents shut off the life support, but after everything their son had fought through in his life, neither of them could do it. They just believed he would come back to them.

Jake, true to his word, had left the police force; after all, it had almost destroyed him. Monique had suspicions about Austin's involvement in what had happened at the house of the 'Ukrainian Monster', but Jake knew there was little evidence to pursue it further. Monique was the chief inspector within the homicide department where Jake had worked.

Jake had received the all-clear from Monique only weeks after the shootout at the Ukrainian Monster's house. The internal investigation was now closed. While the Police Integrity Commission investigation had had suspicions that others could have been involved in the shootout at the Monster's, they hadn't been able to prove anything. Thus, they had found that Jake and Brodie had acted reasonably while conducting their investigation.

Over the past eleven months, Monique had made several attempts to get Jake back on the force. Jake had declined every time.

With Hayley pregnant, Jake was finding it harder and harder to visit Brodie, but as he always had, he made sure he found the time. Even after their daughter Indiana was born, Jake still visited.

Being a new dad didn't stop him.

When Jake visited he made sure he was as normal as possible. He would always remain upbeat, treat Brodie the same as if he was sitting in his lounge room. Jake would simply have a one-way conversation. He would update Brodie on all the happenings of the NBA, the trades, how poorly the Knicks were still going (despite signing Rose), and how the young Wolves were still on the rise. Jake knew Brodie loved his Wolves.

Sometimes Jake would read the paper or do the crossword. On some occasions he would even ask Brodie for the answer to the trivia question; of course, no answers were ever supplied. As the months went on, this became more difficult as Brodie's body had clearly deteriorated.

As the days, weeks and months passed, Jake's mood remained upbeat in front of Brodie. Jake didn't dare let his demeanour slip once while he was in his presence.

After Ryan returned from the abyss that he described only as the in-between (a place between heaven and earth), it provided Jake with hope. Hope that Brodie would also find his way back. According to Ryan, he had been able see and hear everything, but he was trapped and couldn't find his way back into his body.

Jake had begun his new job. It was a lot more boring than the police force, but that suited him just fine. Most cases he was investigating were wives asking for their husbands to be followed, as they suspected them of cheating. Most of the time they were right. It was a girl at the office, someone at the gym, a neighbour, or a mum at the school. Occasionally it wasn't an affair but a gambling addiction. On the rarest of occasions, a man would request his wife be followed, and yes, sometimes they cheated too.

The most excitement Jake had encountered was when he had been confronted by a husband he was trailing. Somehow, Jake had become lazy and been spotted, the first time in over fifteen years. The husband had assumed Jake was the other man. Jake had learnt one thing quickly since starting in the private detective business; those who cheat assume everyone else is cheating too. It's their justification.

Conscious of not wanting to put the wife in any danger, Jake had to think quickly. He was lucky he knew his subject well.

"You fucking my wife?" the large, fat, sweaty man yelled as he ran out his front door towards Jake's car. "Why are you following me?"

As the man bashed on Jake's window, his sweaty, hairy belly rubbed against the glass.

Jake pulled his gun and tapped it on the window. "Step back, sir," Jake replied.

The slob saw the gun and backed away immediately. Jake got out of his car and towered over the sweaty unkempt man who was only five foot three, or five-five at a stretch.

"Sir, I am following you. I am hired by the department of Human Services to ensure you're not claiming your welfare benefits illegally," Jake answered.

The man stood there, mouth gaping, unsure what to answer.

Jake didn't wait. "I have found nothing to report, I am pleased to say." He paused. "I'll make sure you won't need to worry about this again." Jake was about to get back into his car, as if he was in the clear.

"Not so fast, fella," the slob replied, grabbing hold of the door before Jake had a chance to close it. "What benefits you got me down as claiming?" the man asked, belly hanging over one side of his grey trackpants, his butt cheeks poking out the top.

Jake knew he was being tested. "Your disability benefits, Tony. It's clear you're suffering severe injuries from your work accident. When you came out the front door, you could barely muster a jog, even though you were full of adrenaline. In the three days I've been following you I haven't seen anything that raises any suspicion. I really am sorry for the invasion of your privacy, but unfortunately some people cheat the system and then the good people like yourself end up missing out."

Tony looked at Jake. Jake returned a polite smile and tugged on the door for a second time. This time Tony let Jake close it.

Jake had no concern about taking Tony down. It would have taken little effort, but he couldn't blow his cover. If Tony had found out his wife had hired him, or worse still, thought Jake was having an affair with her, who knew what Tony might have done to his own wife. This way at least he would think it was unrelated.

Chapter 3

Picton December 1916

Anne couldn't get the thoughts of last night's visitor out of her head. She had to tell Stanley. At first, she thought it was just a dream, well, a nightmare. Now she didn't know what it was.

It was the night after the séance. Anne had almost put Stanley's stupid games behind her. She was tired and with classes to teach again the next day, she needed an early night. She had decided to read only a couple of chapters of her latest book on loan from the school library. *The Rainbow Trail* was a western. She loved to read, and she loved to teach. English was her favourite subject.

She had been sound asleep. It was the smell that woke her; the same smell as that night at Stanley's.

Then, when her eyes adjusted, a dark shape, a creature of some kind, was there standing at the foot of her bed watching her. It resembled a man, with head bowed, a wide-brimmed hat covering its face, and it was wearing a long black trench coat. Without obvious movement, it slipped to her side, its head raised, its face with eyes blazing fiery red, shaped like a cat's. The rest of its face had no discernible features. She couldn't even tell where its mouth began or ended or how it spoke; yet words came out. There was no real nose. She could see no nostrils, only snake-like holes.

Anne went to move but couldn't. She was paralysed. The only part of her body she could control were her eyes. She looked at the mantel clock that sat ticking on her night stand. The small hand was on the 3 and the large hand was just past the 6. It was slightly after 3.30 in the morning. This thing in the hat hovered next to her. Was it a man, or was it a creature? She wasn't sure.

Anne tried to move her hand to pinch herself. She must have been dreaming, she thought. She couldn't move. A dream, she told herself. *Wake up!* Anne screamed to herself. The scream echoed through her head, as if it confirmed her nightmare.

The thing reached into her bed, taking Anne's arm. The smell intensified. Its hands appeared out from under the sleeves of the long jacket. The fingers were long and bony with long grimy nails.

Anne remained paralysed in her bed watching the creature out of the corner of her eye run its disgusting fingers down the side of her stomach.

"Soon," rasped out of his invisible mouth. "Soon." It sounded again before he simply vanished into the shadows.

Anne sat bolt upright, her paralysis gone. Her heart was pounding. It was about to explode through her chest. What had just happened, where had it gone? The door had remained closed. It hadn't exited via the door. The creature had simply vanished. Anne began to wonder if it was a figment of her imagination. Must have been, she thought. It must have been a strange dream where she was dreaming while she was awake.

Only one way to tell, Anne thought, and quickly looked to her right. Her clock showed just past 3.30. The hands continued to tick away. It wasn't a dream. The creature in the hat was real, and he had been here for her.

Anne didn't sleep much the rest of the night. In fact, she didn't sleep at all until the first glimpse of daylight broke through her window at 6.10 am. It was only then she managed to gain an extra forty-five minutes before the sunlight woke her.

With the dream still reverberating through her mind, Anne headed to the bathroom, collecting her clothes that were laid out across her dresser-chair, ready for the day ahead. She placed them in a pile neatly next to her at the bathroom basin. Anne placed the plug in the basin and began to fill it with cool water. There was no time to heat the water on the stove this morning. She took a fresh hand towel from the rack on the wall and dipped it into the cool water. It was cool against her skin without being cold. Anne unbuttoned her nightgown. It softly dropped to the floor leaving her standing in only her white underwear. She washed her face and neck. Anne dunked the washcloth in the water and began on her arms. Before she pulled the cloth from the water for the third time, her eyes caught their refection in the mirror. They were showing signs of tiredness and stress. The dream last night certainly hadn't helped.

She washed her face again to try and freshen up some more.

She put her fresh singlet on and as she pulled it down over her breasts, she noticed marks on her side; three of them to be exact. They looked like burn marks and they were where that man had touched her stomach in her dream. Had he been real after all? She inspected the marks closely. They looked as though she had touched a hot oven. It was as if Hat Man's three nails had burnt her as he stroked her.

The man in her room had been real after all. What had he said to her? "Soon?" What did that mean?

Anne finished getting dressed. She was panicked now. She needed to speak to Stanley. After work would be her earliest opportunity. She knew the thoughts of Hat Man would consume her mind for the day.

Was this the man they had summoned? Surely not. Who else could it be?

Chapter 4

Picton 1916

Ruth had begun the first stint of her double shift at the tuberculosis hospital at 7 am. She would work until 3 and then return at 11 for her first night shift until 7. She was on night duty for the next three days, followed by four days off. Nights were always the worst shifts, but they were always followed by the days off. The nights dragged, and the days off flew past.

Ruth wore her required striped nurses' uniform, with accompanying hat, her watch pinned to her left breast. Her first job of the morning was to take the morning obs.

There was nothing she could do for her patients. There was no cure. They were all dying, some sooner than others. They had all contracted the 'white plague', TB as it was commonly known. Her patients came to the hospital not to get better but to die peacefully without spreading the disease to the wider population. Ruth made sure she always wore a protective mask to cover her mouth. The most common way the disease was spread was by spittle from person to person.

This was a horrible disease; it infected the lungs of the patients and caused them to eventually cough up their lungs piece by piece.

Her first patient was a lady in her mid to late fifties, June. She had contracted TB while returning from England on a ship. The disease was in the late stages, she was coughing up blood with nearly every cough.

"Morning," Ruth said through her mask.

"Morning," June coughed back to her, spluttering into her handkerchief.

"How did you sleep?" Ruth asked.

"Not very well, a lot of coughing," June replied. This sentence came out cough-free which was a real rarity.

Ruth smiled sympathetically. "I'll get you some breakfast shortly."

"I had a visitor last night," June replied.

"Oh, lucky you. Your family came to visit?" Ruth asked as she checked her chart for the previous night's baseline readings.

"No. I had never seen this man before, strange looking fellow, came in after midnight, seemed to come out of the shadows." Her talking was interrupted by a fit of coughing and her handkerchief was again smeared in blood. She took a sip of water from her night stand leaving a trace of blood on the lip of the cup. "He was a tall lanky man, long bony fingers, no real face, no real mouth. He wore a long coat and a wide-brimmed hat, which was quite strange for this time of year, don't you think?" she asked.

Ruth frowned. "Visiting hours finished at 7. I'll check the logs to see who visited. Maybe it was a dream?"

"He was here, my dear, I can assure you of that."

Not wanting to upset an already dying patient further, Ruth just agreed and added, "It was probably another patient's visitor looking for the way out. Now, what do you feel like for breakfast?"

Ruth waited for June's latest coughing attack to subside, before being told, "Toast and tea."

"Once you have had a shower and breakfast, I'll bring you your first glass of milk for the day, then we will pop outside for exercises before it becomes hot."

"I think the milk and the exercise is really helping at keeping the TB at bay; maybe soon I'll be well enough to go back home?" June asked.

"Possibly, if you keep improving," Ruth answered noncommittally.

June got up and headed to the bathroom down the hall, nightgown almost touching the floor. As June entered the cubicle, she immediately noticed her reflection. She had become even more pale and gaunt than the weeks before. Death was closer now. Her hair had turned another two shades of grey, or so it seemed, although her hair colour was the least of her worries. June wiped some dried blood from the corners of her mouth.

On the underside of her forearm she noticed three burn marks. How had they got there? She didn't know. She hadn't cooked anything in a very long time.

She rinsed the burns under some water. They stung a little, and she quickly tried to dab them dry. The skin around the red marks began to fall away.

Who was the man in the wide-brimmed hat and trench coat, and what was he doing in the hospital?

Chapter 5

Picton 1916

Anne felt the entire day at school was a waste. Her mind had been elsewhere. She was sure the children hadn't learnt anything. She had not told a soul about her 'Hat Man' visitor from the night before; not even her mother. After all, who would believe such an absurd tale?

She had to speak with Stanley as soon as possible. It was that simple. She left the schoolhouse as soon as the bell rang and began the one and a quarter mile walk to Stanley's house. She had plenty of time between the 4.30 train and the 5.20 train, neither of which carried passengers. She would need to cut through the Redbank Range Tunnel to save more walking.

The wind flared up as the afternoon went on. The dust swirled, and Anne dipped her hat to try and avoid the dust. She arrived at the entrance to the Redbank Range Tunnel.

She heard the steam train, but with so much going through her head she just assumed the train had passed through the tunnel. After all, it was 4.39. Anne wasted no time and headed into the tunnel.

She walked into the darkness, and the small arch of light at the other end guided her way.

As she walked she tried to rehearse what she would tell Stanley of last night's events, but it didn't even sound believable to her. She hoped he would understand.

She was almost a quarter of the way into the tunnel when a whistle of the train startled her. It was close, but it hadn't gone through the tunnel yet; it was still behind her. The end of the tunnel was still at least a hundred yards away. Anne turned to see the train approaching. There was no way she could make the end of the tunnel in time. Anne panicked. She hitched up her dress and sprinted onwards. After a few good strides Anne caught a glimpse of the halfway alcove. How had she forgotten it? This was the very purpose of the alcove, to provide refuge in case someone got trapped inside the tunnel with the train bearing down on them. It was only twenty yards. She would make it. She would stand in the alcove, wait for the train to pass and continue on her way. She would be safe.

She darted into the alcove, breathing heavily as she caught her breath and waited for the train to pass. A waft of sulphur arose from behind her. It was a smell that immediately brought back the horrors of her nightmare. She turned to see what was emitting the foul odour. The darkness of the alcove met her with blazing red eyes and a wide-brimmed hat. "I told you I'd see you soon," the creature with no discernible mouth said, grabbing her by the arms.

He towered over her small frame.

"You were just a dream," she faltered.

"No, I am very real; I have come for your soul."

Anne wondered why she hadn't felt the train pass. It wasn't that far behind, was it?

Was the train even real, or was it another trick by this thing, this Hat Man? A trick to lure her into the alcove. Anne shook her head. How could he invent a train? This man was real; he was standing right in front of her, holding her. But he wasn't a physical form, he was more like a shadow of a man at best with no discernible features apart from the hat and the red eyes and the long yellow fingernails.

"Soon I'll taste your fear," Hat Man said through a hole in his face that he used for a mouth.

Before Anne had understood what Hat Man had muttered, she was hurled into the air from the alcove and onto the front of the locomotive, hitting the attached cattle catcher. She died almost instantly.

The engineer had no idea where she had come from. One second the tracks were all clear, the next a girl had dived in front of the train. He had no time to react.

It would have to wait until they arrived at the next station. He would need help from the local constable.

Why would a young girl with her whole life ahead of her jump in front of a train?

Did she jump or was she pushed?

Had someone been in the alcove with her? The engineer thought he had seen the shadow of someone, but he couldn't be sure.

Chapter 6

Picton 1916

Ruth had returned for her second shift in less than twenty-four hours. It was just after 11.30 when word came to her that Anne had been hit and killed by a train and her body was now in the hospital morgue beneath the wards in the south wing.

Ruth was shocked when Beth, the night supervisor, broke the terrible news about Anne. Beth had offered her the opportunity to go home but Ruth thought it was best to keep busy and had decided to stay at work.

She couldn't understand why Anne would kill herself. She had been so happy only days ago.

Had she now thrown herself in front of a train?

Beth had given Ruth some time to compose herself and freshen up. Even after the tears had gone, revisited and gone again, Ruth still couldn't believe her friend was dead.

Maybe it was a mistake. That was it. The authorities were wrong. It was someone else. After all, a train would cause a lot of damage to a human. Maybe mistaken identity? It was likely.

She needed to see for herself. She needed to be sure it was Anne lying in the morgue.

She headed down to the south wing. The buildings between the tuberculosis hospital and the southern wing of the hospital were connected by a covered breezeway. Even though it was summer, the cool night air hit

Ruth as soon as she stepped outside.

She walked along the cobblestone path lit by a few smaller street lamps. She reached a sign:

Southern Wing

< Pathology

Morgue >

The south wing was almost deserted. As she passed the corridor that led to pathology, she could see a pathologist walking between rooms, holding some samples. Probably another case of TB, she thought.

As she descended the hall that led to the morgue, the drop in temperature hit her. Goosebumps covered her arms and shoulders. She should have brought her cardigan, she thought, as she drew closer to the morgue and the temperature continued its decline.

She had only visited the morgue once before but couldn't remember the hallway being this cold. As she approached the entrance she could see the icy air of the morgue escaping into the hall; someone had left the door open. That would explain why the hallway was so cold. The morgue itself was in complete darkness.

"Hello? Anyone here?" Ruth called out as she stood in the doorway.

There was no response; only silence.

The gas lamps along the wall were out. She only had her kerosene lamp to see by.

Ruth held out the lamp and moved it in a circular direction to survey the room. For a second, she thought she glimpsed a man in a hat standing in the corner to her right.

She quickly swung her lamp back. It first glowed on a pair of feet that hung out from beneath a sheet on a nearby table. She continued around to the right side of the room. Had she seen a man? As the lamp brought light to the room, Ruth saw that the thing she had thought was a man in a hat was in fact a simple coat stand holding what it should, a long coat and a hat.

Normally the morgue smelt of death, but today it smelt like bad eggs.

Ruth entered the room, the lamp glow guiding her way. She was hoping the body she was looking for was on the left side of the table, close to the door. She didn't fancy walking across to the far side of the room. Ruth was convinced her friend wouldn't be here. There had to be a mistake. Anne wouldn't jump in front of a train. It just couldn't be true.

She read toe tag after toe tag until she had checked all the bodies on the left side of the room.

She crossed to the darker side of the room and began at the first table. Her dusty lamp glow shone the way. She stood at the foot of the furthest table from the door. She lifted the sheet and inspected the toe tag.

'Anne Cornwell', it read.

It couldn't be. Ruth thought this simply couldn't be happening. It must be a mistake. She felt hot and flushed. Her emotions were about to take hold once more; soon the tears would be flowing. She had to keep it together; after all, it still might be a mistake. She had to confirm it was in fact Anne lying on the table; she would have to identify her for herself from other than a toe tag.

Ruth took the cloth sheet between her fingers and steeled herself for what she might see. She took a deep breath and drew the sheet back.

The body hadn't been cleaned yet, and the mangled mess that lay in front of her was more horrific than she could ever have imagined. The body barely resembled Anne; it was a mess of flesh and bone. One eye was missing, and the right arm was gone from the shoulder. Her hair was matted and torn away from her scalp, and the right side of her face was almost missing. It had taken the full impact of the train.

Ruth moved the sheet down a little farther. The damage was just as bad. A couple of ribs poked out of her side just below her missing arm. Both her legs were intact, although the right was severely broken in several places; her right foot was at right angles.

Ruth had confirmed her worst fear. This torn and crumpled mess lying before her was Anne and she was dead.

Her shock at the sight of Anne's mangled body finally found its voice and Ruth wailed.

After several minutes of standing in the darkness crying over her lost friend, Ruth tried to compose herself.

Seconds later, the questions came.

Did she really kill herself?

Why?

Ruth drew the covers over Anne. She had seen enough. The vision of her shattered remains would live in her memory forever.

As she pulled the sheet over her deceased friend's head, she noticed burn lines running horizontally, wrapping around the left arm.

Intrigued, Ruth lifted Anne just enough to see the back of her arm and shoulder. The lines continued.

What could have burnt her in such a fashion?

The train wouldn't have been hot?

It was the most puzzling thing she had ever seen.

She would have to ask the medical examiner, once he was done with the autopsy.

She finished covering Anne and began to leave the morgue.

Suddenly, the coldness she felt in the hall was back.

Her spine tingled.

Her arms suddenly exploded in a forest of goosebumps. She felt someone watching from the darkness.

A being.

She flung the lamp around, and each wave of the lamp arrested her fears. Nothing but the empty room showed itself in the light.

Ruth calmed her nerves, and headed for the door, all her fear gone. There were no ghosts. It was just her imagination running wild.

By the time she reached the door, her sadness had returned as had the questions about Anne's final moments.

She dragged the door closed behind her but before the door shut completely, the dark room spoke one word. Ruth heard it loud and clear.

"Soon."

Ruth freaked out, and fear now encompassed her whole body. She screamed, almost dropping her lamp.

She ran all the way back to the breezeway.

Something had spoken to her.

A ghost was the most likely answer, as ridiculous as that seemed.

Did she even believe in ghosts? She slowed to a brisk walk in the breezeway.

Beth welcomed her back to the ward with, "Oh my God! You look horrible. Are you all right?"

"Just a bit shaken," Ruth replied.

"I shouldn't have let you go down there. Why don't you just go home?" Beth suggested, for the second time that night.

"No, it's all right. I'll finish my shift," Ruth replied.

"Then go make yourself look a little better and get back to your rounds," Beth instructed.

Ruth gathered herself and made her way to the bathroom. She wiped away the running make-up and applied a fresh coat. She undid her bobby pins, redid her hair and pinned it back into place. She looked at herself in the mirror and was pleased with the improvement. She smiled a fake smile and the mirror smiled back.

The hurt behind her eyes remained.

The question her eyes held remained.

Why? Ruth went from patient to patient checking their blood pressure and pulse. Her lamp provided enough light to do her duties without waking the patients.

She arrived at June's bedside. There was no doubt she had begun to love this patient, a lady in the last days of her life and all alone, yet she always provided her with nothing but kindness.

Ruth could see June wasn't in a deep sleep and she would probably wake when she started taking her obs. Ruth quietly and softly rolled her nightgown sleeve and began to apply the blood pressure cuff, while at the same time listening for her pulse through the stethoscope. One-thirty over seventy. All good, she thought.

She placed the lamp on the table next to June, so she could remove the stethoscope from her ears. Then her eyes caught sight of the marks in the dim light, marks that seemed burnt into June's skin.

The resemblance to the marks on Anne's arm was incredible, if not identical.

Ruth quietly shook June. "June, wake up."

"What is it darling? What the matter?"

"How did you get these marks?" Ruth asked.

June looked at her arm, still half asleep. "Sometimes when he touches me he burns me a little."

"When who touches you?"

"The man in the hat and long coat that comes to visit me. Don't worry, they don't hurt," June replied. Her cough had woken with her.

"How many times has he visited you?" Ruth asked.

"About five times. You know what's strange? While he's here I don't cough at all. I feel twenty again," June replied.

June reached for her hanky, ready to deposit the blood she had just coughed up.

"Is he coming to visit again?" Ruth asked.

"He said he would come back, soon."

'Soon.' That was the word she had heard in the morgue. Had she seen Hat Man? Had he been there?

She needed to find this man.

Chapter 7

Melbourne 2016

Jake sat in his new office situated in Port Melbourne. It was a lot more lavishly furnished than the one he was used to at homicide. He had just finished his report on Tony Aldrich. He was cheating with a lady who frequented the local watering hole. He had suggested his client, Samantha Aldrich, get a divorce and an AVO. Jake was worried her husband would become violent, considering the way he'd approached Jake outside his home earlier.

Jake had even offered to be there while she packed.

While she appreciated his caring, she shrugged off his concern saying that Tony was too weak to become a wife-beater.

Samantha said that next time he left for the pub, she would pack her car and go. He would never see her again.

Jake placed his report into a large yellow envelope along with the photos of the women to whom Tony had taken a liking. Samantha was going to come in, pay her bill and pick up her file.

Jake wanted to see her, but unfortunately, he had an appointment with a new client so on the way he delivered the envelope to the reception area, leaving it in the 'to be collected' tray.

His appointment wasn't far away; only a few minutes' drive.

Jake pulled up at the kerb. The home was one that only the affluent could afford. It was a big home, behind black wrought-iron gates, with a circular driveway and a buzzer at the front path.

Jake pressed the buzzer.

"Yes?" an unfamiliar voice replied.

"It's Jake Miller from Elite Detectives. I am here for an appointment with Mrs Bassil," Jake said into the metal box.

The gate popped open and Jake stepped through onto the brick pathway and headed for the door.

Jake was met at the door by a tall thin woman, attractive, yet she came across to him as very cold and indifferent.

"I am Mrs Bassil, but you can call me Karen. Please come in."

Jake followed her down a tiled hall to a hexagonal dining room. Everything in the home was immaculate. Not a single thing was out of place. The house reminded him of a display home.

Jake sat where Karen directed. She sat opposite.

The table was a dark mahogany with a high sheen; recently polished, Jake thought. In the middle of the table sat a large jug of iced water with slices of lemon and lime floating amongst the ice.

"I asked you here because I need you to find out who killed my daughter," Karen said. She was calm and matter-of-fact.

"Mrs Bassil, we don't usually do that sort of work. We generally focus on missing persons, insurance and adultery investigations."

"It's Karen."

"The police are the best ones to handle homicide investigations," Jake added before she could continue.

"The police have investigated. In fact, the coroner has even handed down his finding."

Jake was a little puzzled. "Why don't you start from the beginning, and I'll see what I can do to help you."

Karen poured herself a glass of water. "Would you like some?"

"No, thank you."

"In July 2014," Karen began, "my twenty-one-year-old daughter Gemma went to a small town in NSW called Picton Town. It was the weekend starting Friday the 4th."

Jake had heard of this town, but he couldn't remember from where or how.

"Gemma was there with a friend on a girls' weekend, as many college kids do. While she was there, she had a terrible car accident. Her friend Paige, who was the driver, was killed. While Gemma survived, she was never the same. She blamed herself. She was already going to counselling due to the death of her father but despite all the help, a month later she returned to Picton Town, rented the same room as she had the month before, and according to police, killed herself."

"You say Gemma was already in counselling because of her father? What happened?" Jake asked.

"In late October 2013, my husband of twenty-two years suddenly died in his sleep. He was fit and healthy. It was totally out of the blue. Gemma was nineteen going on twenty. It hit us all very hard. To help her cope the doctor offered free counselling," Karen replied blankly.

Karen took a drink to clear her throat and prevent the tears. It was still a raw subject, all these years later.

"Sorry for your losses, I really am," Jake said.

Karen could feel the sincerity in his tone.

"Have you spoken to the counsellor about her state of mind? Had she been concerned about her depression?" Jake asked.

"According to the psychologist, Gemma blamed herself for what happened, but never showed any signs of self-harm. She wasn't on any antidepressant medication," Karen answered.

"Were you told how Gemma died?"

"I was told Gemma was found in the bathtub with a radio," Karen replied. "The radio was found at the bottom of the bath next to her feet, and a wash cloth was covering her face."

"I can see why you're puzzled. It's a hard position to get yourself into, that's for sure," Jake replied. "Did you know why Gemma went back to Picton weeks later?"

"No, I don't even know why they chose to go there the first time."

"Were you given Gemma's belongings after she died?" Jake asked.

"Yes. They sent me a bag of her personal belongings; jewellery, phone, wallet, keys. But I sold the car. Easier than having it trucked down here. I didn't have anyone to help me collect it, so I sold it; got a fair price for it," Karen answered.

"Do you know if the police investigated the phone and her social media accounts?"

"Yes, they did, but she hadn't made any posts or sent any texts or even called anyone since the day she left," Karen replied.

Jake was taking notes.

"Do you still have the phone? Do you know if her Facebook page is still active?"

"I have the phone. It was one of those new iPhones. We closed the Facebook page just after she died."

"Can I look in her room?"

Karen sat shocked, looking at him.

"Have I said something to upset you, Karen?"

"No, but how did you know her room was still, well, the same?" Karen asked.

"I just assumed. Generally, parents leave the room exactly as their child leaves it, until they have closure. It's normally more consistent with missing children, but I can see you haven't reached closure yet," Jake explained.

Karen stood up and headed down a side passage that adjoined her living area. The door to the room was shut. Jake had expected it to be a shrine, and he was correct.

"Excuse the clothes on the floor. I just couldn't bring myself to tidy up," Karen said.

Jake stood in the doorway and observed the room. The walls were covered with photos and twenty-first birthday cards, and there was a double bed, covered in heart-shaped throw pillows of assorted colours. A beanbag sat in one corner, and a desk with a mirror in the other. On the desk sat a silver Mac laptop, and a jewellery box. Next to the desk was a large matching bookcase, full of books and magazines.

Karen stepped into the room. "This was Paige," she said, plucking a photo from Gemma's wall. "They'd been best friends since year seven, inseparable they were."

Jake took the photo. They were both attractive girls, with big smiles and their whole lives in front of them. Paige had long, flowing, brown hair while Gemma wore her reddish-blonde hair in a shorter, punkier cut.

"May I have a look around? I don't mean to pry, but it's important that I try to find out as much about Gemma as I can," Jake said.

"Sure thing. However, please excuse me." Karen left without another look into her daughter's room. Jake wondered about her quick exit. Maybe she doesn't like being in here, he thought, but almost instantly dismissed that idea. No, that couldn't be it. The room was immaculate, everything in its place. She was obviously in here often. Maybe she didn't like watching a stranger in her daughter's room, a room that had now become sacred to her.

Jake stood in the middle of the room and tried to absorb all that was Gemma; everything she had been and everything that had made her tick. His attention was drawn to the desk and the bookcase. What a person liked to read often provided a good insight.

Jake began to look through the books. A lot of Stephen King, Dean Koontz, Joe Hill, and others. Jake removed one book he hadn't seen before, something that interested him. It was an older book according to the cover; published in 1959. *The Haunting of Hill House* by Shirley Jackson.

Jake read the blurb. It was a horror story, a story about a poltergeist living in a haunted house. It sounded very similar to Stephen King's *The Shining*.

She liked horror stories, Jake thought. So did a billion other people. Nothing unusual there. He was about to put the book back when something caught his eye. It was a second row of books hidden behind the front row of novels. The hidden volumes were not published books, but handwritten journals with a gold spine. They were A5 size, lined up in year and month order. Jake removed the first one and turned to the first page.

1st Jan 2014.

It's New Year's Day. I can't believe I'll be twenty-one this year. I can't believe you have been gone 4 months already. Time has gone so quickly, since you passed. I swear the funeral was only yesterday. Mum has struggled, but I suppose you can see that from 'up there'. If there is an 'up there'. I used to have such faith. Now I don't know what to believe. The last 6 months has left me asking so many questions about faith. How does a man as healthy as a bull die in his sleep? Where was God to protect you?

Anyway, enough about God, last night was the first New Year's since I was 16 I didn't go to a party. Paige and I just stayed home and watched movies. It was a good night. Paige suggested we go to Picton in NSW. Apparently, it is a well-known Australian ghost town. (I had never heard of it.) She thought having evidence of the afterlife might help me renew my faith in God. I am not sure I am ready for such an adventure, yet. Maybe in July when I get to the mid-year break? If I make it, that is, even though this is supposed to be my second-last year at uni, it might be my last. I am really not enjoying it. I love the law, but the theory is so boring. I don't know if I can grind it out for another two years.

As always... until tomorrow. Thanks for listening, love you with all my heart.

Love Gemma xxx

Jake took one last look around her room. He now had an idea of who she was and why she had gone to Picton Town. He doubted Karen knew about the diaries and was probably too upset to be in the room to search for them. She had stood back from the doorway the whole time he was in the room.

"Would you like that water now?" Karen asked him as he returned to the dining area.

"That would be great, thank you," Jake replied, approaching the table where he had sat only minutes earlier.

"Karen, obviously I would have to do further investigations, but from what you have told me and what I have seen in her room, Gemma didn't appear suicidal. However, that doesn't mean she wasn't suffering depression. Suicide often occurs after the person suffers a depression that is so dark most of their family is totally unaware they were suffering, until the body is discovered."

Karen gave him a look of contempt, as if she had been told this before. Jake knew exactly what the look meant.

"Now, I am not saying she was depressed or suicidal, but you asked me to investigate and find the truth about Gemma's death. If the truth is that she killed herself, are you going to be prepared to accept it?"

Karen looked at him. It was a gaze that Jake thought would burn through his flesh. "Yes, I'll accept whatever the investigation finds," she answered.

Jake could tell it was hard to say, but he believed her. She would accept his findings.

"Here is what I think we need to do," Jake began. "We need to go back to when she began therapy after her father's death, all the way through to the car accident and Paige's death, and then look at the reason she went back to Picton Town. Do you have any idea why she went back?" Jake asked straight out.

"No, she didn't talk to me about it at all. On August 15th, it was a Friday morning if I remember correctly, she got up early and left. I thought she was just going shopping. She never came back."

"Didn't she have a bag with her?"

"She did take one, apparently, full of clothes. The police returned it to me, but I never saw her put it in the car. Maybe that's why I just assumed she was going shopping," Karen replied.

Again, Jake believed her.

"Whatever the reason she went back to Picton Town, we need to know," Jake said.

One thought ran through his head; not many people pack a bag of clothes when they plan on killing themselves. Usually, they take nothing.

"I don't know why she was there. All I know is, Saturday lunchtime I got a knock on the door by two uniformed police officers. They passed on the details about Gemma's death. I was told to contact Inspector Connolly for further information. Right there, my world stopped," Karen replied.

Jake let her compose herself before he continued. "I'd like to involve a friend of mine, Lucas Taylor, who worked in homicide in NSW. He made detective and more importantly, he is a good guy. He specialised in missing persons and homicides, including the infamous backpacker murders, and like many ex-cops he now does private sector work. I'm sure he would be willing to help with the Picton side of the investigation. It would definitely speed things up. He would have connections," Jake offered.

"Is this friend of yours going to cost me a lot extra?" Karen asked.

"By the time you deduct all the travel I would save from my end, it will probably work out even, and you have the bonus of two of us working on Gemma's case for you."

Jake didn't think Karen was concerned about the cost. He thought she was just ensuring she wasn't being ripped off.

She thought about it, as she sipped what was remaining in her glass.

"Very well then, that will do fine," she replied formally.

"I'll organise a contract for you and I'll also need you to sign a release form authorising me to speak to Gemma's psychologist," Jake said, only pausing to finish his own glass of water. "The contract will have our fees and the estimate for the first fourteen days' work and then we'll review. How does that sound?"

"Fine. How long will it take to get started?"

"I'll have the forms to you tomorrow, so the day after. I'll also give you a list of things I'll need for the investigation."

"Such as?" Karen asked.

"All Gemma's journals, all the items from that night, the jewellery, and a photo of her and Paige."

"I don't understand. Why do you want the journals? They are private between her and her father. I haven't even read them." Karen wasn't angry, but she was getting irritated.

"I understand how emotional and personal all this is for you, I really do. This is the worst thing a parent can experience, but if you want the truth, you need to let me in so I can do my job. You need to think of me as a lawyer, a priest and a doctor. What you tell me, stays with me and will die with me."

Jake stopped speaking, sat back in his chair and waited. She needed to decide what she wanted; the truth, or the fantasy of her daughter that currently existed in her mind.

"Okay – I'll organise what you need. You can pick it up tomorrow when you drop off the contract," Karen agreed.

Jake thanked her and headed for the door.

All night, he expected to get a call from Karen cancelling the investigation. Jake could tell her memories of Gemma were clearly beautiful and untainted, and he thought she would probably choose to preserve those over finding the truth.

It was a rare occasion for Jake. He was wrong. No such call came.

Chapter 8

Picton December 1916

The day of Anne's funeral was a humid overcast summer's day. It was a day that Ruth knew was coming, yet one she dreaded more than any other day she could remember.

She hadn't been asked to speak at the funeral. Those privileges were left to the parents, aunts and uncles and the school headmaster for whom she had worked. However, Ruth felt compelled to say a few words about her best friend, whom she had known for many years.

She needed to say goodbye.

She approached the iron gates of the St Mark's cemetery. High on the hill within the grounds were the chapel and adjoining graveyard. Tombstones were set amongst weeping willows and several large oak trees. A small stream flowed beyond the graveyard but within the grounds.

The chapel was filling fast. While Ruth didn't know some of the mourners by name, she recognised them from the school where Anne had worked. Even from the gate she could make out Anne's mum, whose head was covered with a black veil, leaning against the shoulder of her taller, thinner husband. The local hardware owners, the O'Brians, entered. He tipped his hat. They shook hands. The wives hugged. Next to offer their sympathies were the Woodstocks, the town's stock and feed owners. Even the local publican Mr Doyle had closed the pub and was in attendance. He dipped his hat.

"Condolences, Miss Ruth," he said, as he passed her on the path and headed towards Anne's parents at the chapel.

Ruth had taken only two steps when a voice called her name, stopping her in her tracks. Ruth spun back towards the gates. Stanley stood there, tall, strong and strapping, dressed in his black slacks, shoes and hat. Even his shirt was black. Maroon braces held his slacks up.

"Sorry. I didn't mean to startle you," he offered.

"It's all right, it's just such an awful day. I think I'm on edge. I haven't been getting much sleep this last week," Ruth replied, watching the wind blow the loose leaves around the graveyard.

When Ruth's eyes finally met Stanley's, she could see he too was sleep deprived.

"How are you coping?" she asked.

"I can't believe she's gone," Stanley replied quietly.

"I know. Such a tragedy."

"I was going to ask her to marry me, on New Year's Eve. Well, that was the plan. Now it's all gone. Why would she have done this? She was happy, wasn't she?" Stanley asked.

Ruth sighed. "As far as I knew she was. I don't understand it either."

Silence filled the air between them.

"How have you been sleeping?" Ruth asked after a short pause.

"I haven't been getting much at all," was Stanley's quick response.

"Same here."

They continued walking up the hill towards the chapel. Ruth stopped and took a breath. "This may sound weird, but have you seen a strange man in a hat around town?"

Stanley froze. "I had what I thought was a drifter break into my house two nights ago. He said he would be back soon."

"Was he wearing a long black coat?"

"Yes."

"What did you do?" Ruth asked.

"I couldn't do anything. I was paralysed. I think he drugged me or something, because I couldn't move. I'll be ready for him next time, though, I bought myself a Colt six-shooter. If he shows up again he'll get all six, for trespassing," Stanley said.

"Don't go doing anything silly."

Stanley frowned down at her. "Silly! Why are you asking about this guy? Has he been bothering you too?"

"I haven't seen him, but he's been visiting one of the patients at the hospital, and no one knows who he is," Ruth replied.

"Maybe that's where he got the drugs he used on me." Stanley sounded as if he had just put two and two together. He added, "You know, the strange thing was, the next morning, when I woke up, I had these marks on my stomach." He untucked his shirt, revealing three horizontal burn marks about two inches long that began just above his hip bone.

Ruth's jaw dropped.

For a split second she thought she was in the morgue again, looking at Anne's body.

The marks on Stanley were identical to those on both Anne and June.

"I have seen those marks on other people. Those exact burns, same length, same direction," Ruth replied, dumbstruck. "Do you think this mystery man may have had something to do with Anne's death?"

"I don't think she jumped in front of the train, that's for sure," Stanley said.

The church bell sounded. The service was about to start. Stanley straightened his tie and they hurried up the gravel path to the church.

After the funeral, the mourners were invited to join the family at the pub for the wake.

Ruth couldn't handle any more sadness that day, and instead gave her apologies to Anne's parents and made an early exit.

She needed to find out about this man in the broad-brimmed hat and the long coat who had been visiting her patient.

Chapter 9

Picton December 1916

By the time the wake was over, Stanley was slightly drunk and totally exhausted.

He had to be at work in just over twelve hours. He couldn't afford to give up another day's pay.

Once home, Stanley prepared an egg on toast and a cup of tea to settle his stomach and took two aspirin to clear his head. After dinner, he headed straight to bed. As he had done since he bought the pistol, he checked and double-checked that it was loaded with the safety off, and then slid it under his pillow. He hopped into bed and turned out his kerosene lamp. The glow of the glass dissipated after a minute or two but by then, Stanley had already fallen asleep.

During the early hours of Tuesday morning, Stanley was woken by a rancid smell. Whatever it was stank to high heaven. Stanley initially thought something was burning. He sat up and sniffed repeatedly, trying to identify the smell.

After a few second his eyes adjusted to the darkness. At the foot of his bed he could see a man in the wide-brimmed hat and long coat. It was as if he'd appeared out of the shadows, as if he had drifted in through the wall.

Hat Man's eyes were red and fiery, his face pale with no discernible features apart from those piercing red eyes. What man had red eyes? Was it a man or some sort of creature? He wasn't sure.

Stanley slid his right hand under the pillow. He could move. Tonight, he had not been drugged.

Tonight, this stranger, this 'Hat Man', would experience the power of his Colt first hand.

"What do you want? I have no money if that's what you're looking for." Stanley's hand wrapped and then tightened around the mahogany butt of his hidden pistol.

"I want your soul," Hat Man replied in a voice that was deeper and more evil than anything Stanley had ever heard.

"My soul?" This man standing before him had either been smoking the mushrooms near the tunnel or had escaped from an asylum. Either way, he wasn't right in the head.

"Get out of my house, you bum, before I kill you where you stand!" Stanley demanded.

He tried to sound strong and authoritative, yet his voice quavered a little upon the delivery of the message.

"Stanley, do you really think that Colt under your pillow is going to stop me?" Hat Man asked softly.

At first, Stanley wondered how he knew his name, then something else struck him. How did he know that he had a gun or what make it was?"

"How—?" Stanley began before he was cut off by Hat Man.

"How do I know all these details? It's like I am reading your mind, isn't it Stanley?" Hat Man questioned, giving a sinister grin.

For the first time, Stanley saw the semblance of a mouth and what appeared to be teeth. They weren't pearly white either. From his quick glimpse, they looked yellow and jagged.

Stanley removed his hand from beneath his pillow, clutching the Colt, and pointed it straight at the Hat Man or whatever the thing standing in front of him was.

Stanley expected Hat Man to run or duck, at least dive away from the pistol's barrel. Hat Man however, didn't even flinch. He stood his ground at the end of Stanley's bed.

With the gun pointed directly at the stranger, Stanley was surprised at how steady his hand was. Stanley aimed the sight at the man's chest and without thinking any further, he pulled the trigger.

A loud crack filled the quiet night air. A quick flash of light momentarily brightened the bedroom and the smell of burnt gunpowder briefly replaced the sulphur stench that had permeated the room.

A split second after the flash, Stanley expected to see the intruder fly backwards and then fall lifelessly to the hardwood bedroom floor.

Yet no fall came, no blood, no injury. Instead, there was a second smaller yellow flash where the bullet should have hit its target. It was as if the bullet had simply vanished.

Instead of letting out a cry of anguish as Hat Man should have done when the bullet struck, he simply smiled, this time giving Stanley a full view of his jagged yellow teeth.

It must have been a misfire or a dud bullet, Stanley thought.

Stanley wasted no more time trying to determine what had happened to the first shot and squeezed the trigger for a second time. As soon as the shot rang out, he fired again and again. Each time, the end of his barrel blazed, the smell of burnt gunpowder filled his nostrils, and the bullets flashed yellow and disappeared. There was no impact on the target whatsoever.

Hat Man stood firm as the shots burst into small balls of yellow light in front of him, just before they were destined to hit him.

Hat Man snarled hideously and gave another sinister smile.

Stanley sat in his bed, frozen with fear and disbelief. Surely, they all couldn't have been duds? Maybe the mystery man was wearing a metal plate over his chest like that Bushranger Ned Kelly had done back in 1880. Maybe that would explain the yellow flashes. Maybe they were the bullets hitting the metal.

As soon as that thought had entered his brain, he dismissed it. There was no sound of bullets hitting metal, no ting, or ricochet.

Stanley adjusted the aim of his Colt just in case there was a metal plate protecting his chest. Stanley aimed right between the intruder's eyes, dead centre of his forehead, just south of his brimmed hat.

Again, his arm was steady, again he squeezed the trigger. There was another crack and again, a split second later, another burst of light at the end of the barrel, just as it had done on the previous four occasions.

This time there was no smile, no sinister laugh. Hat Man stood his ground, unshaken.

They must be duds, Stanley reaffirmed to himself as his fifth shot failed.

"Now, you will be mine." Hat Man spoke in a deep horrifying voice.

Stanley had his finger firmly on the trigger, and he was ready to fire his sixth and final shot. Stanley pressed down hard, squeezing as he had done five times before, but the trigger didn't move. It was as if the safety had been engaged.

Stanley squeezed harder, but the trigger didn't budge. Stanley panicked, quickly looking at the side of the revolver to check the safety.

It was off.

Stanley looked up, fearing Hat Man had advanced on him. Instead he was standing patiently with his right hand up like a stop sign. Stanley froze, although he didn't know why.

Hat Man pointed his finger and thumb into the shape of an imaginary gun and placed the tip of his finger against his forehead.

He gave a beaming smile, revealing those horrible teeth once again.

Stanley's hand mimicked the Hat Man's gun finger and he placed the barrel of his Colt against his own temple. The warm metal barrel nestled firmly against his skin.

Stanley quickly grabbed his gun hand with his left hand and tried to lever the gun away from his own temple. It was immovable, like a rock. He tried a second time. pulling his arm down with all his weight, yet he could not stop himself.

Still smiling, Hat Man created an imaginary trigger finger with his third finger, which he began to squeeze.

Stanley could feel his own trigger finger beginning to constrict. He was now applying pressure to the trigger, with the barrel resting against his temple.

Stanley knew he didn't have the strength to pull the gun away from his head; the power Hat Man was using was too strong. Stanley thought if he couldn't move the gun away from his head then maybe he could move his head away from the gun.

He shifted his head backwards, but the gun remained pressed against his head.

As Stanley moved his head forward trying to get it away from the barrel, he noticed Hat Man compressing his trigger finger even further. He felt his own finger apply more pressure to the trigger. No matter how much he tried to prevent it moving, it did as Hat Man instructed it.

Stanley knew he didn't have much more time before the gun would fire. He quickly shoved his left thumb behind the trigger, in an attempt to prevent it depressing any further. He cried in pain as the trigger depressed further, in the process cutting into Stanley's left thumb. This thing was no man, Stanley thought.

The house began to tremble, and the windows rattled as if an earthquake was coming.

"Please stop this, please don't!" Stanley cried.

"I'm sorry, but you summoned me, so I have come for you. Soon you will be part of me," Hat Man replied.

"Part of you?"

"That's what happens when I collect your soul," Hat Man said, smiling.

Before Stanley could mumble a response, Hat Man pulled his trigger finger and touched his palm.

The trigger on Stanley's Colt depressed further, and the back of the trigger began to cut into his thumb again. The pain was excruciating but it ended quickly for Stanley.

The last of the bullets in the Colt fired, spraying Stanley's brains and skull fragments across his bed and his room.

After everything went black, Stanley found himself staring at Hat Man. What had happened? Did the gun misfire again? Then he gazed back at the bed. He could see himself there, dead. He was now a translucent representation of his body.

He stood over his bloody body trying to reconcile what had just occurred.

A cold breath that tickled the back of his neck interrupted his thoughts.

Stanley turned to see the thing, the Hat Man, standing toe-to-toe with him. His bony fingers unfolded from his hands into ten tiny spears and before he knew it they were inserted into his translucent stomach. Hat Man's mouth opened up.

Everything Stanley had inside him was being drawn out, all the love, all his memories were being taken. He was being taken with them; Hat Man was digesting him head first. The last thing he saw, before being swallowed by the darkness, was a bright, incredibly warm light that seemed to be calling for him; a light he would never reach.

Chapter 10

Picton December 1916

Five hours after Stanley had been killed, Ruth sat down next to June as she ate her breakfast.

"How did you sleep?" Ruth asked.

"Wonderfully well." June sat up in her bed, her tray table in front of her. She began with her toast and poured her tea. June liked her tea strong, so she only added a smidgen of milk.

"Have you had any visitors recently?" Ruth asked, wanting to get straight to the point.

"As a matter of a fact I saw Scat last night, before he had to go to work," June replied.

"Scat?" Ruth recognised the name from the séance.

"Yes, that's what he calls himself," June replied placidly.

Maybe it was a coincidence, Ruth thought. Unusual name to be a coincidence…

"Do you know what Scat does for work?" she questioned.

"Oh, um he did tell me…let me think." June paused. Her eyes went to the right and up as if she was searching her brain for the answer. She took a gulp of her tea. As she placed the cup back on the tray table, a bit spilt over the lip, staining the crisp white sheet.

A few seconds later, her eyes returned to centre. She had found the answer. "He is a collector," June stated.

"Do you know what he collects?" Ruth probed.

"I don't think he has ever said…but it must be something rare. He always seems to be working long hours."

June could feel her cough building. It was about to erupt the way it did each morning, once she became active. June retrieved her handkerchief from the bedside table and placed it next to her tray.

"Did he say anything else to you last night when he came to visit?" Ruth asked.

"Yes, quite a lot. In fact, most of it was about you and your friend."

"What about me, what friend?" Ruth asked quickly, desperate for June to spill the beans.

"Your friend Stanley." June's first cough came; it was coarse and full of phlegm.

Ruth waited eagerly for June's cough to subside.

"What about Stanley? How does he know Stanley?" Ruth asked impatiently.

"He said he needed to collect something from Stanley. Something very rare, then he said, he was coming to see you." June coughed again.

Ruth sat in the chair beside the bed, trying to comprehend what she was being told. What could Stanley have that a collector would want? She knew for certain he didn't own anything rare or of great value.

"Do you know where this Scat was going after he left you last night?" Ruth asked, still trying to get a handle on what Stanley might have.

June thought, trying to recall. Her eyes went back to their search mode. When her eyes returned to their normal position she said, "Now that you mention it, I think that's when he mentioned Stanley; I think he said he was going to collect something from Stanley."

Ruth was becoming frustrated now. "June, this is really important. Can you tell me what he said, word for word?"

"Sorry dear, but I don't remember everything like I used to."

"Please try?"

June sipped the remaining tea. "To the best of my recollection, as Scat was leaving I asked him where he was off to this late. It must have been 2 am. He replied by saying, 'I'm off to collect some goods from a man named Stanley. He is a friend of Ruth, your nurse. Matter of fact I need to collect something special from Nurse Ruth soon too.' That was it. I'm sorry; that's all I remember."

Ruth decided she had to speak to Stanley, but it would have to wait until after work. She had no way of contacting him out there on the railroad.

"Thank you. It's a big help," Ruth said to June.

"What does he need to collect, dear?" June asked.

Ruth ignored her question. "Before I take your morning obs, is there anything else you would like to eat or drink? How about a glass of milk?"

"No thank you," June replied as she pushed her tray table away.

Ruth spent the rest of the day wondering what on earth this man could want with Stanley and herself.

Nothing came to mind.

At the end of her shift, she passed Nurse Mary Crankshaw in the lunch room where she was making herself a cup of coffee before her shift began.

"You worked graveyard shift last night, didn't you?" Ruth asked Mary.

Mary turned from her coffee and biscuits. "Yes, I certainly did. I'm back to do the afternoon shift already."

"June told me she had a visitor at 2 am, but there was no one listed in the visitor's log, and to be honest I can't imagine you allowing visitors in at that time of night…"

Mary frowned. "She didn't have any visitors. Hasn't had any for weeks, not since her son came up from Melbourne. And you're right; I wouldn't allow anyone in at that time of night. I need this job. It keeps food on the table. If I did that, management would surely send me packing."

"I didn't think so," Ruth said.

"You know, she may be beginning to lose her marbles. She's been telling me all sorts of stories. She even said her friend was looking forward to meeting me," Mary said.

"Did she mention a name for this friend?" Ruth asked.

"She did. It was a peculiar name. Um…what was it?" Mary pondered. "Scar I think. No, that's not right, I can't recall, sorry."

"Scat?" Ruth questioned.

"Scat, yes that's it. She comes up with some whoppers all right. The other day she told me Scat was going to take her out of here. Free her from this prison, she told me, or something absurd like that."

"Maybe she's already lost her marbles?"

"Looks that way. Let's hope we never get like that, hey?" Mary replied.

Ruth felt much better after speaking with Mary, yet how would June know about Stanley? She had to speak to Stanley as soon as possible, and decided she would head over to Stanley's straight after work. She only had handover to do and then her shift would be finished.

Handover seemed to take a month of Sundays. Those last fifteen minutes seemed like an eternity.

The walk to Stanley's house was forty minutes, if she used the Redbank Range Tunnel. She doubted she would be able to go through that tunnel anytime soon. She knew she would have to go the long way, which would add an extra twenty minutes, but she thought it would be better than facing that dark tunnel where Anne had met her fate.

Chapter 11

Melbourne 2016

As soon as Jake arrived at the office the next morning, he began on the investigation contract for Karen. He also placed a second call to Lucas. Jake assumed he was swamped in cases and that was the reason he hadn't returned his call yesterday afternoon.

Jake had his list in front of him, tabulating the most important things he wanted Lucas to follow up first, although he assumed Lucas would know exactly where to start.

Jake removed his brown leather jacket, hung it over the back of his chair and settled into his seat. He was enjoying wearing a leather jacket, shirt and jeans; far more comfortable than the suit and tie required during his years in homicide.

He dialled the Sydney number with the (02) prefix. He had to get in touch with Lucas to prepare the contract. In a worst-case scenario, if Lucas was too snowed under, Jake would make the trip to Picton Town himself.

The phone rang four times and just when Jake thought it was going to revert to message bank again, a muffled voice answered.

"This is Lucas," the voice groaned.

"Is that Lucas?" Jake questioned, thinking he may have dialled incorrectly.

"That's what I said," was the blunt response.

"It's Jake Miller from Vic Homicide. We worked on the Satan's Son's bikie cartel a few years back."

"Hey Jake, my phone didn't recognise the number. How ya doing?" Lucas asked.

"Good, I'm doing private work now. I hear you're doing the same up there." Lucas's northern slang drove Jake crazy. The shortening of words like 'you' to 'ya', Jake could tolerate, but what really irritated him was the mispronunciation of words like 'something' and 'nothing'. Lucas always pronounced them 'somethink' and 'nothink'.

Despite Lucas's Central Coast slang, Jake knew that his detective skills were second to none. Sometimes Jake wondered if Lucas was an even better detective than he was. He didn't think that of many people.

"Yeah, going on two years next January. It beats putting guys away and seeing them out on bail a few weeks later, plus I don't need to wear the suit and tie anymore," Lucas replied. His voice was still a little quiet and muffled.

"Have you got a few minutes or is this a bad time? You sound as if you're in the middle of something."

"Yeah. I'm okay, for the moment. I'm on a stakeout, so if I have to fly, I'll call ya later today," Lucas said.

"Understand. I have a case I need your help on."

"An interstate affair?"

"Suicide."

"Suicide? Why ya investigating a suicide?" Lucas asked.

"Victim's mum has hired me. She thinks her daughter was murdered."

"Guessing the coroner ruled suicide?" Lucas questioned.

"He sure did, and very quickly too."

"What was the cause of death?"

"Electrocuted in a bathtub."

"Sounds like suicide to me," Lucas said.

"That's what I thought at first and it probably is. Problem is, the radio was found in the tub at her feet."

"Hmm, that raises questions. You have sparked my interest here, Jake. So, what do ya need from me?"

"She died in a hotel room in a small town called Picton, not far from you. Her mum doesn't know why she was there. Police believe she went there to commit suicide. I want to know if you would be interested in doing a few days of investigation. Find out what she was doing there. You have a good nose for finding the truth. While you're investigating what she was doing up there I'll start looking into her background from down here," Jake explained. "What muddies the waters even further is this: just six weeks prior to her death on the weekend of the 4th of July, the victim and her friend were involved in a car accident where her friend was killed."

"Victim's name?" Lucas asked.

"Gemma Bassil."

"Gemma driving?"

"No, her friend Paige was. Police reports indicate they were both highly intoxicated."

"So, it ain't her fault. Not like she is going to have the guilts," Lucas mused.

"Wait, there's more. After being pulled from the wreckage, Gemma told police that a drifter in a hat had been tampering with their car, while they were ghost-hunting at the Redbank Range Tunnel."

"What the hell is that?" Lucas asked.

"I don't know; might be worth researching before you leave though."

"Who said I'm going anywhere?"

"When I tell you the fee you will…"

"Why, what's the fee?"

"$15,000 for the first fourteen days, split it 50-50. Then we reassess where the investigation is."

"Sounds reasonable. Do ya have a pen? I'll give you my email." Lucas sounded interested.

"Go ahead," Jake said.

Lucas reeled off his address and Jake promised he would send all the information he had, as well as a copy of the contract by the next day. Jake said goodbye and was about to hang up the phone when he heard a voice say something on the other end. Quickly, he raised the receiver back to his ear.

"Yo, Jake, ya still there?" Lucas was saying.

"Yes…sorry," Jake replied.

"What hotel did she die in?"

"It was the Intercontinental."

"You know that hotel is supposed to be haunted, don't ya?"

"Don't tell me you believe in ghosts, Lucas?"

"N-n-no, not at all, but ya start wondering about all those stories."

"You'll probably only have to stay a few days, just sleep with the light on," Jake advised.

Lucas chuckled. "I'll take my Beretta, just in case."

"I don't think you can shoot something that's already dead," Jake answered, laughing.

"If I see anythink, then I'll find out." Lucas became more serious and asked, "What dates did she stay there?"

"There are two dates I need you to investigate in 2014. The first is when the accident happened, the 4th of July weekend, and the second is six weeks later, on the weekend of the 16 and 17th of August. I believe she was found dead on the morning of the 17th, by hotel staff. Got that?"

"Sure."

"Okay. Thanks." Jake hung up the phone and flicked his track pad. His computer came to life. It sat idle on the Google search page.

Jake typed three words.

'Picton Town Ghosts.'

Chapter 12

Picton December 1916

The December afternoon heat had died down about halfway through Ruth's walk to Stanley's house. It made the longer trip more bearable. Sometimes, she even felt a touch of a cool breeze as she walked down the path that detoured the tunnel where Anne had met her demise.

By the time Ruth passed the tunnel, the cool change had clearly come, and the clouds were rolling in. It made climbing the hill that the tunnel cut through a little easier. There would be a thunderstorm tonight. She hoped she would make it back home before the heavens opened.

Arriving at Stanley's farm, she headed through the gate, which had been left ajar. Luckily, his animals were kept in the back paddocks adjacent to the shed.

The cloth sheets that Stanley used as makeshift curtains were closed, covering the dirty, dusty windows. A couple of flies landed on the inside of the window before disappearing out of sight.

Ruth tried to peer through the gap in the sheets, but the lounge, the same lounge where they had performed that séance, appeared empty. Since then the world had changed.

Ruth stepped off the porch and headed around to the right side of the home where a dirt path had been cut into the brush. The horizontal cedar panels were fading in the summer sun.

Ruth walked around but could see nothing through any window, except when she peered into the bathroom. While the room was empty, apart from a towel crumpled on the floor, Ruth noticed more flies, or probably the same ones, she thought, flying around the inside of the house.

At the back porch, resting against the wall was Stanley's bicycle. He must be home.

"Stanley!" Ruth called.

There was no response.

Ruth moved towards the back door. She knocked loudly and waited.

"Stanley, you home?" Ruth called again.

Still no response.

The sun was getting lower, but it was still an hour or so before dusk.

She knocked a second time, this time, louder, almost thumping on the door. As her hand hit the door, she noticed her arm was covered with flies. She tried to shoo them off, but they clung to her. They were normally bad in the summer heat, especially before a thunderstorm, but this was the worst she had seen them.

Ruth looked at the bike again. It was usually with Stanley. Suddenly she got a bad feeling in the pit of her stomach. She turned the handle on the back door. It was locked.

Ruth turned towards the back paddock. About fifty yards away from the back door was the outhouse, and beyond that, two large paddocks with a tin hay shed in the middle. Ruth stepped off the back porch and walked down the roughly cut path towards the outhouse.

She made it halfway down the path before stopping. The long grass was not an ideal place to be walking on a hot summer's day, especially in her nursing shoes and not her riding boots. She squinted. She could see the horses and cattle in their respective paddocks, but when she turned her focus to the shed, she saw no movement. If he was feeding the animals he would be going to and fro from the shed to the paddocks.

"Stanley!" she yelled as loudly as she could. Again, there was no response, and no one appeared from the shed.

"Stanley!"

She waited. Still there was no movement from the shed.

50

Ruth headed back to the house. She turned to face the road, thinking maybe he had walked to a neighbour's place; his closest was a hundred yards up the hill and across the road.

Ruth's gaze returned to the gate. It was open when she arrived. What if that drifter had paid Stanley another visit?

She needed to get in and check if Stanley was in there. Check if he was all right.

She returned to the first window she had looked through at the front of the house.

Ruth dug her nails in under the bottom of the window, pulled and managed to prise it open enough to climb through. The floorboards inside groaned under her feet.

The house was dark and smelly. A large mat lay in the middle of the lounge room floor and two high-back armchairs faced the window. In the corner sat a guitar and next to the window was a small table holding a radio and a clock, which showed it was just before 6 pm.

"Stanley, you home?" Ruth called out.

She listened for a response as well as any movement.

There was none.

Ruth moved through the kitchen. A frying pan lay in the sink, unwashed, and flies flew from room to room. She could hear them buzzing about the place. A plate sat in the drying rack, ready to be put away. An unlit kerosene lamp sat on the table.

She headed towards the bedroom. The door was shut, and she knocked. More flies lingered around the bottom of the door.

There was no answer and she couldn't hear any movement.

Ruth wrapped her hand around the doorknob. It whined as she turned it gingerly. A great sense of dread came over her.

Flies landed on her face.

Nothing could have prepared her for the sight that awaited her on the other side of the door. Stanley lay dead in bed, his eyes wide open and filled with fear. Blood was splattered across his bed clothes and the floor. Some had even reached the other side of the room.

Flies were not only crawling over Stanley's face, but they had followed the trail of blood across the room.

Ruth approached the bed slowly. She went to the right-hand side of the bed to avoid all the blood. As she reached it, something silver on the floor glistened up at her. She knew instantly it was his revolver.

She passed it by without touching it. She knelt on the bed, careful to avoid his right hand which hung slumped over the edge, and reached across to feel his neck for a pulse. But as she suspected, there was none.

Going by Stanley's expression, someone or something had terrified him.

Shaking with grief and fear, Ruth realised she must get the police and ambulance.

She looked up at the back of the bedroom door. Just to the left of it she noticed there were five holes in the wall. She wondered why he had fired the gun before he'd turned it upon himself.

Had he fired at an intruder perhaps? Maybe the drifter?

She leaned over Stanley's body. The left side of his head was missing, splattered on the floor and wall beside him.

Ruth screamed and instantly felt sick.

She frantically ran to the front door, released the lock and flung open the screen door. She made it down three steps of the front porch before she vomited violently.

Ruth tried to collect her thoughts. She needed to call for help. The nearest phone was located at the general store ten minutes away. As she ran, she wondered if Stanley had turned the gun on himself. Had he been suicidal? Sure, he'd been upset at the funeral, but who hadn't been?

Yes, Stanley was worried about the drifter, the 'Hat Man' that had been around town.

Something was terribly wrong.

Ruth still looked awfully unwell when she arrived at the store because the storekeeper asked her, "Are you feeling all right, Miss Martin?"

"Not at all, Mr Wade. There's been a terrible accident at Stanley's farm and we need to contact the police and an ambulance." Ruth's voice had begun calmly but ended up in a full-on sob.

Mr Wade, who was in his early fifties, placed the cloth he was cleaning the counter with on the till, and called for his wife.

Elsa came running from the back of the shop.

"Elsa, please get her water and a chair, while I call the authorities." Mr Wade headed out the back to the phone.

Elsa nodded and filled a glass from the tap and sat Ruth down behind the counter.

Mr Wade returned.

"They're on their way. What on earth has happened?"

"Stanley is dead; looks like he shot himself," Ruth sobbed.

"Oh, my goodness!" Elsa squealed in horror at the news.

After about ten minutes, the police arrived and a few minutes later the ambulance. Both arrived by carriage. Cars were not available in Picton yet although according to the mayor, they weren't far away.

Ruth tearfully explained to the sergeant how she had found Stanley. The only thing she omitted was why she had come to see him. She thought if she told the police she had wanted to talk to him about a mysterious Hat Man, they would have her on the first bus to the insane asylum.

Instead, Ruth just stated that she wanted to see how he was coping after Anne's funeral. After all, Stanley and Anne had been dating for nearly two years.

The sergeant asked if he had been drinking heavily at the wake. Ruth explained she had left after the service and hadn't attended the wake, so she couldn't say what condition he was in. The sergeant took down everything she said.

"Miss Martin, the ambulance is going to take Stanley's body to the morgue in Picton."

Poor Ruth doubted she would ever be able to forget the image of Stanley in that bed. She feared it was burnt deep into her brain.

"Would you be able to drop me at St Mark's, please? I really think I need to talk to Pastor Dwyer," Ruth said to the policeman.

"No problem. It's on my way back to the station, so hop aboard."

He offered his hand to help her, and she lifted the hem of her uniform and stepped into the carriage.

As they headed back towards town, all Ruth could think of was that maybe, the mysterious Hat Man was somehow involved in her friends' deaths.

Chapter 13

Melbourne 2016

With the contract signed and the initial fee paid, Jake sat in the waiting room of Gemma's psychologist.

From the furniture and the décor, Jake immediately concluded that Mrs Jermaine was running an extremely successful business. The magazines were new, the tables were all dust-free, the counter was shiny, and the silver lettering glistened under the lights.

A photo on the cover of one of the gossip magazines caught his attention. It was a photo of two parents, the Walters, who had been investigated for murder. Jake had been a part of the investigation. Early on, everyone thought the mother had murdered her children in their sleep; suffocated all three.

All the investigators wondered how anyone could do such a thing, especially to their own children. Jake always waited before reaching a conclusion until all the facts were in. He felt it affected his ability to stay open-minded. His biggest fear was that his emotions would push him in one direction and he would end up missing vital evidence that would solve the case.

He was especially proud of himself that he had managed to stay focused in the Walters' case. While many in the force had condemned the couple, Jake had just done his job.

When the toxicology reports came back, there were many red faces along the halls of justice. It turned out that the culprit was in fact a faulty space heater. Apparently, it hadn't been serviced and was leaking carbon dioxide. The deadly gas had killed the children in their sleep.

While there was no crime, the Walters' lives were changed forever.

It was another ten minutes of patiently waiting before Mrs Jermaine called Jake into his office. She wasn't what he expected at all. She was dressed very casually and looked every bit the caring mum. She wore a long black skirt below her knees, long black boots and a white shirt and cardigan. Her hair was brown, short and tucked behind her ears.

The office had the usual armchair, located opposite an urbane-looking black and silver couch. Her desk was opposite, with two chairs in front of it. She took her seat behind it and offered Jake one of the chairs.

"Apparently you're investigating the death of Gemma Bassil?"

"Yes, that's correct."

I have told everything I know to the police. I don't see how I can help you any further, Mr Miller."

"Please, call me Jake."

He noticed she didn't offer her first name in response. She wanted to keep this formal. He doubted she would be anything like this with her clients.

"I'm not conducting a police investigation, just trying to ensure the police investigation was accurate and provides closure to the family."

"Was it accurate, Mr Miller?"

"I haven't completed my investigation yet, but on the surface, it appears so. Mrs Jermaine, may I ask you a few questions about Gemma's treatment?"

"I'll answer what I can, but some topics may be privileged. I am sure you understand physician–patient privilege."

Jake couldn't understand why she was being so evasive. It was more than patient privilege. He wondered if she was hiding something.

"Firstly, privilege dies with the patient and if I have to get a court order to release your file on Gemma then I will, but I would prefer not to. This is not a witch hunt, Mrs Jermaine. I am not here to cause trouble, or to cast doubt on your expert opinion. I just want your help to put this case to rest," Jake said firmly.

She leant back in her chair and thought for a second, before unclipping a set of keys from her office key chain. She huffed, stood up, retrieved a file from her cabinet, and returned to her desk.

She slid the file across the desk.

"I'm not trying to be difficult, Jake, and while I know I did everything I could to help Gemma, it doesn't stop me from feeling responsible. I always wonder if I missed something."

"I wouldn't beat yourself up about it. One thing I have seen in my time on the force is people are very good at burying dark secrets deep inside themselves. I'm not here to lay blame for her suicide. I am here just to confirm that it was suicide, that's all, Mrs Jermaine."

"Please, call me Kelly."

He nodded.

"You think she died some other way?" Kelly asked.

Jake shuffled in his seat and opened the folder she had slid to him. "It's possible it was an accident, or even foul play."

"You think someone killed Gemma?"

"I don't, but I don't rule anything out until the evidence suggests otherwise."

He had flicked through three pages of notes, scanning them as he went. Nothing abnormal caught his eye. To him it was a typical psychologist's patient who was suffering depression from the recent loss of her father followed by the tragic loss of her best friend.

"Do you mind if I ask you a few quick questions?"

"Of course, although all the notes are in my file there."

"Some of this may not be in the notes. Did you know that Gemma was writing a daily journal?"

"Yes, I was the one who suggested she begin a diary. It was done as a coping mechanism for the loss of her father. I suggested she talk to her dad by writing the journal."

"Have you read any of the entries?" Jake asked.

"No, it was her personal diary. She didn't offer to show me, and I didn't ask to see it. Have you read them yourself?"

"Some entries, but not all of them," Jake replied. "How emotionally stable did Gemma seem to you, when you last saw her?"

"The last time I saw her was two weeks after the car accident that killed Paige. Gemma came in to see me. She was on the mend physically, but she was still a mess mentally. Even though she was extremely upset by Paige's death, I never saw the symptoms of self-harm. Depression yes, self-harm, no."

"That would have been late July 2014?"

"Correct." Kelly flicked through her file. "It was Monday the 28th to be exact. From my notes here, Gemma said she planned to go back to Picton. She told me it was no accident."

"The crash?"

"That's right. Apparently, before they had the car accident they were being followed by a man who had scared them."

"What would going back achieve?" Jake asked.

"Apparently, he was a local. Gemma had told the police after the accident that they were being followed. Somehow, I don't think the police took her information too seriously. "

"Did she say how the accident happened?"

"No. Just that they were being followed."

Jake finished writing notes and laid the pen and his notepad on his lap.

"Maybe she wrote about it in her diary," Kelly suggested.

"I could find no diary for July 2014. It's like that month never existed for Gemma," Jake replied.

"Maybe it's because she had the accident that month," Kelly offered.

"But I don't even have the July diary. You would think there would be entries up until the time of the accident. The August diary is also missing."

Jake continued, "So, Gemma saw you on the 28th of July 2014 and then a few weeks later on the 17th of August she was found electrocuted in a hotel bathtub?" Jake confirmed.

"Sadly, that's what happened. Yet none of us knows why." Kelly sighed.

"I wonder what changed between those two dates?"

Kelly shrugged. "We all ask that question."

Jake put his pen in the inside pocket of his leather jacket and closed his notepad. "Thanks for your help." He extended his hand and shook Kelly's firmly but gently.

"Jake, let me know what you find, please."

Jake, who was halfway out the door, turned and answered in the affirmative as he left her office.

Chapter 14

Picton December 1916

Two gas lanterns at the entrance to St Mark's Anglican Church lit Ruth's path.

Pastor Joseph Dwyer was only twenty-one. He was a baby-faced pastor with pleasant facial features, of small stature and slight frame. He always appeared happy and at peace with himself, as if he didn't have a worry in the world.

Stationed at St Mark's, he worked under Pastor Philip Fletcher who was due to retire in the next few years, and who provided sound guidance in Joseph's spiritual development.

On the night Ruth came bursting through the doors of St Mark's, Joseph was about to prepare for a date; his second with young Laura Hayfield who was three years his junior.

Ruth had tears streaming down her cheeks, her eyes red and bloodshot.

"Are you all right my dear?" Pastor Dwyer asked.

"No, I've had a terrible week," Ruth replied.

Joseph knew exactly what she was talking about. He had performed the service at Anne's funeral after all. He could tell, yesterday at the service, she wasn't coping well.

"Sit please." He motioned her towards the front row pew.

She sat, as he took up a seat beside her.

"Did you want to talk about Anne?" Pastor Dwyer questioned.

"Anne and Stanley." Ruth dabbed a tissue to her eyes, trying to dry up the flow of tears.

"Stanley? Is he having problems dealing with Anne's death too?"

"He's dead!" Ruth blurted. "The police say he may have killed himself sometime last night. I just found his body in his bedroom." Ruth burst into another flood of tears.

Pastor Dwyer sat on the pew, stunned by the news of Stanley's death.

"How did he die?"

"Suicide apparently; shot himself." Ruth sobbed.

"I spoke to him yesterday at the wake, and he didn't appear suicidal. In fact, considering the occasion, he was quite calm," Pastor Dwyer said.

"He appeared fine at the funeral, when I saw him. I should have stayed for the wake, but I just needed to go home and have a good cry."

"We all need a good cry sometimes. There is nothing wrong with that. Nothing to be ashamed of," Pastor Dwyer soothed. "I'm sure they are in a better place. They are with the Lord now."

"I came here because I don't think Stanley or Anne killed themselves. Something strange is going on in this town," Ruth said.

Pastor Dwyer looked at her with an expression of confusion. "I don't understand what you mean, Ruth. Anne stepped in front of a train. Maybe it was a tragic accident, but it's clear that's what happened. As for Stanley, I understand that his death is raw but if the police say he killed himself then they are usually right, my dear." He placed his hand on hers. "Death is a very hard thing to understand. It is what tests our faith the most."

Ruth looked up at him. Kindness shone in his eyes. "Yesterday, Stanley told me he was having trouble with a drifter in town."

"A drifter?"

"Apparently the drifter has been visiting a lady I care for in the hospital as well."

"What sort of problems was he having with this drifter?" Pastor Dwyer asked.

"Stanley told me he had broken into his house. That's why he had bought the gun; for protection."

"Have you informed the police of this person?"

"No." Ruth hesitated.

"What is it, my dear? Is there something else you want to tell me?" he probed.

"I'm afraid you'll think I'm crazy. In fact, I think I'm crazy," Ruth replied.

"I'm sorry. I don't follow. Why do you're think you're crazy? I promise I won't judge."

"When Anne died I saw her body in the morgue. She had an expression of fear that was so intense, it was like she had seen the devil himself. She looked horrified. While I was there I noticed that she had these strange horizontal lines on her stomach. There were three of them. They were like burn marks. Anyway, while I thought it was strange I didn't think any more of it until…"

Pastor Dwyer sat on the edge of the wooden pew, listening intently. "Until?" he prompted.

"Promise you won't think I'm crazy?"

"I promise."

"Until I did my rounds and found that the patient who has also been seeing this man, 'Scat', or whatever she calls him, also had the marks. Then to add to my concern…" Ruth looked up.

Pastor Dwyer's mouth was agape, his hands trembling.

"Pastor, are you all right?" Ruth asked.

He sat glued to his pew edge, unemotional, frozen.

"Pastor?" Ruth asked. She touched his shoulder. "Pastor?" she called again.

"What was the name you said?" he asked quietly.

"Scat."

"The church speaks of the seven deadly sins. Well, each sin has a demon. A demon is often referred to as Satan or Scat."

"Why would a demon be here on earth, and what would he want with us?" Ruth asked.

"If it is a demon, then he would be on earth to collect souls. That's what they do," Pastor Dwyer said quietly.

"How and why would one be after them?" Ruth asked.

"Usually demons only come to earth if they are called upon, summoned, if you will." Pastor Dwyer sounded grave.

Ruth tried to place her hands over her mouth before the gasp came out, but she was too late.

"What have you done, Ruth?"

"Stanley, Anne and I did a séance last week. We thought it was harmless. We were just fooling around," Ruth explained.

"Messing around with the dark powers is never a good idea," Pastor Dwyer chided.

"I see that—now. How do we kill this demon?"

"I don't know if we can, as he is not human. Only something of pure good can destroy something of pure evil."

"You're pure and good, Pastor."

"Thank you, my dear, but I think it may take more than me to rid the town of his presence. I'll need to write to the church and seek counsel from my superiors. A demon is beyond my experience," Pastor Dwyer admitted. "Until I get a response from the archbishop, I suggest you wear this. It will give you some protection, help keep you safe."

Pastor Dwyer rose and walked to his dais. He took a silver cross and necklace from a box and placed it around Ruth's neck. "It was what I wore before I was ordained," he said, offering a half smile.

Ruth thanked him and relaxed a little.

"How many marks did you say were left on Anne?" Pastor Dwyer asked.

"Three...why?"

"It could be his mark. Most people think of this as the 666, but during my studies I learnt that each sin has a specific demon.

"The demon for Pride is Lucifer. That's why everyone refers to Lucifer as the devil: really, he is just the first demon on the list.

"Envy is Beelzebub. Wrath is Sathanus or Scat, and so on: every sin has a demon. I think it is this demon we are dealing with and he is leaving three lines because he is third in line, so to speak."

"In line for what?" Ruth asked, confused.

"To rule hell, I suspect. If he is a demon of some kind, as we suspect, I would think you would be safe within these walls, as we are on sacred ground.

If you ever feel he is after you, get here, or to any church. I'll telegram my superiors, and in the meantime it's probably best you don't discuss this with the townspeople. We don't want to unnecessarily scare anyone, and we don't want you taken away to the loony bin." Pastor Dwyer gave a grim smile.

Ruth nodded but didn't answer. What would the townspeople think of her story?

"Do you know what this being looks like? I assume he has taken on a human form of some kind?" Pastor Dwyer asked.

"According to Stanley and the lady I look after, he wears a long coat and a wide-brimmed hat. Shouldn't be too hard to spot, in this heat."

"He might look out of place, but he won't feel the temperature. The only thing he is after is souls."

"What does he do with the souls he claims?" Ruth asked nervously.

"He feeds on them: they become a part of him."

"Thank you, Pastor, please let me know when you hear back from the church. I'll keep you updated if I see anything," Ruth said.

The pastor again put his hand on Ruth's. "Stay strong. The cross should keep you safe," he encouraged.

Ruth stood, preparing to leave the security of the church. She made her way down the aisle and headed towards the wooden arched doors.

"Would you like me to walk you home?" the pastor offered.

"No, thank you. I have troubled you enough already. It's only a few minutes away. After all, I have this to protect me." Ruth rubbed the cross between her fingers and them tucked it in under the top of her dress, so it rested against her skin.

Her emotions were running wild as she stepped out of the church. She was full of sadness and disbelief over Stanley, thankful for Pastor Dwyer's cross and fearful of the unknown demon. Of all the emotions, fear was the most prominent one running through her.

She walked the whole way, continually checking that the cross was still nestled between her breasts.

Chapter 15

Picton January 1917

Ruth had spent the two weeks since seeing Pastor Dwyer on holiday. She had taken a week off for Stanley's funeral and another week for the Christmas break.

Today was her first night back at work. As usual, her first point of call when beginning work was to do handover at the nurses' station followed by patient observations.

"Good to have you back," Beth said, giving her a hug. This was something Ruth had not experienced from her matron previously.

"Before you start, I have something to tell you," Beth said.

Ruth could tell Beth was unsettled but did not know why. Maybe she was about to fire her…no, she'd just said it was good to have her back.

"June passed on last night. I was going to contact you, but I thought no point disturbing you when you would be in today," Beth said.

Ruth stood there, a little shocked. Sure, June had TB but compared to some other patients, she was in reasonable health.

Ruth didn't feel much of an emotional reaction. She thought there would be sadness, yet no tears came. Maybe she had exhausted so much sadness over the past three weeks, she simply had none left.

"How did she die?" Ruth asked.

"In her sleep, peacefully," Beth replied.

"Has her family been contacted?"

"The hospital called them first thing this morning. They are organising the funeral."

Ruth hadn't noticed that Beth still had hold of her shoulders.

"One other thing. You will need to take June to pathology," Beth continued.

"Why can't the orderly take her?" Ruth asked fretfully.

"Ray is not back until tomorrow and as you know, the pathologists need to do the blood tests within twenty-four hours of death. Because Ray is not here you will have to take her," Beth replied.

Ruth sighed, but agreed.

Beth gave her another quick hug and then picked up the patient charts and began discussing them one by one.

Over the last few weeks since seeing Pastor Dwyer, she had thought very little about Hat Man, or the absurd possibility of a demon strolling her town. Yet walking down the hallway that led to the morgue, the thoughts flooded back, and the possibility of a demon Hat Man again seemed very real. All the fear she had felt that night at Stanley's came rushing back. It was as if fear had replaced blood in her veins. The closer to the morgue Ruth came the more uneasy she felt.

Without any conscious effort, Ruth's hand clasped her necklace. It wasn't until her fingertips touched the coldness of the cross that she realised she was playing with it.

Where had the fear come from?

She walked closer to the morgue door. She passed the corridor on her right that led to the pathology centre. A breeze from the empty hall hit her. Fear built with each step she took. She took a deep breath, trying to calm down, trying to reassure herself that everything would be all right.

The morgue was dark, cold and quiet. The lamps were again out. Ruth's only light was her hand-held lamp.

Goosebumps instantly rose all over her skin as soon as she entered.

She was hoping June's body would be located on the entrance side of the morgue yet somehow, she felt it wouldn't be. The bodies were always lined up in order; the newest ones awaiting autopsy, or if the cause of death was under investigation, were together, while the ones ready for burial were normally in the fridges nearest the door. As Picton was a small town, it only had three fridges. With the TB outbreak, this was far short of what was required. As a result, many of the deceased were lined up on trollies throughout the morgue. Ruth looked to her right where she thought she had seen the shadow of Hat Man last time. She moved her lamp in that direction. This time she could clearly see the coat rack was empty, which helped ease her tension.

She guessed June was the most recent death in the hospital, so she went to the furthest trolley on the far side of the room, the darker side, the same place where Anne's remains had lain just weeks ago. The lamp glow led the way through the trollies of the deceased. She came to what she thought would be June's body, only to find it was an elderly man; in his eighties, by the look of him. DOA was written on the toe tag. Ruth recognised him as a local but couldn't remember him by name. She moved along to the next trolley in the queue. She removed the sheet and June was staring back at her. Beth had said she had died peacefully in her sleep, yet the look on her face resembled horror or fear, rather than uninterrupted peace. Her expression seemed odd.

She drew the sheet further down and inspected her arms and stomach with the torch. Ruth could see the three burn marks she had witnessed earlier. They had faded somewhat. Maybe it was due to no blood being pumped around her body, she thought. Ruth brought the covers back up. As they reached June's chest, she had once last look at her face. It certainly was a fearful expression rather than one of peace.

Ruth swung the lantern around the room just to double check she was still alone, make sure there was no Hat Man, make sure none of the deceased had woken.

Everything was as it should be. Nothing had moved, nothing had changed.

Ruth hung the lantern on the end of the trolley and went to flick the trolley's brake off with the top of her foot, only to find air. There was no brake. This was a new scissor-lift trolley, which had the brakes on the other wheel. She again used her foot and disconnected the brake. The trolley glided as she pushed it past the lines of deceased patients and headed out into the hall, towards the pathology corridor. There were no dodgy wheels on this trolley—not yet anyway. Ruth pushed the bed back the way she had come, turning left at the corridor. The goose bumps had left her, at least for the moment.

She manoeuvred the trolley through the twin doors into pathology.

"Hello?" she called.

"Right with you," came the reply from behind the reception counter.

Ruth waited. She had stood away from the trolley and away from June. She had been as close as she needed to be and closer than she wanted. She would be so glad when this job was done. She had seen enough death to last a lifetime. Lately, she had begun to feel like a mortician rather than a nurse.

"So, what we got here?" the abnormally tall man asked as he emerged from behind the desk.

Ruth went through June's details with him while the pathologist checked the wrist and ankle bands in order to confirm the details were correct. Ruth stuttered nervously a couple of times, trying to sound more professional than she felt.

"Where is the orderly? Normally he brings the bodies," the man said. He must be over seven feet tall, Ruth thought, as he spoke.

"Holidays," Ruth replied.

"Ahh, the luck of it, off on holiday while we're stuck here, hey?" he asked rhetorically.

"Oh no, we're the lucky ones. I'd rather be here than at some resort," Ruth joked.

The tall man laughed a snort of a laugh, followed by a little giggle that didn't belong to a body of his size. "You got the chart?"

Ruth took it from the end of the bed and handed it up to the tall man.

"Thank you."

As she headed for the door, a loud voice from above called her back. For a second, she thought it was God speaking to her. "You need to stay here with me. It's against protocol to leave me with the body."

Ruth turned and stood in the doorway, unsure what she was supposed to do.

He moved June into the room, pulling a second trolley by her side.

"This will only take a minute."

The tall man placed the large needle into June's wrist and it filled with bright red. In all he took seven vials of blood.

Ruth watched.

"You can take her back now. The blood results will be back from the lab late tomorrow."

According to the tall man's signature, his first name was William, but she couldn't make out his last name.

Ruth had started wheeling June back through the double doors when she realised she was holding her necklace again.

She had the crumpled chain pressed tightly between her hand and the silver handle of the scissor trolley.

Since Pastor Dwyer had given it to her, she had hardly thought about the Hat Man and she still hadn't seen him. Whatever had happened was over now.

She entered the dark morgue, wheeling June back to her original position, with one hand on the trolley and the other already clasping her necklace. Her lamp swung as it dangled from the end of the trolley. As she crossed to the darker side of the room, the hairs on her neck stood up as if they were all screaming at her. She instantly stopped, turning to looking over her right shoulder.

She clearly saw a man in a long coat and a wide-brimmed hat. The eyes burnt at her.

She screamed.

She was still holding the necklace and screaming when the chain broke as she reeled around in fright, and the cross fell from her hand to the floor. Seconds later, she felt it make contact with her foot. Where it was now she had no idea.

Ruth stood, feet pinned to the floor as if they had been nailed to the spot. She turned her body from the waist, removing the lamp from the trolley and holding it out towards where she thought she had seen the man.

Nothing!

No one was there. Except for the dead, she thought.

Jumping at shadows, she thought again.

Her thoughts returned to her necklace. Where had it gone? She hung the lamp back on the trolley. The lamp provided just enough light under the trolley for Ruth to see her necklace. She bent down to collect it. As the tips of her fingers gathered the chain off the floor, she remembered the chain was missing the most important part. The cross. It had fallen from the chain.

Down on hands and knees, beneath June's cold lifeless body, she searched the floor trying to locate it. The lamp flickered, and Ruth looked up. It was as if a strong wind was trying blow it out.

Maybe it was running out of kerosene.

A cold breeze blew up from behind, causing her goosebumps to return. Her lamp flickered again. Just a few more minutes, she begged. Her prayer went unanswered as her lamp flickered again. Seconds later, a loud bang came from behind her. She jumped up and spun around at the same time.

Her fear had returned, as she could see the door had closed. Just a breeze, she thought, but without her lamp she couldn't see anything.

All she wanted was to get her cross and get back to her ward. She'd had enough frights for one night.

Ruth turned her lamp down to try and save fuel, but she was nearly in pitch black and she could barely see the floor.

She knelt and resumed her search. Almost instantly she located the cross on the other side of the trolley. She tried to move the trolley, but it wouldn't budge. She clicked the brake with her toe, but it was already released. She pushed harder the second time but still it wouldn't move. Something was wrong.

Before she could bend down to see what the problem was, the corpse at the end of the line sat straight up, opened his eyes and screamed.

Ruth screamed back.

Then the female corpse opposite sat up and screamed.

Ruth screamed again.

They were alive.

She needed her cross to protect her. Pastor Dwyer had said she would be safe with it on. She fumbled on the floor beneath June. She climbed halfway through the scissor lift; her fingers touched the edge of the cross trying to bring it closer to her.

The screaming continued. Ruth finally clasped the cross between her thumb and forefinger.

"He's here for you," June said, leaning over the bed.

Ruth screamed again and scrambled backwards, dropping her cross once more.

June's eyelids were wide open but the eyeballs themselves were rolled back.

Ruth could feel feet behind her, but she was too scared to look. She wanted to remove herself from under the scissor lift but couldn't take her eyes off June who although dead, was leaning over the bed speaking to her.

"He is here. Scat is here for you."

The other dead bodies that had been screaming moments ago were now chanting, "Scat, scat, scat."

She knew exactly who Scat was.

Still crouched under the scissor-lift bed, Ruth looked over her shoulder. She could barely make out a pair of legs and what appeared to be the bottom of a trench coat.

Her whole body began to shake. Terror ran through every vein. Her heart was racing. She could feel a pulse throbbing in her neck. Frantically she again looked for the cross, but she couldn't locate it.

She turned back to where June had been hanging over the side of the trolley. She was still there, smiling now.

"Time's up!" June screamed

"Time's up!" The other voices joined in this new chant.

A pair of claw-like hands with long yellow nails grabbed Ruth's ankles and pulled.

Ruth was dragged along the floor. Whoever was here for her, wanted her out from under the bed. She grabbed onto the base of the trolley bed, trying to prevent herself from being dragged out.

Her legs were high off the floor. She could feel someone's fingers burning through her stockings. Soon the fingers would burn her legs.

Her shirt had become untucked. Ruth was losing her grip. Whoever had her legs was yanking hard.

Her hold on the trolley gave way.

There was nothing to hold onto.

Her nails dragged along the concrete as he pulled her out.

Ruth flipped over, kicked hard and screamed as loudly as she could. "Help!"

How could the pathologist not hear her screaming?

Couldn't hear with the morgue door closed, her brain answered immediately.

She screamed louder.

"Help, hellllp!"

"Time's up," the chorus of the dead replied from above.

She could see the man pulling her, the drifter or demon in the hat. What-or-whoever it was, really wanted her. She had no doubt it was the one that had killed Stanley and now it wanted to kill her.

Still sliding, Ruth grabbed another of the bed's arms and held on for dear life.

Her attacker yanked once more. Ruth's grip held firm.

The trolley wobbled and groaned as the tug-of-war continued with Ruth underneath.

Suddenly the scissor lock gave way, sending the bed crashing to the floor.

The scissor arms acted exactly as they were designed and folded onto themselves, crushing Ruth's throat.

The pressure on Ruth's throat was enough to crush her windpipe. For the next few frantic seconds, Ruth desperately struggled to free herself from under the fallen trolley, but she failed.

Ruth thought she had just passed out. It wasn't until she saw her lifeless body lying tangled with her head trapped under the scissor-lift stretcher that she realised she was dead.

She stood motionless, staring at her corpse. A loud snarling noise bellowed from the shadows behind her. She spun, still disorientated, unsure as to who or what she had become. She turned, only to find herself face to face with the creature that had been chasing her. The Hat Man.

Hat Man moved so quickly Ruth didn't even see it happen. It wasn't until she looked down that she saw Hat Man had stabbed her with his fingers. Hat Man's fingers were woven around her invisible insides and back out like shoelaces.

A bright light appeared near the door, strong enough to illuminate the whole morgue. It was warm and inviting. Ruth tried to move towards it, but Hat Man's grip was strong. He ran his face up and down her neck. When he brought his face level with hers, he opened his mouth. The first thing that hit her was the rancid smell, a smell of decomposing flesh. The second was his teeth, which were yellow and oddly shaped.

Without any warning the jaw unlocked, its teeth protruded from its face, and a whirlwind of air began to pull at her, dragging her into Hat Man's mouth.

Into a dark abyss of screaming souls.

Chapter 16

Picton December 2016

Lucas passed the sign that read 'Welcome to Picton, the Stone Quarry Town'. In front of the brick and stone sign was a flowerbed full of annuals, mostly yellow. The Mazda 3 he drove was a lot smaller than the police Commodores he was used to as a detective, yet it was more economical and a much nicer drive. Lucas hadn't quite made the jump from a suit to casual wear. He still wore the slacks and the business shirt, but no tie, and on hot days he rolled up his sleeves.

He slowed to fifty ks as he entered the town. It was the first time he had been in Picton. There was so much of Australia he still hadn't seen.

As he passed the sign from the north, the road slowly descended around a long sweeping bend. In a few kilometres, he would be in the heart of Picton. His first impressions of the town were nothing like he'd thought they would be. Before he'd left, he had done his online research of the town and the Picton Intercontinental Hotel where Gemma had died, and he'd been expecting something far different. The town was represented as one of Australia's most haunted towns, with numerous ghost sightings including in that hotel. In the early 1900s, the hotel had been used as a tuberculosis hospital. According to the internet, a ghost still roamed the halls. Other reports and sightings included a woman who had been hit by a train on the way to visit her boyfriend, now haunting a local disused railway tunnel, and two young teenagers who were seen from time to time roaming the graveyard of St Mark's cemetery, hand in hand.

Lucas didn't believe in ghosts and he wasn't about to start now. After all his years in New South Wales Homicide, he was more concerned about the crimes committed by the living. Even in the weird cases that involved ritual killings and black magic, the investigation always revealed a human was responsible. Sure, he had a few criminals who claimed they were possessed and couldn't control their actions, but he had never arrested a ghost.

The closer he got to the town centre the more normal it appeared. It was a bright, vibrant, quaint little town that seemed to be a hive of activity. He pulled up at a set of lights at Menangle Street. One way was the Picton Intercontinental Hotel, the other St Mark's cemetery. Lucas had booked the same hotel room where Gemma had stayed, hoping to start investigating from where she had been found and work backwards.

The hotel was on the high side of the road. It was an old two-storey Victorian building painted white, with a beautiful wrought-iron balcony. He guessed from the outside it had thirty or forty rooms maximum.

Lucas parked his car in the nearby vacant parking lot, retrieved his bag from the boot and headed inside the hotel.

The old-world charm of the building remained despite the recent renovations, with new carpet and drapes as well as a fresh lick of paint.

Behind the mahogany reception desk stood the receptionist, a short elderly lady with frizzy white hair. She was wearing a bright floral blouse with tan slacks and according to her work tag, 'Isabella Elliot', she was the owner.

"May I help you?" she asked with a smile.

For the proprietor of a hotel that was apparently haunted, she did seem surprisingly chirpy, Lucas thought.

"I have a reservation under Lucas Taylor." Lucas removed his wallet to produce his ID and pay the $100 deposit to cover the mini bar. He had been through this process countless times before.

"You're the private detective that rang a few days ago. You requested the same room that…" She didn't quite know how to say it.

Lucas butted in. "Yep, the same one that Gemma stayed in."

"We don't normally let out that room. In fact, I really would prefer if you took another. I would be happy to show it to you during the day. It's the same as all the others on that floor."

"No, that one will be fine, thanks."

Isabella nodded in agreement and grinned widely before continuing with the checking-in process. Her demeanour didn't seem sincere.

Lucas clearly saw her gulp. He had spent many years reading people. "Is there something wrong with the room?" he asked.

"No, not at all. I just don't like going in there ever since I found her," Isabella replied.

"You found her?" Lucas questioned.

"Unfortunately. Such a horrible sight to see someone take their life like that."

"I can imagine. Don't panic, I won't require housekeeping. I'm a bit of a neat freak." Lucas tried to lighten the mood.

"I will be fine. I have to face my fears sooner or later."

Despite the honesty of her answer, Lucas couldn't help feeling there was another reason. She didn't want him in the room either.

"Here you go." Isabella handed Lucas his credit card and ID and a small envelope containing two magnetic cards. "Up the stairs and last room on the right."

There was no offer of help with his bag, not that he needed it, but it reinforced that this was a small hotel in country NSW.

The staircase was carpeted except for the first two steps. The grand and spiral staircase with its highly polished wooden handrail and handcrafted timber supports was quite impressive. The staircase didn't resemble one from a cheap country hotel, that was for sure.

Lucas swiped his card and entered his room. The wall on the left was brick. Immediately on the right was the bathroom, with a vanity opposite the shower and a claw-foot bath along the far wall with a toilet between the shower and the bath. He would take a closer look later.

Beyond the bathroom was the double bed complemented by two side dresser tables. Over the bed hung a large chandelier. Opposite the double bed a TV hung on the wall, under which sat a set of drawers. To the left was a freestanding cupboard. Out of curiosity, he opened the cupboard. It was empty but for some coat-hangers swinging on the rail.

Jake had mentioned to him that there were two of Gemma's journals missing; July and August. If the room had been sealed since her body was removed, then maybe the diaries were still here. He would look for them later. First, there was something he needed to see.

He stood beside the vanity. There was a gap of about eighteen centimetres between the vanity and the edge of the claw-foot bath. Lucas searched through the cupboards under the vanity, looking for the radio that had fallen into the bath. He wasn't surprised it wasn't there; probably taken away by the police for evidence.

He wondered if a radio that toppled from the vanity edge would fall into the bath. From what he could see, it would have fallen through the gap between the bath and the vanity. The gap seemed too big for the radio to reach the bath.

He needed to test his theory.

Chapter 17

Picton January 1917

The sergeant had seen many deaths in his time as a police officer, yet the suicides of Anne and Stanley had been two of the most gruesome sights he had ever witnessed.

That was until he walked into the morgue late on a hot Thursday afternoon in January. He had been called in by the hospital director, Mr Richard Lumley, to investigate a fatal work accident.

Mr Lumley met the sergeant at the door. "Thank you for coming so quickly, Sergeant."

Richard had known Sergeant Lee Amly for many years, but he thought under the circumstances he'd best use protocol.

"It's all right Richard, you can call me Lee," Lee replied, trying to ease the situation. "Tell me what happened."

"Well, William from pathology saw the morgue door wide open. He went to close it and he found, well, um…" Richard stopped.

"It's okay, take it slowly."

"He found her crushed on the floor."

"Is William still here?" Lee asked.

"Yes, he's in the tea room."

"I'll need to take his statement. I'll look at the scene first, then have one of my men take his statement so he can go home. Sounds like he's been through a lot," Lee said. "Has anyone apart from William been in there?"

"Just me, but I made sure no one touched anything. We didn't even go near the body. What we saw from three paces was enough." Richard swallowed.

Lee took a step towards the morgue. Richard put a hand on Lee's chest. "It's bad, really bad," he muttered, as if to say, don't go in there. They locked eyes for a second or two before Lee brushed him off and headed inside. It was his job.

The morgue was bright and clinical; all the gas lamps were on and in full glow. The light bounced off the white walls and the concrete floor. Corpses were laid out on the trolleys; four rows of four. The last row, the one furthest from the door, was a little askew. It had three bodies in the row and one trolley sitting in the aisle.

Lee took three steps inside the morgue before stopping. Richard was correct; the sight was horrendous.

A nurse was lying half under a bed, her fear-filled eyes staring at the underneath of the trolley. Blood had pooled on the floor from a cut in her head and dried in her hair. Upon closer inspection, he saw her throat had severe bruising consistent with strangulation.

He knelt, but he couldn't quite see under the bed without lying down on his stomach, and that was out of the question unless he wanted to drag himself through the crime scene.

He rose and stepped back so he was level with the third row of corpses, and then lay flat on his stomach. Under the trolley that the nurse was propped up against, he noticed a small pool of blood.

Behind her he could see a shiny silver necklace. Half the chain was clasped in her hand while the other half was curled up on the concrete floor. A cross lay not far from the end of the chain. He noticed dry blood around the nurse's nose and mouth. Her face was aghast, eyes and mouth wide open, shock and horror written all over it.

Had she seen her impending death?

It looked like a fight.

An attack.

Had the chain fallen off before she died? Was that the reason her head was under the scissor function of the bed? Or had someone killed her?

Had it come off in a struggle?

It looked as if she had collected the chain before the struggle. Maybe she was under the bed when William came across her?

Maybe the pathologist William had had other ideas for the nurse. Maybe that was why there was a struggle, Lee thought. Possibly.

He looked at her legs. Her stockings had runs in them, as if someone's long nails had caused them. He would check the skin for scratches.

It was time to see William.

Lee walked in and sat on the chair opposite him. William looked tired and scared. In the middle of the table sat a barrel of biscuits and around the edge were strewn a few cups.

Sergeant Lee introduced himself.

"You found Ruth, William?" Lee asked.

"Yes sir."

Lee noticed that even when seated William towered over him.

"How tall are you?" Lee asked.

"Six-ten," William replied.

"Wow, big boy! Can you show me your hands? Just put them out for me." Lee demonstrated, holding his hands out, palms facing upwards.

William complied, and Lee noted he had long fingernails for a man. His hands were clean; no cuts, no abrasions.

"Can you tell me what happened?"

William spoke slowly and quietly. "I went to put some bloods in the lab fridge— that's where the lab collects them from. Ruth was going to take the deceased back to the morgue. When I was coming back from the lab I felt a cold draught up the morgue corridor. I went to check it out and saw that the door was wide open. People forget to close it sometimes. When I arrived at the door, I saw her there on the floor. It scared me. I thought she was dead. I didn't intend to go near her but...I thought I better check her pulse."

"Go on."

"When I checked her, she was already gone," William said, his complexion becoming paler.

"Did you touch her anywhere apart from her neck?" Lee asked.

"No, I don't think so, maybe I might have placed my other hand on her leg while I was taking her pulse. I can't remember."

"Did you attack Ruth, William?" Lee asked.

"What! No sir, definitely not. I just said I found her like this. I didn't kill her. I only checked her pulse. I don't know how she died. I didn't hurt her, I swear."

Lee wasn't sure he believed him.

"William, we are going to run some tests on your hands, so you won't be able to leave until we have the results back. One of our officers will take you to the courthouse for the night," Lee said.

William nodded and put his head in his hands.

Lee called Richard into the lunchroom. "How long has William worked here?"

"Only a few months. He just moved over from South Australia," Richard replied. "He had impeccable references."

"Did you check them?"

"As best I could, yes."

"I'll have the coroner look over the body, but my initial thought is, this was no accident. To me there was a struggle. The victim grabbed onto the trolley to try and get away from her attacker when the scissor mechanism malfunctioned."

"You think William was the attacker?" Richard asked.

"It appears that way, I'm afraid. We're running some tests, but let me finish the investigation before we make a firm finding. We're going to have to close off the morgue for the next few hours, while we finish our investigation."

"Sure, no problem. Let me know if you need anything," Richard replied.

"Thank you for your cooperation."

"Would you like us to inform Ruth's family?" Richard asked.

"It's best if we do it. If you could just provide me with Ruth's details, I'll send my men to inform her family in person."

Chapter 18

Picton December 2016

Lucas had done a quick search of the room, but had come up short on locating any diary. He headed back down the spiral staircase towards the reception area.

Isabella was at the desk attending to a young couple who appeared to be checking in for a dirty weekend away. The guy had his hand down the back of his blonde girlfriend's jeans, playing with her pink thong, while she was nibbling on his ear between each conversation with Isabella.

Lucas remembered when he was that young and in love. It seemed a lifetime ago…or was it just a different life? A life where he had been truly happy, a life before the cancer hit and took his love from him.

Isabella handed them the key envelope as she had done with Lucas. "Don't let the ghosts scare you," Isabella said.

The ghost rumours of this town were obviously good for her business. Encouraging them made her a bit of a charlatan, Lucas thought.

The couple were so excited they almost snatched the keys out of Isabella's hands.

Lucas thought the excitement had more to do with the pink thong than the possibility of seeing a ghost.

The guy hoisted his girlfriend over his right shoulder and picked up his wheelie case in his left hand. He took the steps two at a time. The girl squealed, and slapped his back, giggling all the way up the stairs.

"I hope they're not in the room next to me," Lucas joked.

"Right next door," Isabella replied. "I could move you, if you like?"

Lucas knew it was her ploy to have him switch rooms.

"No, thanks. I'm sure I'll get used to their rumbustious frolicking," he said, smiling.

"Something else I can get for you?" she asked.

"I have a couple of questions for ya, if you have time."

"Sure, fire away."

"The first time Gemma and Paige stayed here, did they say they were having any problems?"

"When they weren't in the bar they stuck to themselves pretty much. On the first night they were here, I think it was the Friday night, they were asking about ghost tours. They were keen to try and see a ghost. Mind you, most of our tourists are here for the ghost tours," Isabella replied.

"Which are?"

"I suggested the three most common places tourists go to see ghosts."

"Where are they?"

"Well here, obviously. This place used to be the old tuberculosis hospital. Rumour has it, there is a nurse that still haunts the halls. Although I haven't seen her, some have. My staff claim to have had her visit.

"Second is the Redbank Range Tunnel, or the Mushroom Tunnel as locals refer to it now. Some believe a girl on the way to visit her boyfriend tried to cut through the tunnel, only she misread the train timetable and was hit by the train. Her mangled body was carried on the cow-catcher all the way to the next station.

"Thirdly is the cemetery at St Mark's. It used to be the town church. Now it's a private residence, owned by the church, occupied by the former pastor, Elijah Dwyer. His father was also a pastor of the church. He lives there with his granddaughter, Olivia. They are very rarely seen outside of the church grounds. People have claimed to see ghosts of children running through the graveyard. One of them is supposedly Elijah's brother, who died when he was twelve, playing with a friend on a pile of sleepers."

"How does a twelve-year-old die playing on a pile of sleepers?" Lucas asked.

"Apparently the pile collapsed on him and his friend, crushing them both."

"Do ya know if the girls actually went out ghost-hunting?"

"I assume so, but they were in the bar when I last saw them."

"What about the Saturday? Did ya see them that day at all?"

"No, but they were in the bar again Saturday night. Garry had to stop serving them. They got a bit narky. He's working tonight if you want to ask him the details. He starts at 7. I'd hate to give you information that was wrong or misleading," Isabella replied.

"I'll catch up with him later then. Oh, do ya have a radio that was the same as the one that ended up in Gemma's bathtub? I want to run some tests."

"The police have done all those tests, hun. You'd be wasting your time."

"Yeah, well. I'm employed to run my own investigation, not just concur with the police findings." He could see she was put out by his comments, but he stood firm.

"I could borrow one from another room for you," Isabella offered.

"I'm pretty sure I'll end up with the same results as the police, but at least I'll be able to tell Gemma's mother I tested every theory." He tried to soften the blow. He realised he might need more information and there was no point getting her offside unnecessarily.

"What theory is that?" Isabella asked.

"She had the radio on too loud and it vibrated off the edge into the bath."

"That's what the police think happened too."

"Speaking of police, who is it best to speak to about the deaths?"

"They were both handled by Inspector Mike Connolly, except he's stationed in Thirlmere, which is just south of Picton. I used to have his card, but I think I chucked it out about a year ago. I didn't think I would need it again."

"That's okay, I'll track him down."

It was too late in the day to speak with Connolly. He'd save that task for first thing in the morning.

It was probably best to get his bearings around town, then come back and grab some grub and speak with Garry in the pub, before going ghost-hunting.

He stepped out into the December heat. He could almost see the heat smouldering off the tarmac of the carpark. He noticed a black Mercedes packed two spaces over from his Mazda.

No wonder the girl checking in had been excited; her man had money and looks.

Chapter 19

Picton January 1916

Pastor Joseph Dwyer, upon returning to the church after grocery shopping, found Sergeant Lee waiting.

"Sergeant, what do I owe the pleasure on this fine morning?" he asked.

"Unfortunately, it's not pleasure. It's business, Pastor," Lee replied.

Dwyer's smile faded. "Please come in."

The St Mark's Protestant Church was unlocked, as always; people in this town were good, honest folk.

Pastor Dwyer held the heavy wooden arched door open for the sergeant and then followed him inside.

It was only a small church. It would seat about seventy-five people, with standing room at the back for another twenty-five.

"What is this about then, Sergeant?" Pastor Dwyer asked.

He had taken a seat on the altar step, so he was facing Sergeant Lee who was sitting in the first pew.

"I was hoping to speak with Pastor Philip."

"Unfortunately, he has gone to Sydney for some tests."

"Oh, I knew he had been unwell, but I didn't realise he was that sick; please pass on our prayers."

"I'll pass them on, thank you. Is there something I can help you with?"

"Do you recognise this?" The sergeant extended his hand, showing the pastor a silver cross in his palm.

The pastor took it and rubbed his thumb down it from top to bottom, before flipping it over to look for the church's inscription.

'ST. MARKS' was engraved on the back.

"Yes, that's one of the church crosses," Pastor Dwyer replied, handing him back the cross. "Do you mind if I ask where you found it?"

"At a murder scene, I am afraid."

"Not Ruth Martin?" Pastor Dwyer cringed.

"I am afraid so… How did you know?" Sergeant Lee asked.

"A few weeks ago, after Stanley's death, one of your men brought her here. She was scared someone was after her, so I gave her the cross."

"Did she say who that might be?" Lee questioned.

"She told me he was a drifter who had been following both her and Stanley. She said he wore a wide-brimmed hat and a long coat and that he called himself 'Scat,'" Pastor Dwyer replied.

"What type of name is Scat?" Sergeant Lee joked, beginning to chuckle.

"It means devil," Pastor Dwyer replied, instantly silencing the sergeant's chuckles.

"Why would someone call themselves that?"

"Maybe he is a man with mental issues, maybe he is a devil-worshipper, who knows?" Pastor Dwyer replied.

"Well, we caught him," Sergeant Lee said.

"What do you mean, you caught him? I thought Stanley killed himself…"

"Stanley did kill himself, but maybe the drifter followed Stanley to find out more about Ruth. I mean, we found Ruth's killer. He worked at the same hospital where she worked."

"Are you sure it was him?"

"Evidence suggests it was. Ultimately, it will be for a jury to decide. Thanks for your help, Pastor. I needed to confirm this cross was Ruth's before the trial. Her parents couldn't identify the necklace as hers, but if you say you gave it to her, your word is good enough for me."

Chapter 20

December 2016

The temperature was in the mid-30s and despite the strong northerly wind, the heat was becoming unbearable. Lucas's shirt was damp down the centre of his back and under his armpits.

He was standing out the front of the church grounds. The church had been fenced off from the cemetery and a 'Trespassers will be Prosecuted' sign hung on the church side. Lucas ignored the sign and headed into the church.

A gust swept across the graveyard, taking the loose leaves and twigs with it. Lucas made his way on to the slate stepping-stones leading to the church doors. The wooden arched doors were closed. He turned the old black wrought-iron handle to the right and pushed. The door was unlocked, but heavy. It opened inwards, revealing a small standing area at the back of the church. Straight in front of him, about twelve rows deep, was the altar.

The altar was on two levels. On the first lower step were candles and candelabras. The second held the podium.

The church was empty; not a soul around.

"Can't you read? This is a private residence. It's no longer a church," a voice uttered from the rear of the stage.

"I just wanted to ask the father a few questions," Lucas replied.

"The father, as you call him, is long gone, I'm afraid," the old man replied, coming into view. Lucas guessed him to be in his early to mid-eighties.

"I want to ask him about some ghost sightings. Do ya know anythink about that?"

"I am not a tourist guide, so please leave."

Lucas thought about pushing the issue further, but he had other leads to follow before he began causing trouble around town. "Sorry." Lucas raised his hand, as if to say, 'my fault', and headed for the heavy timber door.

By the time he had made his way out of the church gate he could see there were people in the graveyard. Normally he wouldn't have noticed mourners, but these weren't normal mourners. They were tourists looking for ghosts.

It would have only been just after 5 pm but they were out getting their photos before dark. Lucas assumed they would be taking more during their night ghost tour, but these were the before shots so to speak, before the town became scary, or spooky or whatever it became at night.

Lucas assumed it would be like every other town at night and just become dark.

He approached the three chattering women taking photos of the old gravestones.

"Excuse me?"

"Hi," the youngest of the three women replied.

"Do you mind If I ask why you're taking photos of a graveyard?"

"We're hoping to capture the ghosts of the children playing," she said, smiling. "I'm Ellie."

Lucas hadn't intended to chat up Ellie, but she seemed to find any conversation flirty.

"Lucas," he replied, offering his hand. "I hadn't heard of the ghost children in the graveyard. I have heard of the nurse at the Intercontinental and the lady in the Redbank Range Tunnel, but nothink about any children."

"Oh, you're staying at the Intercontinental?" Ellie said, smiling.

Lucas didn't reply. He just smiled back.

"Legend has it that three children were killed when a pile of sleepers collapsed, crushing them. Apparently, two of them, a boy and a girl, have been photographed running through the graveyard, hand in hand," Ellie offered.

Her friends had moved deeper into the graveyard without her. "I'd better go; are you going on the tour tonight?" she asked, stepping away from him slowly.

"No. No tour for me, although I'll probably see ya at some of the sights," Lucas replied.

"Well, maybe I'll catch you in the bar at the hotel later tonight. I'm sure that's where we'll end up," Ellie replied, smiling again.

"Sure."

He stood and watched her run a little to catch up to her friends. She turned once to see if he was still there, and grinned when she saw he was. He supposed that meant something. At least it had when he was last dating.

He guessed Ellie was in her early thirties. That's how old Tara, his wife, was when the cancer finally took her life. He hadn't even thought of dating anyone else since. As far as he was concerned, his love life had died along with the love of his life.

As much as Lucas enjoyed a little flirting, he would never have considered anything physical. He still considered it as cheating.

He may not have been the best husband in the world, worked too much, maybe neglected his wife too often, but one thing he had been in his marriage was faithful.

Every time he thought of Tara, the image that came to his head was her at her absolute worst. It was just hours before she'd lost her painful year-long battle with the big C. Her face was pale and drawn, her eyes dark and hollow, her breath shallow. She looked as if she was at death's door. She was. Yet it was this memory that stuck with him the most. Maybe because it was the last time she told him she loved him. While he could clearly see her ruined cancer-riddled body, he could just as clearly remember her sweet soft voice, and the last words she spoke. 'I love you.'

These words replayed many times in his head as he walked out of the graveyard.

He didn't have time to go to the Redbank Range Tunnel before dinner. He would just have to see it at its scariest in the dark. He needed to test his radio theory before he went out tonight. He needed to know if this had been just an accident or someone wanting to make it look like one.

Lucas was extra hungry. Maybe skipping lunch had something to do with it.

He headed back to the hotel for an early dinner.

As he pulled away from the kerb, he could see the three ladies of Ellie's party taking a selfie in front of the St Mark's sign.

Everyone was taking selfies these days.

Chapter 21

Picton December 2016

When Lucas arrived back at the hotel, Isabella was still at the desk. Lucas wondered if she ever left.

"I have that radio for you," she said as he came through the door.

She held it out in her hand for him.

"Do you mind holding it for me? I'm going to grab some dinner first," Lucas said.

"Sure, no problem," she replied. "I'll be here. Just collect it when you're ready."

He turned and headed to the bistro on the right.

At just before 6, the place was almost empty. The only other people there were two elderly couples, one at each end of the bistro. Here for the 'early bird specials', he thought. I must be getting old, eating dinner at this time of day.

Lucas did not go out much since his wife's death, as he hated sitting at a table by himself, being judged by all the other couples, not to mention the restaurant staff themselves. They were the worst. They treated him as if he had the plague.

He preferred just to eat at home and while he couldn't cook, he could heat a frozen meal in the microwave. Macaroni and cheese was his favourite and for the times he required something a little more substantial, he could always dial a pizza.

He sat down at the bistro, flicked through the three-page menu and while there wasn't a lot of choice there were some classic dishes: roast of the day, bangers and mash, steak. Lucas ordered a steak, chips and salad. He hadn't eaten a steak in months.

While he waited for his meal to arrive, he headed up to the bar for a drink.

"You Garry?" he asked, ordering his Coke.

"No, I'm Ben. Garry comes in after 7. Does the rush hour with me, then takes over the evening shift," Ben replied.

Lucas turned looked again at the two old couples in the restaurant and wondered about the rush hour.

"Rush hour?"

"It gets crazy busy in here between 7 and 8. We're booked solid every weekend," Ben replied.

"I'll come back after 8 then. Thanks for ya help," Lucas said.

Lucas tried to eat the steak slowly to savour the taste, but he was so hungry, he ended up scoffing it down, every last skerrick of it. He only took a break mid-meal to grab a second Coke from the bar. The food was good. Maybe the place would get busy.

Lucas wiped his mouth and waved at Ben as he left the bistro. Ben waved back, holding a white towel in his hand.

"I'll take that radio now, if it's okay?" he asked Isabella.

She reached down under her desk without replying and lifted it onto the counter.

"Where's the radio's normal home?" Lucas asked.

"Usually they're on one of the bedside tables."

"When you found Gemma, was the bed made or unmade?"

"Ohh…" Isabella stood for a while, rapping her fingers on the desk. "You know, I honestly can't remember."

"It's okay. I'll ask the detective tomorrow."

He collected the radio from the desk and headed upstairs.

From the moment he stepped into his room he could hear his neighbours and clearly, they were enjoying themselves. Lucas suspected they had been in bed all afternoon.

He plugged the radio in and switched it on and sat it as close to the edge of the bathroom vanity as possible, without it toppling over.

He removed the towels from the rail and placed them in the bath to ensure the bath was dry. He knew water and electricity didn't mix. He folded the towel to provide a cushion for the radio. He didn't want to damage the bath or the radio itself if it happened to fall into the bath. He doubted it would happen.

Lucas turned up the music, drowning out the screams and moans of next door. The radio blared. It was set on some local pop station that played a variety of music; some new, some old.

By the third song, the radio was vibrating on the counter, but not enough to send it off the bench and into the tub.

He hung the cord over the edge, switched off the radio and hopped into the bath. He lifted one leg out of the bath and dangled it over the edge. He then swung his leg to see if accidentally, it would catch the cord. It did. He pulled, the radio fell, but not into the tub. It fell between the vanity and the tub.

Lucas set it up again, with the same result. He tried the leg experiment a further twenty-seven times, before the radio hit the side of the tub and bounced in. So, it was possible; unlikely, but possible.

The more likely option was someone had purposely pushed the radio into the tub and then left.

He would find out more once he had spoken with Inspector Connolly. The crime scene photos would reveal a lot. He doubted they had investigated it in any detail. If it looked like suicide and there were no other suspicious lines of enquiry, that was usually the conclusion.

Lucas lifted himself from the tub and turned down the radio. He was surprised when he couldn't hear his neighbours.

Lucas decided to give Jake a quick call with his preliminary findings.

The number rang only three times before Jake answered.

"How is it going up there?" Jake asked.

"It's a pretty quiet town. Not a lot going on, that's for sure. I just wanted to tell ya I tested the electrocution theory. It's pretty unlikely," Lucas replied.

Lucas described to Jake how he had tested the radio, volume up, leg out, twenty-seven times. He went through how he had to hook his leg in the cord.

"So, it's possible," Jake said.

"But not likely," Lucas said. "I'll know more once I've seen the actual crime scene photos, tomorrow."

"Let me know your thoughts once you have," came the reply.

"Oh, before I go, I thought of somethink today," Lucas said.

"What's that?" Jake asked.

"I thought, how come we don't have any photos of before the girls' car accident from their first visit?"

"I don't follow. It was all on Facebook," Jake replied.

"Exactly. We got what was posted on Facebook from Paige's phone, but there was zip posted from Gemma's phone. It's as if she didn't take any pics. I just find it strange, that's all, but maybe it's nothink," Lucas said.

"I'll have a look into it," Jake said.

Jake knew Lucas was right. There were photos missing. How had he not thought of it sooner?

"No problem. I'll call ya when I know more. Probably tomorrow arvo sometime," Lucas said.

"Thanks; speak to you then," Jake said robotically, still thinking about the photos.

Lucas knew it would be a long night. A quick catnap now before he caught up with Garry would be a great idea. At first, he thought he'd have trouble falling asleep by 7 pm but after a long day, waking up was the hard part. He ended up sleeping until 8.30 after hitting the snooze button three times. Finally, the noise of his neighbours woke him.

He swapped his suit jacket for his suede one and headed out to see Garry.

*

Melbourne December 2016

When Jake hung up the phone, Hayley was sitting at the table feeding Indiana some goo from a jar.

"Nmmmm."

"Nmmmm," Hayley repeated as she tried to feed her.

Indiana just babbled. So far, her only words were 'mum-mum' and 'da-da'.

"Everything okay?" Hayley asked Jake.

"Yeah, yeah. It's fine. Just thinking about a case is all. Do you mind if I go do some work for a few minutes?"

"Sure, that's fine. We're finished here anyway. I'll put her down, then our stew should be ready."

"Meet you back here in half an hour then?" Jake joked.

"It's a date," she replied, giggling.

Jake made his way down the hall to the study.

After the slayings case, Jake and Hayley had decided it was best to start again somewhere fresh, together. Hayley didn't really care about the location as long as they were together.

Jake had thought a little more practically, including about their travel time to work. In the end they'd settled on a two-storey townhouse in the Docklands. It was quiet, charming, overlooking the dock, and just a short distance from Etihad Stadium and the city itself.

Jake's study was smaller than he was used to, but it was still practical and functional. Jake took Gemma's phone out of the plastic bag of things Karen had given him. He pulled out the phone. It was an iPhone 5c, the newest model when it had been purchased back in 2014.

Jake clicked on the photos icon. Several folders appeared, with different titles. One was favourites, one titled 'selfies', one 'places' and one, 'my photos'.

He looked through the photos, then began to search backwards. The first photo he found was dated 11 July 2014, a week after the accident that killed Paige.

Jake checked the phone settings. He wanted to see if Lucas's missing photo theory was correct.

He thumbed through the settings.

He then hit the mobile setting, and pressed on the arrow. He looked at the current period; thirty-eight days.

It only had photos from the 11th of July. Gemma had been released from hospital after the accident on the 9th, so Lucas was correct. There was a gap between Gemma's last Facebook post and the new phone. Two young girls would definitely take photos when they went on a ghost tour.

He would have to wait until tomorrow to find out for sure, but he was certain there was an earlier phone of Gemma's still missing.

*

Picton December 2016

Lucas couldn't believe the change in the bistro. It had gone from almost deserted to full within the space of a couple of hours. It was the good food, Lucas thought, but it was not exceptional. Maybe everywhere else was just poor by comparison.

He could see Garry behind the bar from the entrance. He stood out like a sore thumb standing next to Ben.

Garry was in his late fifties, short and fat with grey hair. His arms hardly reached past his belly, and Lucas wondered how he reached the bottles on the high shelves.

Nevertheless, Lucas could see why the hotel employed him. He moved quickly, was always smiling and seemed to be able to joke with the customers easily.

Lucas bustled his way through the queue to the order line. The noise was incredible. It seemed to bounce off the walls and reverberate around the room.

"What can I get you?" Garry asked him, just before he had taken his seat at the bar. Lucas had snared one that had just been vacated.

"Coke please," Lucas replied.

"Sure, no problem," Garry said without hesitation.

"I wanted to ask ya a few questions. Isabella suggested you would be the best person to speak to," Lucas said.

"Sure, what can I help you with?"

Lucas removed the photo of Gemma and Paige from his pocket. "The girl on the right died in a car accident, and the girl on the—"

"I know what happened. I told the police everything I know," Garry interrupted.

"It's been a few years. I wasn't sure you'd remember."

"I'll never forget. I volunteer for the State Emergency Service, and I got the call to come cut her out of her mangled car," Garry replied.

Lucas couldn't imagine him being able to do any physical work.

"I'm sorry. Do you mind if I ask you a few questions about the accident?"

"Shoot, but make it quick."

"Had they been drinking?"

"They'd both been in here on the Saturday night, and neither was fit to drive," Garry replied.

"How did they appear to ya, were they happy, having a good time?"

"The one that died in the car accident seemed a lot happier than the other girl. She was drinking and dancing a lot more than the other girl, seemed keener to go on the ghost tour. The taller redhead just seemed like she didn't want to be here."

"So, they said they were going on a ghost tour?" Lucas asked.

"The shorter girl was really excited, wanted to know the best places to go to see a ghost. I thought they were going on one of those guided buses. Had I known they were planning on driving, I would have called the cops," Garry said.

"So where did you suggest they go to see a ghost?"

"I didn't. I've lived here for fifty-three years and I've never seen anything. Hocus pocus if you ask me, so I suggested they speak to the Brown brothers, Dave and Anthony. They claim to have seen several. Between you and me, I think they use it as a pick-up tactic." Garry shrugged.

"Where would I find these brothers?" Lucas asked.

"You might be in luck," Garry said as he stepped back and looked into the dining area. "There they are, far table. They usually come to the bar after dinner, so if you want to wait here I'll introduce you when one of them comes up next. The big one is Dave. He's a little slow, but the older, smaller brother, Anthony, he's switched on."

"One more quick question. Gemma, the one who survived the accident, claimed to police that a man had tampered with their car while they were in the Redbank Range Tunnel. When you arrived at the scene, did you notice if the car had been tampered with?"

"Mate, I could hardly tell it was a car. It was wrapped around a telephone pole. It looked like an old crushed can. How that Gemma girl lived was a miracle in itself," Garry replied.

"Oh, I see. Thanks for your time." Lucas spun on the bar stool and looked over the sea of people.

It took him only seconds to spot the Brown brothers. They were both big; the shorter one would have been six-five and the other six-seven. Both were dressed in shirt and jeans. The taller one, who had lighter brown hair, was wearing a striped shirt and the shorter one's was checked. They both looked like farmers, big and muscular, with tough leathery skin from many hours spent in the sun. Their hands were rough from all the manual labour.

That was just Lucas's assessment from afar. He always liked to test himself as to how close he could profile someone from their looks.

The brothers were still eating.

He ordered another Coke and again turned to watch the hordes of people scoffing their food. He saw the table with the laughing ladies; the one to the far right was Ellie. She looked up at him with a mouthful of salad, smiled, and blushed a little too.

Lucas returned a smile and then looked away. He didn't want to come across as some creepy stalker. He thought of buying their table drinks, but he wasn't sure, so he didn't. He didn't want to start something he wasn't ready for.

He turned back towards the bar, taking another sip of his drink.

Garry was at the other end of the bar serving the young couple from the room next door. They still appeared to be all over each other.

It's going to be a night of little sleep, he thought.

After about twenty minutes, the shorter brother approached the bar to buy a jug of beer. Lucas could see him talking to Garry, and Garry pointing in his direction.

The brother approached Lucas.

"I hear you're asking about the girls who died here a couple of years ago?" he said.

"Yeah, I'm Lucas."

"Anthony," the man replied.

"Garry told me you and your brother were with the girls that night?"

"We were drinking with them here. Paige, the one that died that night, was asking us about the best place to see a ghost. Where is the scariest place? That's what she wanted to know. We told them about the Redbank Range Tunnel, the cemetery and of course this place."

"Had they had a lot to drink?" Lucas asked.

"They were drunk. I was shocked when I heard that she had driven that night. Especially on P plates." Anthony shook his head.

"You didn't go with them?"

"No, my brother likes to drink too much."

"After the accident, Gemma claimed someone had been tampering with the car and thought it could have caused the accident. Do you know anything about that?" Lucas asked.

"Are you accusing me of tampering with their car?"

"No, no, don't misunderstand me, I meant to ask ya if you had heard of that happening around town." Lucas hastened to calm the situation.

Anthony looked at him without expression, and then seemed to make up his mind. "What I'm about to tell you is off the record, doesn't get repeated, understand?"

Lucas nodded, more than a little curious at what he was about to say.

"This town has a lot of secrets, a lot of ghosts and a lot of demons. Maybe it was Hat Man. He's been killing people in Picton for the last hundred years," Anthony said.

Lucas hadn't read anything on the internet about anyone called 'Hat Man'.

"What do you mean…a hundred years? How's that possible?"

"Some think Hat Man is a creature, a monster, some sort of demon summoned to earth from hell itself. According to town legend, a group of

100

young people did a séance to speak to one of their mothers who had passed. It opened the door. All three died in unusual circumstances. Many other townspeople have died in unusual circumstances over the years, and some think that the Hat Man was responsible. Apparently, he lives in the shadows, or he is the shadows. The town doesn't publicise it because if it gets out, the tourists won't come and our town dies. They promote the ghost sightings…just not the cause of the ghosts." Anthony sounded serious.

"Do ya think Paige was a victim of this Hat Man?" Lucas asked.

"No, she was just drunk, and they shouldn't have been driving. Maybe she was a little freaked out from the Redbank Range Tunnel and, well, when you're panicked and half drunk, accidents happen." Anthony shrugged.

"What about Gemma when she returned in August? Did the Hat Man have anything to do with her death?" Lucas asked.

"I can't say for sure it wasn't, but I don't think so. The last time I saw her she was depressed about her dad. I don't even know why Paige brought her here. It's not like this is the place to bring someone to cheer them up. I would have thought the Gold Coast would have been a better choice."

"So, you didn't see her when she returned in August."

"I didn't even know she was in town."

Lucas had never heard such a bizarre story in all his life. A summoned demon, killing people? It went against everything he believed. There was always a logical conclusion to every death. Demons had never been one of them. He was sure Anthony was having a lend of him.

"Before you go, Anthony, what do you and your brother do?" Lucas asked.

"We run our dad's farm. He retired five years ago, so we've taken it over."

"Cattle?"

"Mostly cattle and sheep, and a few crops."

"Thanks for ya time, much appreciated."

"No problem, if you need anything else, just ask."

Anthony took his jug of beer and headed back to the table to his brother. He was more muscular up close than Lucas expected; not only was he tall but he was very solid.

Chapter 22

Picton December 2016

Lucas sat in his car outside St Mark's cemetery, window down, cool night breeze on his face. It was nearing 11 pm and a busload of tourists had just arrived. Surprisingly, they were mostly women of all ages; girls with small bottles of bubbly, and older women with their Stephen King books in hand, their glasses hanging around their necks, all chattering away.

A middle-aged, curly-haired, plumpish woman stepped off the bus and clapped her hands.

"Hi everyone. I'm Megan Lupia, your spirit guide for tonight. To have the best chance of an interaction with a spirit, it's important to remain quiet and move slowly through the cemetery and stay together, so I can tell you about significant historical events."

She led them in. The chatter continued but at a much lower level.

Everyone joined the group, except for one girl in her late twenties, petite, wearing glasses and kind of cute, in a dorky sort of way. She stayed behind them, busy taking notes, scribbling fast in something that could only be shorthand. A writer, Lucas suspected immediately.

Lucas followed them in, even though he wasn't part of the group.

"Who do ya work for?" Lucas asked quietly, coming up beside her.

"*The Australian*," the lady replied.

"What's your piece about?"

"All the unusual deaths that have occurred in this town over the last fifteen years."

"What do ya mean?"

"There have been nine women who have died in unusual circumstances in that time. All of them were from out of town. All of them came here for ghost tours." She swapped her notepad for her camera as she spoke.

"I'm here investigating the death of Gemma Bassil," Lucas told her.

"She's just one of the nine," was the response.

"What do ya mean—died in unusual circumstances?" Lucas continued.

"Well, three either fell or hung themselves from the Redbank Range Tunnel bridge, and one hung herself from the hotel roof. Police claim they were all suicides." She used her fingers to indicate quotation marks around the word 'suicides'. "Then there was Gemma's 'suicide'. There were even two girls who drowned in Stonequarry Creek that runs at the bottom of the railway bridge, and both deaths were ruled accidental. One apparently tried to save the other and drowned trying."

Lucas wondered if she had heard the rumour about Hat Man. He was close to telling her what he had heard but thought it best to wait until he had a better understanding of what was going on here.

"You know, on top of those nine," she added, "are four women who just disappeared. Came here on ghost tours. Vanished off the face of the earth."

How had he not known this? Lucas wondered. How had it not come up? Had he been too focused on his case and not seen the bigger picture?

"Have you got a card?" Lucas requested.

She took a card from the plastic sleeve at the back of her pocket book. She flipped it over and wrote a number on the back. "This is my room number. For some reason, cell phone service is really patchy in this town. If you get any information you think might help me solve some of these riddles, it would be great."

"I'll call you if I come up with anythink," Lucas replied, handing her his card.

"Nice to meet you, Lucas," she said, looking at the name on the card.

Lucas just replied with, "The pleasure is mine." He hadn't yet looked at her card.

"Are you two going to join us?" said someone at the front in a quiet but firm voice. Lucas and the journalist hurried to join the group.

"Now, on the path just beyond those two large headstones is where people have seen the ghosts of two young teenagers who were killed playing on the railway sleepers. They were crushed to death when the sleepers fell on them. Some wonder why they haunt the graveyard when they were killed on the train line. Well, it's believed this is because one of the boys killed that day was Thomas Dwyer, brother of Pastor Elijah Dwyer and son of Pastor Joseph Dwyer.

"Elijah Dwyer still lives in the church today, with his granddaughter," Megan said, pointing to the church behind the neighbouring fence.

"Now, if you don't see anything, don't get disappointed because many people will take photos and then later on when they look at them you may see the kids in the background," she said, as she moved through the tombstones.

Members of the tour group were all taking photos, not only of the graveyard but of the church next door.

Lucas walked back to the car.

His head was racing. How had he not picked up on the four missing girls, the nine unusual deaths? He couldn't understand. Once a death was ruled an accident or a suicide, it was case closed. But the missing girls…how had they not shown up when he'd Googled Picton?

Maybe they weren't known to be missing here.

Maybe they weren't known to be missing at all. Maybe they were backpackers, and they had been reported missing but just not from here. Possible, he thought.

He needed to talk to the reporter more. He flipped her card over, 'Talia Baxter Investigative Reporter', it read.

She was following something, and it had led her here.

The tour bus took off, leaving a cloud of smoke behind it, heading south through town. The streets were all but deserted.

Lucas watched, ready to follow. He placed the card inside his wallet before starting his car. It was facing north, and he needed to double back. As he turned the car around, his lights flooded the graveyard. He flicked the gears into reverse and looked up out of habit, and there they were, where she said they would be: playing, running, chasing each other, like kids do, except they were dead. He wound down his window, his car idled, but the wind carried their voices above the sound of his car.

They were both dressed in olden-day clothes, the girl in a dress and the boy in shorts and a shirt.

He could hear them laughing, as if they didn't have a care in the world, as if they were at peace.

They ran behind a large tombstone, one first, then the other and just like that, they were gone.

Vanished.

He looked to the right of the graveyard, and a face peered back at him. It was the pastor.

Had he been watching his brother play?

Lucas couldn't be sure.

That was his first encounter with a ghost. He feared it wouldn't be his last, before his time in Picton was up.

He headed south in pursuit of the tour bus. It shouldn't be too far ahead.

He came to the intersection of Menangle and Argyle Street. He looked south and saw the taillights of the bus disappearing around the bend. He punched the Mazda and caught up with it.

He followed the bus for a few minutes before it slowed and pulled off to the right, coming to a stop just inside a side street.

The street that had no name.

Where the street met Argyle Street, a sign read, 'Closed to the Public. Trespassers will be Prosecuted'.

Lucas pulled up behind the bus and watched the women disembark.

The tour guide would get upset when she realised he was piggy-backing on her tour.

"Megan?" he called from his car.

"Yes?" she replied, looking for the voice that had called her.

Lucas approached her and took her aside. "Sorry, I'm investigating a young lady's suicide and I asked my office to book in one of your tours while I was in town. Anyway, long story short, they didn't. Do ya mind if I tag along?" Lucas asked.

He gave her a hundred-dollar note. "For the inconvenience," Lucas offered.

"That's fine," Megan said, smiling, and took the note. "Just follow along." She turned towards the crowd of people huddling at the bus steps. "Okay, local council prohibits vehicles up this road, so we have to go on foot from here. Some people ignore it and drive, but I don't want to be shut down."

Lucas followed the tour group up the private road for about four minutes, until they arrived at a green gate set about a hundred metres in front of the tunnel.

It read 'No Pedestrian Access Permitted Through the Tunnel.'

The gate was only a metre high and did nothing to prevent people from entering the tunnel.

Why did they want to stop people from entering the tunnel? Lucas wanted to know. What was the big deal? Wasn't as if trains still used it.

Megan addressed the group in front of the sign. "This is the most evil place in Picton. The ghosts that haunt the tunnel have a dark, malevolent energy. Bad things have happened in there over the last one hundred years.

"Many people have gone through the tunnel and have experienced nothing. Others have gone through and seen a lady in a dress, running through a tunnel. Some have heard a train or felt a cold chill, or something brush past them." Megan paused and took a breath. "Yet others have seen the dark entity that they refer to as 'Hat Man'. I have not seen this entity myself, but I have had people on my tour come screaming out of that tunnel, who claim he was in there. So, pair up and we will do it one pair at a time. If we all go through at once you won't get anything out of the experience."

Talia Baxter approached Lucas, "Do you mind being my partner?" she asked, peering at him through her glasses.

"Not at all, but if you're hoping for a big strong man to protect you from evil spirits, then I think you're barking up the wrong tree. I might run out of there screaming before you," Lucas teased.

Talia laughed. "I'll keep ya safe," she replied, still giggling a little.

"I'd like that."

They waited their turn to head into the tunnel.

Other members of the group were coming out saying they could feel a presence. Some claimed to have felt something touch their legs or their arms. But no one claimed to have seen a ghost, let alone the legendary Hat Man.

Lucas and Talia stepped over the gate and headed into the tunnel. They passed two elderly ladies who had just emerged from the tunnel. Both shook their shoulders several times as if trying to shake off a chill. They passed Lucas and Talia fifteen metres from the entrance.

"How was it?" Talia asked.

"Really creepy," one replied, but kept walking.

"Sounds like we're in for a treat," Talia said.

This time Lucas was the one laughing.

When they arrived at the entrance they both stopped and looked. They couldn't see to the other end. It was just an abyss of darkness. Lucas and Talia switched their torches on and stepped into the tunnel. To the crowd watching it was if the tunnel had swallowed them, just like the couple before them, and the ones before that.

Lucas found the tunnel cold and eerie when he first entered, but the deeper they walked into it, the more the nature of the tunnel changed. It went from cold and eerie, to a heavy dark feeling, more of a presence.

Anthony's words came flooding back. 'Apparently, he lives in the shadows, or he is the shadow.' This tunnel is one big shadow, Lucas thought.

They continued to walk, the gravel crunching beneath their shoes.

At the midway point of the tunnel was an alcove. It was ten metres ahead, just on the perimeter of the torch glow. Lucas assumed the alcove had been built into the tunnel for pedestrians to duck into and avoid an oncoming train, but he couldn't be sure. It didn't seem like a very practical idea.

Without warning and for no reason, the temperature dropped significantly. It went from being a mild and pleasant summer's night to bitterly cold within a few steps.

"Are you cold all of a sudden?" Talia asked.

"Freezing," Lucas replied. He shone his torch on Talia's face. "Do ya want to keep going?"

"Yes," she replied in a low but excited whisper.

They continued into the tunnel, into the cold, into the shadows.

They arrived at the alcove. It was about a metre and a half deep and a metre and a half wide, enough for two people to step into when a train passed.

Lucas shone the torch ahead. Nothing, only more tunnel and darkness. He turned back towards Talia. She had her back to him, looking back the way they had come. He stood next to her.

"Do ya want to keep going?" Lucas asked again.

There was no response, so he lifted the torch beam to her face. It was frozen in a stare.

"Talia?" he asked.

"Do you see that?" she replied, hardly moving her mouth.

Lucas lifted his torch to shine down the direction they'd come.

She was walking towards them. She was young and dressed in olden-day clothes.

"Is that a ghost?" Lucas asked.

"It's the ghost of Anne Cornwell. She died in here," Talia whispered.

Lucas remembered reading about it, when he'd researched Picton.

"She was hit by the train," Talia said, her voice trembling.

A loud whistle blew, then the sound of an oncoming train filled the tunnel.

Anne appeared to be running, although she had no feet.

She was floating.

She came straight towards them.

Within a second, she went straight through them.

Lucas felt a shiver, as if his soul had just been stolen. Every hair on his body was standing up.

Anne disappeared into the tunnel.

Talia and Lucas both whipped around and looked into the alcove, but she was gone.

"Wow!" Talia said. "We saw her." She was excited.

Lucas's chest felt heavy pressure. The air had grown thick. He felt he was struggling to breathe.

His torch dimmed.

Something was wrong.

All his senses were screaming at him. Every instinct in his body was telling him to run, leave, get out. The messages to his brain were all the same and they were relentless.

But his feet wouldn't move.

Before he could get his feet moving, a tall dark shape appeared from the corner of the alcove.

Out of the shadows, Lucas thought.

Suddenly, it took the shape of a tall man, about six-seven, way bigger than Lucas, and his eyes were ablaze.

Lucas stumbled back, tripping over his own feet and falling to the gravel.

He heard Talia scream as he was on his way down.

He couldn't take his eyes off this thing, whatever it was. It came towards them. Talia turned and ran, stepping over Lucas on her way. As the shadow stepped out of the corner, Lucas could make out it was wearing a hat.

Hat Man, Lucas registered.

He gathered himself. Once he was on his feet, he sprinted to try to catch up to Talia.

"Keep running!" he called out to Talia.

Lucas glanced over his shoulder. The thing, the man, was still behind him and was closing in.

Lucas pushed himself faster, head forward, back straight, knees high, arms pumping. He was going as quickly as he could.

A black mass flew past and stopped in front of him, floating in mid-air.

Talia was ahead of it. She was almost out.

The thing hung there, floating, now more a dark cloud than a man. Suddenly the cloud formed again.

It was another man. Not the one with the hat. This one looked like how he imagined the devil himself would look. It had horns, eyes of fire, wisps of blue steam coming out of its nostrils, claws for hands, and it was skinny. Evil personified.

"Soon!" it screamed at him.

Its mouth opened up, releasing a swam of flies.

The swarm flew straight at him.

They were thick and black, noisy. It seemed there were millions of them. Lucas closed his eyes, covered his face and crouched down.

The sound stopped.

Then nothing but darkness. Lucas looked behind him and saw only his torch lying in the dirt.

For the second time in as many minutes, Lucas got up from the dusty gravel floor of the disused train tracks and headed towards the exit.

He would leave his torch where it lay. There was no way he was going back for it now.

He was never going into that tunnel again!

Chapter 23

Picton December 2016

Lucas emerged from the tunnel to find a pale and panicked Talia on her knees, trying to gather her breath. Megan was there beside her also trying to comfort her, as well as asking what had occurred. After all, it could mean big things for her business. If someone had sighted the mythical Hat Man, ghost-hunters from around the world would come to try and capture a glimpse.

"Are you all right?" Megan asked Lucas, not wanting to leave Talia.

"Yeah fine," he replied, although he was far from fine. He continued walking over to Talia who was trying to recover on a log. She seemed to be in shock. Lucas had seen it many times on the job, usually after a violent crime. The whole bus appeared to have gathered around her to get their fill.

"You got a blanket and water?" Lucas asked Megan.

Someone in the crowd came forward with them.

Lucas wrapped the old checked picnic blanket over Talia's shoulders and sat down next to her. He held the water bottle while she sipped it. Talia was still shaking but gradually settling down.

"So, what happened in there? She came out all frantic. I don't understand what happened," Megan said.

Lucas recounted the events of the tunnel, including Hat Man and his several transformations.

"So, you're a medium, what do you think?" Lucas asked Megan.

"To me it sounds like you met a demonic entity. Generally, they don't want to be disturbed and will do anything to protect their space," Megan replied. "I've only read about them," she added.

"I take it no one else is going into the tunnel?" Lucas asked.

"I think it's best if we cancel it for tonight," Megan agreed. "Would you two mind if we caught up tomorrow just so we can go through what happened? So I can document your experience?"

Lucas shrugged. "That's fine by me."

Talia just nodded in agreement. She was still in her own little world.

"How about we meet for a morning coffee?" Megan suggested.

"I can't do it till lunchtime. I have a meeting in the morning," Talia replied, without making eye contact.

"Lunch is fine. There's a nice coffee shop opposite the church. How about we meet there?"

Lucas agreed, and Talia nodded.

"Are you right to walk back to the bus?" Lucas asked.

Talia nodded again and stood up, holding the blanket tightly.

"Do you want to go back in the bus or would you like me to drop you at your hotel?" Lucas asked.

"Would you mind?" she muttered.

"Of course not."

They headed over the green gate and began the walk back to the car. Megan and her busload of ghost-hunters walked just ahead.

Lucas could hear the crowd chattering. Some of it was downright mean.

"Can't believe we didn't get to go in the tunnel," one of them said.

"Just because a pair of idiots get a bit scared," someone responded.

"Such a rip-off!" a third one added.

By the time they reached the car, they had heard several comments. Talia hadn't said anything, and Lucas wondered if she'd even heard them. He wedged the brochure that Megan had just given him between the passenger seat and the console.

"Where ya staying?" Lucas asked.

"Picton Inn. It's on Argyle, just after the creek." The firmness had returned to her voice. The shock was passing, Lucas thought.

He drove off and a short time later, they pulled into the circular driveway for hotel guest pick-ups and drop-offs.

"Thanks for your help," Talia offered.

"No problem. Are you going to be okay for your appointment tomorrow? Do you want me to take ya?"

"Thanks anyway, but I'll be fine. I just got a little shook up tonight is all." Talia gave him a small smile.

"Where ya going tomorrow anyway?" Lucas asked.

"They don't know I'm coming yet, but I know they'll be home and I want to ask them about some of the missing girls."

"Who is they?" Lucas asked, puzzled.

"Just a couple of locals. I don't want to say too much until I know more."

"Be careful, don't go walking into something."

"I've done this for years. I can handle myself."

Talia sounded confident but after what he'd seen tonight, Lucas wasn't so sure.

"I'll see you at the café, tomorrow," Talia said. "Thanks again," she called on her way into the hotel reception.

Lucas headed off north to his hotel. Finally, he could think over what he had seen tonight. It wasn't the most horrific sight he had seen. The Ling family murders still held that trophy, but it was only one of a few times he had feared for his life.

Generally, he was good at putting bad experiences to one side and moving forward, yet he feared this one would haunt him for some considerable time.

When Lucas walked into his hotel just after 1 am, reception was closed, while the bistro was finishing up. He could see the Brown brothers, standing at the bar talking to a couple of girls.

He gazed around the room looking for Ellie, although he didn't know why. Maybe he just wanted someone to talk to; maybe he wanted more. He decided it was a situation best left alone.

His room was dark and quiet. The neighbours were obviously asleep.

Lucas threw his keys on the bedside table and sat on the bed, attempting to gather his thoughts. Something was going on in this town, something evil, and he had no idea what to do. He looked in every dark corner of his room, expecting some creature to jump out and attack him. Nothing did. He flicked on the TV, something to break the quiet. He needed something funny, something that would take his mind off things, just until he could sleep.

The Exorcist was on the first channel he flicked to. He watched just a split second, but it was enough. The next channel was showing a comedy, an old one but a goodie, more for teenagers than for someone in his early forties, but still it was light, and it was fun.

He watched about ten minutes before he could feel himself drifting off to sleep. Suddenly he was woken by the sound of running water. He sat bolt upright in bed. The sound was clear; unmistakable. It was someone running a bath. He rolled off the bed and dived for his bag. Within seconds the Beretta butt was safely in his palm and his fear dropped a little. His clock read 4.11 and the TV was showing snow.

He approached the bathroom doorway, as he would enter a suspect's home, cautiously protecting his body, gun low, double-gripped and at the ready. He glanced inside the bathroom. No one was there…unless they were hiding in the shower. He entered the bathroom and looked into the bath. It was dry. Had he dreamt about someone filling a bath? Was it his subconscious acting out? Both were possible, but he doubted it. He had clearly heard running water.

Instantly the room went cold, just as he had experienced in the tunnel. Pressure began to build in his chest again. A shiver ran through his body. Lucas could have sworn that something passed behind him, but when he turned there was nothing there. He stepped one foot into the entrance. He could see both rooms without moving. He could see both rooms were empty. This was crazy!

Returning to the bathroom, he placed his Beretta on the vanity and ran some water. He needed to wake up and make and sure he wasn't dreaming this whole thing.

Cupping his hands, he scooped the water and splashed his face. The cool water felt delightful, refreshing. He felt better already. He caught sight of his refection in the vanity mirror.

His reflection sent him stumbling backwards, almost onto the toilet seat. His skin had gone all pale, ashen in fact, and his eyes had huge black rings around them, but worst of all what Lucas thought was fresh water running down his cheeks was in fact blood. It trickled from both his eyes.

He quickly rinsed his face again, splashing his eyes and cheeks several times. He watched the blood drip into the basin. He reached for the towel hanging on the nearby rack. He dried his face. He looked at the white towel expecting to see it soaked in blood. It was clean, like new.

Lucas took another look in the mirror. He was fine. He must be imagining these visions. The shock of the tunnel must have had more effect on him than he realised.

He needed to settle himself down and go back to sleep. His face was fine. He was fine. He just needed to get some sleep.

He went back to his bed, continually trying to tell himself that it was all in his mind; he had been through a traumatic experience. He switched the TV channel, wanting something to calm him. *The Exorcist* was still on, showing the same scene as before as if it had been paused all this time. How could that be?

He flicked again. *Anchor Man* was on, so he settled for that.

After an hour of TV, no sleep and no further visions or noises, Lucas decided to get up and do some research into those missing girls.

He switched every light in his room on and fired up his laptop. He searched for 'Missing Girls Picton'. Nothing came up.

He typed 'Thirlmere Missing Girls' into the Google search bar. Two girls' photos came up. Bree and Natalie had been backpacking from Melbourne to Queensland. They had reached Thirlmere before vanishing. He typed in 'Maldon Missing Girls'. Nothing came up. He tried 'Razorback Missing Girls'. One girl was reported missing. Eighteen-year-old Peta Reid had been driving north in her red Ford Laser (REX 780 was the plate). He would remember that plate. He'd had a dog called Rex once, a beautiful German Shepherd. She had been driving south along the Old Hume Highway just four days before Gemma and Paige's accident. Lucas knew the road well. It was, after all, the same road he used to get into town. He Googled other neighbouring towns but couldn't find any more missing girls.

By the time he had completed his Google searches, it was just after 6 am. Thinking he might try and get a couple of hours' sleep before breakfast, he flicked the TV over to the news and closed his eyes.

Chapter 24

Melbourne December 2016

Jake waited until after 8 before he rang her. He'd had very little sleep and needed some answers.

The phone rang four times before a drowsy Mrs Bassil answered. "Hello?"

"Mrs Bassil, it's Jake Miller here. Do you have a few minutes to talk?"

"Yes, sure Jake, what can I do for you?" Her voice was instantly more attentive.

"I need to know what you're not telling me," Jake said.

"I—I don't understand. Sorry," Mrs Bassil said.

"Mrs Bassil, if you want the truth about your daughter then I need to know everything."

"Jake, I seriously don't know what you're talking about. I have told you everything."

"No, you haven't. Let me start you off. Why did Gemma buy a new phone when she was released from hospital?"

"She lost her last one in the car accident and the police never returned it." Mrs Bassil sounded puzzled.

"Why didn't you tell me that?"

"I didn't think it was important." He could hear the shrug in her voice.

"Every detail, no matter how small, is important to me," Jake said firmly.

"Okay, sorry," Mrs Bassil offered.

"Now, tell me why the girls went there the first time. And don't tell me you don't know, Mrs Bassil!" he added before she had a chance to reply.

"They were going there to speak to her father." Mrs Bassil sounded reluctant.

"But he's dead," Jake said bluntly.

"Apparently there's a place in Picton where you can speak to the dead."

"What do you mean…a place?" Jake asked.

"Paige didn't say. Just that there was a place where you can communicate with the dead. She and Gemma went there so Gemma could say goodbye to her father. I don't know what this has to do with Gemma's death, honestly."

"It may have nothing, or it may have everything," Jake said. "After the accident did she say if they actually went to this place?"

"Yes, they had been there, and she had spoken to her father. She claimed they saw someone tampering with Paige's car, and then the accident happened."

"Did she tell you about the conversation with her father?"

"No. I didn't ask. I don't believe in that stuff, but I know she needed closure, so I didn't say anything to dissuade her," Mrs Bassil said.

"Mrs Bassil, whatever the reason Gemma went back to Picton may be related to why she died. At the moment, we're trying to figure out how Gemma died, and knowing why she was there in the first place is a big piece of that puzzle."

"I'm sorry, but I don't know anything else. I don't know why she went back."

"If you think of anything can you please let me know? No matter how small, okay?"

She agreed, and Jake hung up.

The phone rang instantly.

*

Picton December 2016

Jake answered the phone as if he had been sitting on it.

"Jake, it's Lucas."

"I have some news for you," Jake said.

"Me first," Lucas insisted. "I met a woman named Talia, an investigative reporter for *The Australian*. She said she was looking into the nine recent deaths in Picton that had either been ruled accidental or suicide, and also the four missing girls."

"What girls?" Jake asked.

"That's what I wondered, so I did some research into it. They all disappeared in nearby towns."

"Do you think that the nine deaths and the four missing girls are related?"

"I don't know. It's hard to make a murder look like suicide but it's possible. I don't know how jumping off a roof can be anything but suicide, for example," Lucas responded.

"Maybe they were pushed?"

"Possibly. I do think it's likely that the four missing girls are all related to the same case. It's too coincidental otherwise," Lucas said.

"Serial?" Jake asked.

"I'd say so. I should also tell you that there was an incident last night."

"What sort of incident?"

"Last night I swear I saw the devil."

It wasn't the bar fight incident that Jake had been expecting to hear about. "Go on."

"I went on a ghost tour to the Picton Redbank Range Tunnel and while I was in there with Talia, we saw the ghost of the girl who was hit by the train a hundred years ago, Anne Cornwell. Anyway, just after she vanished, this thing—black, tall, wearing a wide-brimmed hat, appeared from nowhere. Its eyes were red like fire. It reached for us, trying to grab us, and I tripped. Talia just ran for it. Meanwhile, this thing got in front of me, changed from a man to a devil creature, horns and all. Then without warning, it became a swarm of flies. Then it just vanished. Locals call him the Hat Man. Some say he's responsible for all the deaths around here."

"Yeah good one," Jake retorted, expecting Lucas to burst out laughing any second.

"Jake, I'm serious. That wasn't the end of it. When I got back to my room I was woken by someone running water in my bath. When I got up to look, there was nothink. I splashed my face with water trying to wake myself up a little. When I looked up, there was blood coming out my eyes, I looked like a dead man. This place, this town, it's haunted. In fact, I think it's evil," Lucas said.

Jake didn't know what to say. He had never heard such a bizarre story. "It's probably just your mind playing tricks on you. Maybe go stay somewhere else?" Jake suggested.

"I'll be okay," Lucas said. "So, what's your big news?"

After everything Jake had just heard, his news didn't seem so exciting any more.

"Oh, it's nothing really. I just wanted to tell you I spoke with Gemma's mum and found out why Gemma and Paige went up there. They were going, would you believe, to…well…speak to the dead."

"What?"

"Paige had heard of a place that made communication between the living and the dead possible. Don't ask me how, or where it is, but they went to communicate with Gemma's father. According to her mother they had been to this place just before they had the accident."

"But they crashed on leaving the tunnel."

"Maybe that's the place then."

"I'm not going back there. That place is pure fucking evil."

"She also said she met some boys there," Jake continued.

"I have spoken to the boys…men, rather, if you mean the Brown brothers. I met them in the pub. I don't think they went to the tunnel with them, but I'll look into it further."

"Also, Gemma is missing a phone. It's an iPhone 4. She lost it during the accident. The police never returned it and as far as I know it hasn't been recovered," Jake said.

"Okay…tunnel, Browns, phone."

"Are you sure you'll be okay up there?"

"Yeah, I'll be fine." Lucas replied. "Can you ring your cop friend about the missing girls? I've sent you an email with the details of the three I found."

"Sure."

"I'm having lunch with Talia, so I'll ring you when I'm done and let you know what I've found out."

"I'll try and have some answers for you by then," Jake replied.

"Thanks champ."

"Hey Lucas, with what you know, all the deaths, missing girls, haunted hotel, what does your gut tell you?" Jake asked.

"I think there's a killer in town. Who or what that is, I don't know yet, but I'll find out. One thing is for sure; I don't think it's the ghost I saw tonight."

*

It was only a few minutes' drive from his hotel to the town of Thirlmere, just under eight kilometres south of Picton.

Lucas hadn't made an appointment to see Inspector Connolly. That was the way he liked it. He got to see them answering on the fly and was more likely to get a more truthful result. He knew all cops weren't honest ones; he had seen that first hand.

He also knew from experience that a lot of country stations were grossly understaffed. Meaning, they didn't have the manpower to invest in a case where there appeared to be an obvious answer. So often the obvious answer was the answer they settled on. However, it was not always the correct one.

Lucas parked just across the road from the station, which was neither large nor modern, but more substantial than Lucas had expected.

Lucas made his way into police reception. The constable at the desk seemed put out by his request to see the inspector.

"Is he expecting you?" she asked.

"No."

"What's it regarding?" she asked in a huff.

"Gemma Bassil case," he said, showing his PI badge.

She buzzed through to a back room. "Sir, I have a private detective here to see you regarding the Gemma Bassil case; says he needs to speak with you." She listened intently for a few seconds. "Sure thing," she said and hung up. "Take a seat, he'll be with you in a minute."

Lucas looked around and sat on an old hard wooden bench against the far wall. It looked as if it had been donated by a church.

It was about twenty minutes before Inspector Connolly came bustling into the foyer and showed Lucas into his office. Inspector Connolly stood just on six feet, was thick-set, and had greying brown hair. On first impression his appearance was perfect, his uniform immaculate, but when the subject of Gemma came up his eyes started darting evasively.

Lucas needed to dig a little deeper.

"I need to see the case file on Gemma Bassil."

"We don't release police files," Inspector Connolly snapped. "Not without a court order."

"So, you won't provide me with any information?"

"No, we consider the case closed."

"What can you tell me about the seven other mysterious deaths in Picton?" Lucas asked, changing tack.

"There's nothing mysterious about them. I'll grant you, some were unusual, but the cases all came to logical conclusions."

"You don't find seven suicides over the last two years a lot for Picton?" Lucas questioned.

"I don't know where you're getting your information from, but out of the nine deaths, including Gemma and Paige, four were ruled suicide and five were ruled accidents."

"And what did you rule Gemma's?"

"It was suicide."

"What about the four missing girls, what information do you have on them?"

"Not enough; they're missing persons. We're following up all leads, but we've had very little to go on. No sightings. I have detectives working on every one of them," Connolly said.

"Ya don't think they're related?" Lucas asked.

"No; do you?"

"I think they're very similar, so it's possible," Lucas answered.

"I'm sure my detectives will make a connection, if there is one," Connolly said.

Lucas was getting stonewalled at every turn. He had to try a different approach.

"Look, I get where you're coming from. I used to be on the force. Nothing worse than when a relative keeps arguing with the outcome. Let me help you out here… Give me some information from the crime scene. Mrs Bassil won't stop hassling you if my investigation ends in an open finding."

Lucas had given him the old 'help me, help you' argument. Connolly was considering it. He had gone quiet, and was rocking back on his chair, fiddling with his pen as if it was helping him think.

"Giving me zip doesn't allow me to come to a conclusion," Lucas added, trying desperately to push him over the line.

"All right, I'll show you the file, full access to the photos and coroner's findings, on the condition that in your report to family, you acknowledge the assistance my office provided you with the investigation," Connolly instructed.

Lucas agreed, but if the information showed that Gemma's death had just been brushed over, he would have no trouble in detailing the police incompetence.

A few moments later, Connolly returned to his office with a full folder under his arm. On the tab read one word: 'Bassil'.

"Follow me into interview room one. You can take as long as you like to read through it. If you have any questions, well, you know where I am," Connolly said.

Lucas was surprised he had gone from no access, to full access, unsupervised.

He opened the file.

Everything looked to have been done professionally. This was not what Lucas was expecting at all. The death had been reported by hotel management. Isabella had been listed specifically as the person who'd called in. Her statement was attached.

She had entered the room as usual around noon to perform housekeeping duties, whereupon she found the deceased in the bath. She immediately called the police and ambulance.

Lucas looked at the photos. Gemma had a wash cloth over her face. Could that have been left there by the killer, a sign of remorse? Possibly, unlikely: more likely she was trying to relax in a hot bath.

Photos were taken of her feet and the radio that lay in the bottom of the tub. The photo clearly showed the cord of the radio caught under Gemma's heel.

It was as he'd tested previously. Maybe her leg had been out of the bath and when she'd pulled it back in, it had caught the cord of the radio and dragged the radio with it.

With her eyes covered by the face washer, she might not have known the immediate danger she was in.

There were no signs of force, no bruises, no trauma. She hadn't been raped. There was nothing to point to murder, that was for sure. Based on all the evidence Lucas had now seen, he would have deemed her death accidental.

How had they arrived at suicide?

He read through the attached reports.

The radio had been tested. It had been ruled the cause of the electrocution and had damage consistent with being submerged while active. They had even had the radio tested for DNA. Two sets were found, Gemma's and Isabella's. Isabella was questioned about her DNA being present and the answer supplied – that her DNA would be on every radio in every room as she did most of the housekeeping – was ruled reasonable, so she was removed as the one and only possible suspect.

The report then listed the items tested.

Made sense, Lucas thought. Every box had been ticked before Isabella had been ruled out.

The police had even documented a report from Gemma's psychologist which provided a list of medications and her current mental health state. 'Severely Depressed. On desipramine nortriptyline.' She had also been prescribed cyclobenzaprine for back pain since the car accident.

The toxicology report showed elevated levels of desipramine nortriptyline plus a large amount of alcohol, with blood alcohol concentration of.13.

She was seriously drunk, Lucas thought.

He read down further.

Finally, there was the medical examiner's report.

Lucas skipped to the conclusion.

'Due to the high level of prescription drugs and alcohol in the deceased's system, combined with the fact that it took a conscious effort to pull the radio into the bath, and the deceased's predetermined metal instability, death therefore more likely than not was a pre-planned suicide and not an accidental misadventure.'

Lucas closed the file. While he might have favoured accidental death over suicide, he could see how the ME had drawn his conclusion.

Really, only Gemma knew what her intent was.

Lucas leaned on the door of Connolly's office where he was talking on the phone. He noticed Lucas and indicated for him to wait a moment.

"What can I help you with?" Connolly asked after hanging up.

"I'm done. Thank you for your time. I just have one more question. It relates to the accident that killed Paige. Do you recall that car crash?"

"Yes, I know all about it. How does that relate to the suicide of Miss Bassil?" Connolly asked.

"I'm trying to track down a couple of journals and a phone that belonged to Gemma. I know the phone was lost during their first trip here."

"Everything we found was handed back to the next of kin after the accident."

"What happened to the car?" Lucas asked.

"From memory they didn't want to pay for it to be towed back to Melbourne, so I sent it to the wreckers. It was a write-off. No good to anyone. I doubt it would still be there. Compacted by now, I would suggest," Connolly added.

"I'll go check it out," Lucas said.

"The wreckers are on the way to Tahmoor, just off Old Gully Road."

Lucas thanked Connolly for his time again and decided to head out to the wreckers, hoping he would have time before his lunch appointment.

*

The road was dusty, poorly maintained and with the gravel build-up on the sides, it would be easy to skid off into a tree and not be discovered in this remote area for some time.

He snapped the thoughts of his crushed dying body out of his head and focused on the road ahead.

Glimmering, a mountain of metal rose out of the dust ahead. The wreckage yard was enormous; Lucas was heading into a sea of disused, mangled cars, trucks and buses.

A metal chain-link fence bordered the wreckage yard surrounded by neighbouring forest. The gates were open, so Lucas drove in and headed towards an old school portable that had been converted into the office.

The heat had picked up, as had the north wind, and the previously mild day was now unbearable.

The wind blew the dust up around his ankles and he had turn away to avoid getting grit in his eyes.

"Whatya looking for?" a man asked. He was a big guy wearing a blue singlet and matching shorts, clearly a country Aussie, Lucas thought.

"I'm looking for a car," Lucas said.

"We've got thousands of them, none working, but thousands of them." The man laughed.

"It's a particular car."

"Always is, a particular car, a particular part."

The desk was swamped in paperwork and invoice books. Behind him there were hooks holding orders. The office seemed very disorganised.

"It's a blue 2010 Ford Focus I'm after."

"Lots ten to fourteen," the man said.

"Ya have four lots of 2010 Fords?"

"No, I have fourteen lots of Fords but post 2000 are in ten to fourteen," he said. "Take what you need off the car and bring it back here to pay."

"I don't need any parts."

The man stopped shuffling papers and looked at him, somewhat confused. "What do you need then?" he asked.

"I'm looking for some belongings that were left in a car."

"Nothin' in the cars. They're clean when they come here."

"Do you mind if I go have a look?"

"Sure, knock yourself out." The man waved him out of his office. "Just be aware there are a lot of snakes and spiders out there, especially browns. They're all over the place out here; I often find them curled up in boots or under motors, etc."

Lucas acknowledged the proprietor's advice before leaving the shaded office for the heat.

A path was carved out between lots, nothing special, just gravel and dirt, but it was better than walking on the grass. There were wooden signs along the way for different lots. Lucas followed the directions to lot ten.

Every lot he passed was full of cars. Some were stacked on top of others. Some had been compacted by a machine he assumed was somewhere on site.

By the time Lucas arrived at lot ten, he was drenched in sweat. The back of his shirt was all wet.

There were blue Fords scattered over all four lots. Lucas wandered randomly from blue car to blue car, sometimes through the grass, being vigilant for snakes.

Some cars had the rego plates still intact, while others had none, which meant he might need to check the serial numbers. He was looking for a write-off.

He'd been in the yard for a bit over an hour before he located the car he was after. It was sitting in the far back corner near the post-and-wire fence. Lucas could see straightaway why it was a write-off; the front driver's side had been badly crushed.

Lucas guessed it had hit a big tree. Now he knew why Paige hadn't survived. No one would have.

Lucas climbed in from the passenger side. The rear door had already been removed. He opened the console. Inside was a scrap of paper, with the words 'Redbank Range Tunnel after midnight' written in pencil.

It confirmed he had the right vehicle.

The back seat and floor were empty. The glove box contained half a pack of Tic Tacs, a service manual and a can of So deodorant. Lucas sprayed a little on himself. It had a strong, enticing musk smell.

Lucas then knelt down beside the car. He slid the seat back and looked under it. The heat inside the car was intense.

Struggling to see under the seat, Lucas contorted his body to get a look, but it was futile, nothing there, no phone, no diaries. Lucas uncurled himself and stepped away from the car. Next, the boot, and apart from an old tartan picnic blanket and accompanying cane basket, it too was empty.

Only one more place to search; the driver's side. Being so badly crumpled it was tough to access. Lucas returned to the passenger side and slid across the back floor towards the driver's side. The nearer he got the narrower the floor became. The front seat was a buckled mess, and half of it had been cut. Lucas assumed this was the work of Fire and Rescue, trying to remove Paige from the car.

Defying the laws of physics, Lucas managed to wedge himself onto the passenger side floor. Under the front seat was a black rectangular object. It was the phone.

Lucas had to wiggle the phone out from under the front seat track, which was easier than he thought. By the time Lucas was out of the car he was covered in sweat, his shirt almost see-through, but he felt a sense of triumph.

It was an iPhone; what model he wasn't exactly sure. All he knew was it was one of the early ones, with the wide charger.

He held down the power key to see if it would power up. It remained lifeless. Hell, the thing might not even work now when charged.

He headed back to his car, and as he passed the office stopped in to offer the man $50 for the phone. Instead, he ended up parting with $100. Still, it was better than applying for a court order to claim the phone.

A hundred was the cheapest and easiest way out. Lucas wished he had just lied and said he hadn't found anything, but for some reason he couldn't lie; it just wasn't in his nature.

*

Lucas arrived back in town at 11.45 and although his shirt had dried on the drive back, he stopped in at the local chemist for some deodorant to freshen up. He looked for a phone charger, but they didn't sell them.

Arriving first at the café, he took the liberty of ordering himself a tea and a bottle of water. Walking around the junk yard had really dried him out.

He had finished his tea and almost half the water before Megan Lupia arrived and sat opposite him.

Lucas ordered her a coffee. A skinny latté to be exact.

"You look hot and bothered," she said.

"I've been out, gallivanting around."

"How did you sleep after the incident in the tunnel?" she asked.

"I had some bad dreams, or visions, I'm not sure which."

"Visions?"

"Well, I dreamt I heard the bath running, and then I thought I saw blood running out of my eyes when I looked in the mirror. Clearly none of that happened, so I guess it was a dream," Lucas said. "Let me ask you, can you communicate with the dead?"

"No, I'm not a medium like John Edwards. But I can feel their presence."

"Have you ever seen ghosts?" Lucas asked.

"I've seen ghosts here in town. At each place on my tour I've personally seen a ghost; that's why I started the tour," Megan said.

"Have you ever seen the thing Talia and I saw last night?"

"No, I haven't, although many on my tour have claimed to have seen a creature lurking in the tunnel. Up until now, none had reported it interacting with them."

It was 12.25 when Megan asked if Lucas had heard from Talia.

"No, I haven't. She had an appointment this morning apparently, that's all I know," Lucas said.

Megan pulled out her phone and called. There was no answer, so she left a message.

"The thing you saw in the tunnel last night; can you tell me more about it?" Megan asked.

"The more time that passes the less real it feels. I really don't know what I saw except it was some sort of man in a hat. It changed shape and tried to prevent us leaving that tunnel. It spoke, saying something that sounded like 'soon', but I can't be sure," Lucas said.

"I definitely think it was something demonic. I wish I'd been able to see it," Megan said.

"This thing you wouldn't ever want to see. It was evil. Whatever it is, it's best to keep away from it. I wouldn't be sending any more people into that tunnel," Lucas said.

"The tunnel is why they come, and as long as no one gets hurt, I'll keep taking them there."

"Try Talia again," Lucas suggested, unwilling to argue.

Megan did. This time she didn't bother to leave a message. "Voicemail again," she said.

"Well, without Talia, I don't know how much more I can add."

"Yes, it's a shame; I wonder what happened to her?" Megan questioned.

"Maybe call the hotel room to see if she's checked out?" Lucas suggested.

She called the Picton Inn. "Talia Baxter's room please."

The phone rang out before returning to reception.

"Has she checked out?" Megan asked.

"No, she left early this morning after breakfast, but I haven't seen her since," they said.

"So, you expect her to return?" Megan asked.

"Yes, she needs to check out."

Megan turned to Lucas. "They say she went out this morning and hasn't come back. Maybe she got caught up at the meeting."

"Maybe," Lucas replied. "Do ya know where I could get a charger for an iPhone? It's an old style one."

"Maybe try the electronics section at Kmart. Otherwise you need to go to Thirlmere. They have a Dick Smith store there."

Lucas stood up, paid for the drinks and offered to contact Megan as soon as he had made contact with Talia.

Megan said she would ring him if she heard from Talia first.

Lucas was lucky. He found a charger for Gemma's old phone at the local Kmart. The battery symbol came on, which was a good sign and as he waited for it to charge, he wondered if he would find any little piece of information that could be helpful.

The phone finally fired up.

Lucas was desperate to see the photos; the selfies and whatever else it contained. He was right; they had taken photos.

The first photo was taken at the pub. Paige was at the bar talking to the bigger of the two Brown brothers, Dave, if he recalled correctly.

The second photo was later in the evening based on the time stamp and it was a selfie, similar to the one he had watched Ellie take yesterday.

The third was of the green gate and the Redbank Range Tunnel.

The fourth and final photo showed their blue Ford in the background and over to the right appeared the front corner of a red truck; looked to be a Ford F100, possibly early 90s model, but he wasn't sure.

Lucas scrolled through the diary pages, but found nothing, no notes, no appointments. He clicked the Facebook app, but the page no longer existed.

Maybe someone had been tampering with Paige's car? Someone else had been there for sure. Maybe the red truck was significant?

Lucas took the business card he had been given by Talia and called her office number.

"I'm after Talia please," Lucas said.

"I'm sorry; she is out of the office at the moment. Would you like me to take a message for you?" the receptionist asked.

"I've called her mobile, but she hasn't returned my calls and I'm just wondering if you've heard from her?"

"Let me check." The phone went on to its usual hold music.

A few seconds later a male voice replaced the receptionist. "Can I help you?"

"I was waiting on the receptionist. She was trying to locate Talia."

"May I ask who I'm speaking with?"

Lucas gave his details.

"My name is Earl Johnson, I am Editor in Chief here at *The Australian*. We too are concerned about her whereabouts. She was in Picton, working on a story. She believed all the deaths and the missing girls in the area were connected. She hasn't checked in at all today."

"Is it unusual for her not to check in?"

"It's unheard of, especially when I leave a message," Earl replied.

"I take it then you're just as concerned for her safety as I am?"

"Extremely concerned. It's only been five hours, but she told me she was following up a lead that might connect everything. Did she tell you where she was going?" Earl asked.

"No, just that she had a lead to follow up. Tell you what, I'll ring the local inspector and see if he can help. I also know people in homicide. I'll get her phone traced—it might give us a location at least. What sort of car does she drive?"

"It's a silver Toyota Prius hatchback. I'll get you the rego number." Lucas heard the phone being placed on the desk.

A minute later Earl was back on the phone reeling off the rego number.

"In the meantime, if you hear from her, will you call me to let me know she's all right?" Lucas requested.

"Will do, thank you. Keep us updated," Earl replied.

Lucas hung up the phone and wrote down Earl's name next to the details of Talia's car on the pad provided.

Even though it had been only a few hours since contact, the fact that she hadn't spoken to her boss was concerning. Staying in touch with the office when you're an investigative journalist is of paramount importance, Lucas thought.

His gut told him something was terribly wrong, but common sense kept providing rational answers. Maybe her phone died? Maybe she hadn't got the messages because the phone service was so patchy out here. Or maybe her car broke down and she was stranded somewhere.

Then he remembered the nine unusual deaths and the four missing girls she was investigating, and his gut kicked in again.

Something was amiss. Lucas picked up the phone again and got on the line to Inspector Connolly.

The desk sergeant recognised him and put him straight through.

"Connolly."

"Inspector, it's Lucas Taylor," he said, sounding panicked.

"What can I help you with now?" the inspector answered in a tone that was less than helpful.

Hearing the frustration in his response, Lucas apologised before he began. "Sorry to bother you, but an investigative journalist has gone missing and I was wondering if you could keep an eye out for her."

"How long has she been missing?"

"Five hours," Lucas replied.

"Five hours is hardly missing. You know the drill. She has to be missing for twenty-four before I can even open a missing person's file. Give me a call back tomorrow," Connolly replied.

"Wait," Lucas begged. When he realised Connolly was still there, he began again. "I'm not asking you to open a missing person's case, I just think she might have broken down somewhere. If you could get your guys to keep an eye out it would be helpful." He passed on the details provided by Earl.

"Okay, we'll keep an eye out. Do you know where she was going?" Connolly asked.

"No, just that she was following up a lead on the missing girls. She believes their disappearances were linked."

"They are not linked. I've had staff working on them for years. Can't find anything that links them, except that they're all missing."

Lucas didn't want to start an argument about his policing methods, so he held his tongue. Connolly hung up, promising to call him as soon as he had any information.

Immediately, the hotel phone rang, startling Lucas. Calming himself, he answered the phone. "Hello?" He hoped it would be Earl, calling with good news.

"Lucas, it's Jake. I've done some research on the missing girls."

"What have you found?" Lucas asked.

"I've found a lot of angry parents who feel they're being dismissed by the police. It's as if they're not making any effort to look for these girls."

"Inspector Connolly just told me himself that the cases are not related."

"How can they get away with thinking that?"

"The police are claiming there is nothing to connect them," Lucas explained. Before Jake could reply, Lucas spoke again, blurting out, "I'm glad you called. The investigative journalist who told me about the missing girls has now gone missing herself."

"Talia? Seriously?"

"Seriously. She was supposed to turn up to lunch with me and the ghost tour operator, Megan Lupia, but Talia didn't show. I haven't been able to get hold of her and neither has her work. Everyone is worried about her."

"Why were you having lunch with the tour operator?" Jake asked.

"She wanted details about last night's tour, after we had calmed down."

"What do you think you saw in the tunnel?"

"A fucking evil ghost."

Jake didn't comment further. He didn't believe in ghosts and the only evil he knew was in the monsters he chased. "Do you have any idea where Talia was going?" he asked.

"Nup. She wouldn't say. Just that she was going to see a couple of locals and they didn't know she was coming yet."

"A couple? Did she mean husband and wife?" Jake asked.

"Doubt it. I think she meant two people. Her comment to me was she was going to meet a couple of locals."

'A couple of locals that don't know I am coming.' It repeated in his head. He had even warned her.

What had she walked into? His fears intensified.

"You there? Hello, Lucas!" Jake called.

"Sorry. I was thinking. I'm worried what she's stumbled into." He tapped the bedside table with the end of his pen like a drummer from the 80s as thoughts raced through his head.

"Jake, could you do me a favour and run her credit cards and phone? We might be able to find her that way."

"Sure, but it'll take me some time. I'll need to get Monique to do it for me. I don't have the authority anymore. I'll call you as soon as I get something," Jake replied. "Anything else to report?"

"Back on Gemma… I found her iPhone. It was jammed in the car under the crumpled driver's seat. There were a couple of photos on it and one was of particular interest. It was time-stamped just before the accident. It showed a red vehicle near their car. It looks like a Ford F100 but it's hard to tell. The photo only captures the front corner of the vehicle," Lucas said.

"So, someone else was at the tunnel with them?"

"Looks that way."

"Do you think the tunnel could be the place they went to communicate with the dead?" Jake asked

"It's possible. There's a lot of energy in that tunnel. I don't know if seeing ghosts is the same as communicating with the dead, though. Even if they did come up here to try and contact her father the first time, Gemma didn't do that on the second visit. She died the first night."

"Don't ask me why, but I think the two visits are linked. There had to be a reason she came back. We need to know what that was," Jake said.

"What do you think it was?"

"I don't know; maybe she was depressed and wanted to die at the place Paige met her fate."

Lucas thought about it for a while, before answering with a very unconvincing, "Perhaps. I need to try and find out what she did between arriving here and hopping into that bath. All I know to this point is she arrived early afternoon, got a prescription filled, had dinner at the bistro, and was found in the bath the next day."

"Filling in the gaps of that Friday is key," Jake agreed.

"Every time I answer one question, more questions are raised. I just need to continue the process. Like any investigation, all the clues will lead to the answer," Lucas said hopefully.

"The evidence never lies," Jake returned.

"Let me follow up a couple of these new developments. I'll get back to you as soon as I find out anything new."

"Okay, Lucas. I'll get onto Talia's phone and the credit card usage."

Lucas placed the hotel phone back in its cradle. He sat on the bed, notepad and pen in hand, and wrote himself a list.

Red Truck F100?

Gemma's Friday afternoon?

Talia?

He was starting to get the impression that all these little things were pieces to a bigger puzzle.

Chapter 25

Melbourne December 2016

Jake didn't even hang the phone up, he just clicked the receiver and dialled again.

Monique answered in her usual 'head of homicide' way. "Monique."

"Monique, it's Jake."

"You wanna come back yet?"

"Not yet," Jake said.

At least he hadn't said 'No'. It sounded like he was considering it.

"I need your help," Jake continued.

"Sure; what do you need?"

"I need you to run a credit card and a phone number. As you know, we're investigating a suicide in Picton. Talia Baxter from *The Australian* was also looking into some missing girls there, and well, she's now gone missing."

"I know Talia. Why do you think she's missing? No one has opened a missing person's file on her. How long has it been?" Monique asked.

"Only a few hours, but her boss is concerned," Jake said.

"It's a bit premature to do a phone and card check after just a few hours, don't you think, Jake?"

"I agree, but Lucas was supposed to meet her, and she didn't show. He thinks something is wrong and I trust his judgement."

"You got Lucas working for you too?" Monique asked.

"Just on contract," Jake said.

"He was a great cop, almost as good as you. I trust his judgement too. You'd better give me the details."

Jake gave her the phone number; the credit card she would obtain from the bank on her own.

Jake expected that Monique would get back to him within the hour. While he was waiting, he walked back out into the lounge and found Hayley unpacking Indiana's day-care bag.

Indiana sat on her play mat playing with all the colourful toys hanging from the rainbow bar criss-crossing the mat.

Hayley looked amazing today, although, come to think of it, he thought she looked amazing every day. He'd loved her from the instant he had met her; it was love at first sight.

"Hey you," she said, hooking her arms around his shoulders and dragging him in for a kiss. He was bigger than her by a fair margin, so she had to stand on tippy-toes and he had to stoop.

"I think I might need to go to Picton, to help Lucas," Jake said after their lips finally parted.

"Why? What do you mean…help Lucas?"

"There's more to follow up than we first thought. I'll be away two or three days maybe. Your mum could come to stay and help you out with Indy."

"I'll be fine. It's no problem. It's what you have to do. When will you be leaving?"

"Not till the morning. How about we go out for dinner tonight?"

"That would be great." She smiled, and added, "Maybe tonight we could get an early night, if you know what I mean?" Still holding him, she kissed him again. This time it was long and passionate. Both of them wanted it to last forever.

*

Jake had finished packing for his trip the next day when Monique rang back.

"I've done the searches. The credit card hasn't been used since yesterday. Her last purchase was $98 to a company called Lupia Tours. I looked it up; it's the ghost tour company," Monique said.

"Lucas went on that tour with her. Anything on the phone?" Jake asked.

"Nothing concrete, I'm afraid. There have been no outgoing calls since yesterday. We even triangulated her last known call. At 9.30 this morning she received a call from her work. It went unanswered, but the cell tower it came from was just outside Picton on the corner of the Old Hume Highway and Mount Hercules Road," Monique said.

Jake jotted down the details. "What about the later calls?"

"There has been no more communication with that tower or any tower since 9.30, which means it's switched off, dead battery or…"

Jake butted in "…or the sim has been smashed."

"Exactly," Monique said.

"It doesn't necessarily mean that something bad has happened," Jake said.

"You've been in homicide long enough, Jake. You know that when someone is taken or killed nowadays the perp always destroys the phone."

"I know, I'm just saying, it could be other things."

"We're opening a missing person's file for Talia. Get things moving as quickly as possible," Monique said. "We've already put out an APB on her car. It's a silver Toyota Prius." She reeled off the rego.

"I'll be heading up there myself in the morning so call me if you get anything more," Jake said.

"Always," Monique agreed.

Jake dialled Lucas's room number to relay Monique's info.

*

Picton December 2016

Lucas hung up from Jake and immediately wanted to go to the Old Hume Highway and Mount Hercules Road to the phone tower to see if Talia's car had broken down nearby. He knew the chances of finding anything were slim, but he had nothing else to do.

He drove out of town, heading back the exact way he had come.

The T-intersection appeared out of nowhere and if he had blinked he would have missed it. He turned right and headed up the hill towards the horizon. Farmhouses were scattered. He had hit farmland now. There was one house on the right corner, one on the left halfway up the hill, and a third home on the right set far back from the road on the hilltop.

The dry open paddocks reminded him of his childhood; of visiting his grandparents on their farm. He used to roam it from sunrise to sunset, playing with his brothers and cousins. Their land wasn't as barren as this. Their farm was more treed, with more places to play hide and seek and build forts.

Just past the house on the corner, he saw the telecommunications tower, the owners having leased part of their land to the phone company. Lucas imagined the owners had been well compensated for it.

He hoped to find Talia's Prius, but there were no cars anywhere in sight. He continued his drive up the side road towards the top of the hill.

He looked down the other side of the road; nothing there either. Maybe she hadn't taken this road, but had headed further out of town, back towards Sydney.

Just as his thoughts had begun to explore other possibilities, something caught his eye; a red truck behind a barn on the hill. Even though he couldn't be sure, he thought maybe it was a Ford F100. The design of the vehicle was distinctive.

He turned onto the potholed dirt drive and followed it up the hill to a large garage. Lucas guessed it would hold six or eight cars. As he drew closer to it, he realised his estimation was way off; it resembled a hangar rather than a garage. The brakes on his car squeaked from the dust as he stopped just below the garage.

Directly in front of him was the shed. To his right and further up the hill was the farmhouse, with a barn behind that. In the distance a tractor moved back and forth across the horizon.

He stepped out of the car, his black leather shoes now covered in dust.

His sunglasses shielded his eyes from the rising dust whipped up by the wind. He could see a large heavy-set man working away in the garage. As he approached him he recognised him; Dave Brown.

Suspicion ran through him. All his internal sirens were going off. When he had spoken to Anthony in the bistro, he was told they hadn't been with the girls before the crash, but he now doubted their story.

"Excuse me?"

The man in the shed who was stooped over the workbench tinkering with something mechanical turned and stood up straight. He towered over Lucas.

"Hey," he said offhandedly.

"Sorry to bother you, but I was just wondering if you've seen a silver Prius broken down around here earlier today?"

"No, sorry mate, been working in here all day. Haven't seen anyone," Dave answered.

Lucas introduced himself as a private detective and apologised for being rude.

"I spoke with your brother the other night at the bistro. I was asking him about the night the two girls, Gemma and Paige, had the car accident. Do you remember that at all?"

"No, not really. I was pretty drunk in the bistro that night; I heard about the crash after. You never miss out on gossip in a small town," was the reply.

"Gemma said she thought someone was tampering with their car, and they were being followed before the accident, apparently by someone in a red Ford F100."

Dave was wiping the grease off his hands with an old flannelette shirt that had now become a rag. "What's that got to do with me?" He sounded annoyed.

"I notice you have a red Ford F100 parked up behind your hay shed."

"Oh that. It was my dad's. We've been trying to rebuild it since he died."

"Anthony told me that your dad had retired."

"He says that sometimes. He's still pretty devastated by his passing. Being the older one, I think he had a stronger relationship with Dad than I did," Dave said.

"So, you're rebuilding the Ford. Does it go?" Lucas asked.

"Come and I'll show you, then you'll understand it can't be the same one," Dave said. He led Lucas out of the shed and up the hill towards the barn.

"How long have you guys lived here?" Lucas asked.

"All our lives. Dad owned this place since before we were born." Dave's huge frame cast a large shadow over Lucas, momentarily blocking out the sun.

The barn ran across the top of the property east to west. They reached the barn and turned down the far side. Lucas saw Dave had tucked the greasy towel into the back of the pants.

The F100 was red, old and slightly rusted but didn't look as if it needed restoration.

"So, this is her," Dave began. "She needs a lot of work." He lifted the bonnet, showing an empty engine bay. "See what I mean?"

Lucas saw the big hole.

"No motor, no go." Dave laughed.

"Unless you're Fred Flintstone," Lucas quipped. Privately, he thought that Dave was probably strong enough to pick up the truck and run with it.

"There's the engine over there," Dave said, pointing to a pile of tyres and spare parts resting against the side of the barn. "Over there in the milk crate is the carburettor."

Lucas looked further up the garage wall to the milk crate, which had a large metal box sitting inside it. Behind it were a few old number plates. One in particular drew Lucas's attention. The first three letters read REX-7 and even though he couldn't see the rest of the plate, he was confident it was the letters of Peta Reid's red Laser. Lucas didn't believe in coincidences.

Lucas realised he had been staring at the plate for a few seconds; probably a few seconds too long. "That's one big carburettor," he said, turning back towards Dave.

Dave was right there, just feet way. His demeanour had changed, and he was looking at Lucas suspiciously.

Lucas wondered if Dave had realised his sudden insight.

"Don't think I don't know what you're doing here," Dave said.

Lucas immediately felt uneasy. The investigator in him put the pieces together in a second; the Brown brothers were involved. Somehow, they were responsible for the missing girls. Why the hell had he left his Beretta in the car? he asked himself. Now he needed to get the hell out of there. He had to play super dumb.

As good a street fighter as Lucas was, he knew he wouldn't be able to compete with Dave's sheer bulk. Dave looked as if he would literally be able to tear him apart, limb from limb. He had to bluff his way to safety.

"I don't know what you mean. I was just looking for a friend who was having car trouble," Lucas bluffed.

The giant didn't say anything, just stared.

The silence was concerning. He had always been told, don't worry about the guys that are threatening and mouthing off; they usually aren't capable of carrying out their threats. However, always be wary of the quiet ones, they're the dangerous ones.

For the first time since leaving the police force, Lucas seriously feared for his safety.

He stepped away from the truck and turned to go, saying calmly, "I'll try the other neighbours; see if they've seen her."

Before he could get any further, Dave stepped into him and punched him in the chest and stomach twice. They were fairly soft punches for such a large guy.

If this is the way he fights, I'm in with a chance, Lucas thought.

Lucas kicked him back in the chest, as hard as he would kick in a door when he was on the force. The big man staggered backwards. As he regained his balance, Lucas brought his hands up ready to fight.

Then Lucas saw it; a long thin screwdriver.

He hadn't even seen Dave grab the screwdriver. Where had it come from?

Lucas looked down at his shirt, which was now covered in blood. Everything seemed to instantly slow down once he realised he'd been stabbed.

He looked up towards his attacker, who seemed to be enjoying Lucas's current state way too much. In fact, Lucas swore this was exciting him.

Lucas stepped away and attempted to make his way to his car. He only made it a few metres before his breathing became shallow and he began to cough. He could taste blood. Gasping for air, he staggered forward a little more before falling to his knees, face first into the dust.

*

Anthony had seen Dave talking to the investigator and noted his brother was now standing over the body on the ground. He stopped the tractor, turned off the spray unit and made his way towards his brother. Dave was still standing behind the investigator's body.

"What the hell are you doing?" Anthony asked.

"He knew," Dave said.

"How do you know that?"

"He saw the licence plate; he stood there staring at it as if recalling the number."

"That doesn't mean he knew. What if someone else knew he was coming here?"

"He would have worked it out eventually. I had no choice," Dave said flatly.

Anthony glared at him. "If anyone comes sniffing around he was never here, you understand?"

Dave stood there transfixed, still holding the screwdriver so tightly his knuckles had turned white.

Blood had dried along the screwdriver and on his hand, but a final drip fell from the screwdriver.

"Get inside, now. Hat Man will be here soon. We don't want to disturb him while he feeds."

The brothers, cowering inside, watched as Hat Man appeared out of thin air, took hold of the investigator's stunned soul and consumed him head first. The investigator didn't even move. He just stood there staring at his corpse in bewilderment.

Neither of the brothers made a sound. Once Hat Man had eaten and left, Anthony slapped his brother hard across the back of the head. "Fuck, you're an idiot. That's why we don't kill them here. I told you that last time. We don't need that thing coming to us. If we kill them in the tunnel, we can leave while it feeds. Now, take him and bury him behind the hay shed. Make it deep, you hear me?" Anthony shouted.

Dave didn't answer. Instead he headed outside to do as he was told. Anthony followed.

Dave heaved the investigator off the dirt drive and hoisted him over his shoulder. Blood now dripped down the front and back of Dave's overalls. The investigator's lifeless face had blood and dust encrusted on it.

Dave expected the investigator to be heavier dead, yet he seemed to carry him with ease.

Anthony searched the investigator's pockets for the keys to his Mazda which he found in his right pants pocket.

After sliding the driver's seat back a little, he drove the car into the hay shed so it couldn't be seen. Anthony made sure he wiped it clean before he got out.

Dave laid the investigator's body out next to the milk crate and junk pile, while he dug the hole. Anthony joined him and started digging.

The dead investigator's phone rang. Dave and Anthony stopped their digging and quickly searched the body for the phone. By the time they found it in the breast pocket, the call had gone to message bank.

"Before you take the chip out, find out who was calling," Anthony instructed his brother.

"Some bloke named Jake," Dave said.

Dave took the iPhone and went searching through his tool box for a pin to eject the chip. A paper clip would do, he thought, although finding one of them in his tool box was highly unlikely. Dave ended up settling on a small piece of wire. He pushed in the wire and out popped the chip holder. Dave took the chip, placed it into the back of the truck's tray and smashed it into pieces with his hammer.

He then rejoined his brother digging the grave.

It took them about forty minutes to dig the hole. Dave scattered the pieces of the phone on top of the body the way a relative would place a rose or a picture onto a deceased after they had been lowered into their final resting place.

Once the body was completely covered, Dave merely patted down the soil, scraping some loose dirt and grass on top to disguise the grave.

"I'll go call Dad and tell him what's happened. Then I'll put a couple of steaks on the BBQ. All this digging's made me hungry," Anthony said.

"What about the girl?" Dave asked.

"We'll have to move her soon, don't want anyone else snooping

around…tomorrow perhaps. Till then, we make sure she's well cared for."
Anthony wiped the sweat from his face with his sleeve, leant the shovel up
against the truck and headed indoors.

Chapter 26

In-Between December 2016

I hardly paid attention to my body where I lay in the hospital bed in the world below. Every time I looked down at it, I was drawn to my name on the wall above the bed. Brodie Foxx. The admission date was printed underneath, but I'd lost track of how long I had been lying there.

I always watched and waited for Jake to come and visit. I missed him a lot. I have no doubt that part of the reason he left the force was the fact that I got shot. I don't think he ever got over taking the vest, even though I had insisted.

He came in to see me a lot earlier than usual this day. It would have been 5 in the morning. He read me the trivia as per our usual ritual. He answered most of the questions correctly. He didn't really need my input anyway.

He told me about how my NBA team was doing, which was terrible as usual. He then told me about the Knicks, and how their season had started to derail so soon after it had begun.

"I've got to go away for a few days, or maybe a week," Jake said.

This comment got my immediate attention.

"Hayley said she'll come in and see you while I'm gone." His head dropped. He looked worried, a little upset.

I wondered what was wrong with him. Something was obviously troubling him.

"I need to go to Picton Town to find out what happened to Gemma."

He had told me about the case previously, and how Lucas had gone to investigate it further.

"Lucas doesn't think it was suicide. He thinks it was more of an accident if anything, but he's far from convinced. Since being up there he's uncovered a lot of unexplained disappearances and deaths. I'm going to help him try and put all this to bed once and for all."

Jake sat as if he was waiting for my response even though he knew one wasn't coming. It seemed he was hoping that talking about his latest case would magically wake me.

Of course, it didn't.

Jake slid a book out from under his newspaper. It was a journal. He turned towards the back of the book.

The front cover was plain except for something written in Texta.

Jake found the page he was looking for and began reading. It was as if he was reading me a bedtime story.

"This entry was from the day before she left for her first trip to Picton Town. It's the last entry we have before the accident and the last entry we can find. We don't know where any subsequent diaries are."

Thursday 3rd of July 2014

Tomorrow we're heading to Picton for a girls' weekend away. Paige is really excited to go to a town that might have ghosts. I'm not so sure I want to go anymore. For some reason it doesn't feel right. I don't even like horror movies. Since your passing, it just seems all too real, too close to home. Maybe it's because it's still raw. You know I love Paige, but she just seems to think going there will bring back the bubbly, happy Gemma. I don't know if that girl will ever be back. The world just isn't as bright since you left.

I miss you more than anything.

I never used to believe in ghosts or even in an afterlife, but with Paige showing me all these ghost stories – I'm not sure what to believe.

Paige says that Picton is a spiritual hub and that because it seems to have so much paranormal activity the chances are high that we might be able to communicate with you...summon you, so to speak. Apparently, there is a tunnel up there where you can talk to the dead.

I'm not sure that's something I want, but Paige says it will do me good. Maybe she is right. I don't know.

Maybe we'll get to speak to you. I would love the chance to tell you how much I love you.

If not, let's hope you can see these diary entries, from wherever you are. Love you Dad. Miss you.

"So, what do you think?" Jake asked me.

Of course, I gave no response.

He went on as if I had answered. "I agree. Sounds like she went to see a ghost to prove to herself there is an afterlife; prove that her dad was in a better place."

I could tell as the words left his mouth that he wondered where I was, for I was neither dead nor alive. I appeared to be a vegetable, a lifeless body lying in the bed. Except my spirit was somewhere else, not in heaven, not on earth. I was in the in-between apparently, waiting to finally let go of earth, I assumed.

The white door behind me shook as if it was about to fly off its invisible hinges. I was even more terrified of it than I had been before. Yet for some unknown reason I was still drawn to it. I could feel some magnetic force pulling me towards the door.

I turned away from the door and focused back on Jake. He had stopped at the doorway of my room and turned to me before leaving.

"I love you mate. If anything happens to me. I'll see you in the clearing at the end of the path."

He was quoting Stephen King, from our favourite series *The Dark Tower*.

As he left the room, the door shook again. For a brief second, I thought I heard a muffled scream from far beyond it.

Maybe the door leads to the clearing? I thought.

Maybe once I stepped through the door there was no coming back, no visiting earth again.

Melbourne December 2016

Jake stopped by his office after the hospital visit to finish some paperwork on a new case. He was keen to get on the road but was not looking forward to the ten-hour drive ahead.

By the time he got through the city traffic congestion, it was already nearing 10 o'clock. Jake had already placed another call to Lucas; his mobile was going straight to voicemail. Jake even tried his hotel room, which just rang out. He was becoming more concerned. Something was wrong.

He drove until about 2 o'clock before stopping in Gundagai for lunch. The town was small and charming. The pub food was pretty good too. He had heard of this town but had never actually been there before.

He placed another call to Lucas. Again, it went to voicemail. That was now three unanswered calls, including the one yesterday.

Jake reached the outskirts of Picton just before 6.30 pm, which wasn't too bad considering the delays and the stop for lunch. Even though he had eaten only four hours before, he was hungry again, which was pretty standard for him.

He saw a sign that read Dream Catcher B&B, although he couldn't see any establishment from the road. As he headed into the narrow hairpin bend and up the hill, all the hairs on his arms stood up. His neck and arms had come alive, and his hunger seemed to turn to nausea, the feeling coming deep from the pit of his stomach. A cold shiver ran across his shoulders. It felt as if he was coming down with food poisoning. Maybe the food in Gundagai wasn't so crash-hot after all. But as suddenly as it had come, the sensation disappeared. Was his body trying to tell him something? During his years on the force he'd had a similar feeling once before. It was during a raid on a drug house. Everything was going well until he found himself on the wrong end of a shotgun.

Jake had only stared at the barrel for a split second, but it was long enough to realise he was about to die.

On that occasion, the gun had backfired, taking the drug-dealing hand of its owner with it.

Jake often wondered if in that split second, he'd had an out-of-body experience, not that he would ever admit it to anyone.

Was this the same?

Was his soul trying to warn him?

A loud thudding noise suddenly came from the left-hand side of the car as if the front tyre had exploded. Shaken back to reality by the noise, Jake became aware that he had drifted to the side of the road and hit the sleeper bumps, as he called them. They were designed to make a loud noise, loud enough to wake a sleeping driver on a long trip.

They certainly worked, Jake thought. He had lost concentration and had drifted into dangerous territory.

He immediately focused back on the road and the traffic in front of him, refreshing himself with water he had on board.

The township of Picton really surprised him. It was a lot more modern than he had imagined. As he headed towards the hotel, he occasionally saw an old heritage building surrounded by new additions. The town clearly had tried to retain its past and its history.

Despite his body's earlier possible warning signs, the town appealed to him.

*

Picton December 2016

Jake pulled into the hotel car park. Most of the other cars were old and didn't look like what a private detective would drive.

Jake removed his bag from the boot and headed through the door marked 'Reception'. It was a dimly lit area with a small chest-high counter located beside the stairs.

"Welcome, sir," the middle-aged lady said from behind the counter.

"I've a booking under Detective Miller," Jake said. He wasn't yet used to not calling himself detective. It was an old habit that was proving hard to break.

"Ah yes, here we are," the lady said after fiddling about on her keyboard.

She placed two cards in a folder on the counter in front of him.

"You here on holiday, or business?" she asked.

"Business, I'm afraid."

"We don't get many detectives around these parts. I hope it's nothing serious?"

"Just looking into a possible suicide. Nothing too exciting," Jake said.

"What a coincidence. We had a PI up here for a few days looking into a suicide as well."

"Would it have been Lucas Taylor?" Jake asked, knowing full well Lucas was staying there.

"Is he a friend of yours?" she asked.

"Colleague, actually."

"I'm not supposed to give out information on other guests but as you're a police detective, I think it's okay?"

Jake nodded, indicating it was okay to talk about him.

"Yes, it was Lucas who stayed in the room next door to the one I just gave you. He was a bit of a strange character. He asked me for a radio, so he could run some tests— seemed weird to me, but I just did as he asked."

"You're talking as if he's already left."

"He checked out yesterday."

"Checked out?" Jake questioned.

"Yesterday afternoon," she clarified.

Jake stood there tapping the hotel cards against the counter, reassessing whether he should check in at all.

Where had Lucas gone?

Why hadn't he called him back?

"I've his room tab receipt if you want to see it," the lady offered.

Jake looked at the receipt; paid at 4.18 pm.

He'd paid for some chips, three bottles of Coke and a charge for a lost card.

"What's this lost card charge?" Jake asked.

"He lost one of his key cards," she said.

"How did he pay?"

"PayPass."

Jake wasn't sure what had happened to Lucas, but he knew this wasn't right. Something had happened.

"Can I have the same room Lucas was in?"

"No problem," she said.

She took the cards back off the counter and reissued ones for the room Lucas had occupied. "What is it with you guys? It's the same room the girl killed herself in. I don't know what you're expecting to find in there. It's just a room, same as all the others. I'm sorry, there's still only one card. I haven't had time to re-magnetise a new one yet."

"There's only one of me so I'll be okay with just one. By the way, did Lucas say anything when he checked out?"

The lady stood looking at the ceiling, as if she was trying to remember the exact conversation. "No, nothing really. He just thanked me for his stay. I didn't get to speak to him very often. He was always out."

"What do you know about the girl?" Jake asked.

"Only what I told your friend. She seemed nice. I had met her before when she came here the first time— the time they had that terrible car accident. You know about that?"

Jake nodded.

"When she came, she had dinner and a few drinks in the bistro. The next morning, I went into the room to clean it as I do for all my guests and found her dead in the tub. It was horrific!"

"You found her?" Jake asked, surprised.

"It was horrific to see her like that, I really don't like talking about it," she said, looking to the floor.

"Okay, thanks for your help," Jake said.

"No problem, Detective, just up the stairs. By the way, my name is Isabella. If you need anything, just let me know."

Chapter 27

Picton December 2016

Talia had spent two days captive in the large metal box, unsure of her fate. She thought her prison was a shipping container or something similar. It was hard to know exactly. She wasn't sure why they were keeping her alive. She thought of rape but dismissed it almost instantly because after two days, they hadn't even touched her.

Maybe it was a human trafficking syndicate. She had investigated some in the past; they definitely existed. Usually they involved small children of twelve and under.

Something didn't add up; if they were going to kill her why hadn't they done it already? The longer she was held captive, the higher the risk of her captors getting caught. Maybe they were waiting for the interest in her disappearance to die down before they killed her.

The only thing she knew now was the brothers were responsible for the four missing girls. This room was proof of that. She didn't know what had happened to the girls. She guessed she would find out their fate because it would soon become her own.

She had to get out of this box.

Talia stood up from her brown, woollen blanket and foam makeshift bed. There was no handle on the door, no instrument she could use to facilitate an escape. There were air vents above square grates. If she could get to them, she might be able to fit through them. At a guess, the roof of the container was a couple of metres above her head. There was no way she could reach the grates. At the other end of the box there was a small bucket. This was her toilet.

Talia walked end to end looking for any break in the metal, even just a glimpse of the outside world. Was she still on the farm? Or had they moved her to a different location after they'd knocked her out? She couldn't be sure. There were no cracks, no gap to see out through. She reached the bucket at the far end of the box. It had been emptied yesterday, but it still smelt disgusting. She headed back to her blanket and sat back down in the corner.

The blanket looked fresh and was free of dust. The mattress was free of stains and discolouration; in fact, it was near new. Whatever they had done with the girls, they hadn't killed them in here. Talia sat back down on the mattress, legs crossed, back against the metal wall, to consider her predicament.

She sat staring upwards at the vents, trying to imagine herself up there squeezing through. She would fit. She knew she would. She shook her head, closed her eyes and her inner self screamed, *there is no way up, so think of something else, you stupid bitch.*

She banged the back of her head against the wall in frustration. She drew her legs up and placed her head on her crossed arms, like a six-year-old. Then she noticed it. At first, she thought it was just a scratch. Then she realised it was more.

On the opposite wall, lettering was scratched into the metal. It looked at first like initials, then she realised it was a message, a simple message.

PR was scratched on the first line, and below that, what looked like a date: *4/ 7/14.*

PR? Talia racked her brains for a few seconds before the answer came to her. Peta Reid, one of the missing girls, had been here. She had been reported missing on 5 July 2014, so it made sense that she could have been here on the 4th.

They had held her here too.

Maybe others had been held here also.

The thought of whatever had happened to them happening to her, sent her mind racing.

Somehow, she had to get out of here!

Chapter 28

Picton December 2016

Jake stood in the doorway of the room that only twenty-four hours before, had been occupied by Lucas Taylor. The place was bare. It was as if Lucas had never set foot in it. The bed was made, a chocolate mint sat upon each pillow, and the room was clean and tidy, spotless, in fact.

Jake rested his luggage against the mirrored wardrobe door before sitting on the bed.

He dialled Lucas's number. It went straight to message bank; didn't even ring this time.

So, this was what it felt like being on the other end of a missing person's case, Jake thought. He had to switch into detective mode, otherwise it might be too late for Lucas too. If it wasn't already.

Jake removed his jacket and placed it at the foot of the bed before going to the bathroom. It wasn't a big room. Vanity. Bath/shower and a toilet. Jake's focus was immediately drawn to the power point above the vanity. Lucas had run tests on the radio and while he had said it was highly unlikely to have been the cause of Gemma's death, it was possible, but he hadn't believed it was suicide. So why had he now disappeared? What had he stumbled upon?

Jake knew Lucas was following up on Talia's disappearance. Had he found her? Had what happened to Talia happened to Lucas too?

Many puzzling questions ran through Jake's mind as he paced up and down the room.

"What do we know?" he mumbled to himself to focus his thoughts.

Talia had suggested a serial killer was working the area.

Talia had been going to see 'a couple of locals' about the disappearances.

Lucas was more concerned about Talia's whereabouts than with Gemma's case.

Did the other disappearances have something to do with Gemma's death? Had Lucas found a connection?

Jake stopped mid-step at the foot of the bed. What did Lucas know that he didn't?

He needed to find out who Lucas had called, and who might have called him just before he disappeared.

Jake sat on the bed and called Monique.

"Monique, it's Jake. I need you to run a trace on Lucas's phone."

"What, why?"

"He's missing."

"What do you mean, missing?" Monique asked disbelievingly.

"I spoke to him yesterday afternoon and relayed the information you gave me relating to Talia. I haven't been able to get onto him since and when I arrived in Picton this afternoon, he'd checked out," Jake answered. His response was rushed, as if he was trying to get all the information out at once.

"Slow down, Jake. Did the hotel management say where he was going?"

"No, he didn't say. Apparently, he just paid his bill and left," Jake replied.

"He never called you to tell you what he was doing?" Monique asked.

"No, the last time I spoke to him I gave him the trace information on Talia's phone and her car details. I'm thinking something else came up since which has sent him off in another direction."

"I'll get the trace done on his phone, as soon as possible," Monique replied.

"Thanks. Can you also give me his vehicle details? I have no idea what he's driving these days."

"Consider it done."

Jake removed his laptop from the bag resting against the mirror. He needed to speak to the lady who ran the ghost tours. She was the only one Jake knew of who had spoken to both Lucas and Talia.

Jake searched 'Picton Tunnel Tours'. The page loaded several articles and dozens of pictures of Picton, in particular of the tunnel.

In the middle of the page was a name he recognised. Megan Lupia.

Chapter 29

Picton December 2016

Despite the disgusting odour of the bucket, Talia managed to remove its handle. She tried not to let the destiny of any of the other girls enter her mind. No matter what had happened, she couldn't help them now and she certainly wouldn't be able to save anyone else from suffering the same fate if she too perished.

She took the end of the metal handle and began to carve into the container. She wasn't going to settle for initials; she was going to make sure that if anyone ever found this place, they would know who had been here.

She began with her name followed by her date of birth followed by the previous day's date. Talia's next priority was to set about figuring a way out of here. There had to be an answer.

Still wearing her watch, she knew it was over twenty-four hours since she had been taken. By now, her work mates and family would be worried. Alarms would have been raised, maybe bank accounts checked. Phone records would be investigated.

But no one knew she had been coming here.

Earl had always told her never to go chasing a lead without telling someone where she was going. It was a rule. The most important one, and she had ignored it. Now look at the consequences, she thought.

The container was beginning to cool as the afternoon progressed towards sunset. Soon she would need her blanket. In the early hours of the morning, it was cold.

She heard a noise from outside. She couldn't decipher exactly what it was. She tried to imagine what the sound could be.

Was it the latch on a gate? It had to be, Talia thought. Then a second sound came, this one directly outside the box. She guessed one of the brothers was unlocking the door. There were three locks in total, she now recalled.

The door opened outwards. The shorter of the two brothers entered. He was so bulky he almost filled the whole doorway.

In one hand he had two bottles of water. In the other he had a bowl. She couldn't see what was in it from where she was sitting on her mattress.

She just hoped it was food; she was starving.

"Got some grub for you." He placed it on the floor in front of her. The food looked disgusting. At first, she couldn't even make out what it was. She must have frowned in disgust.

"You one of those vegie chicks, are you?" the brother asked.

"No."

"You better eat up. There's nothing else till morning," the brother said.

Talia remembered hearing something similar from her stepmother when she was a child. "If you don't finish your dinner now, you can have it for breakfast," she used to say.

Talia realised the brother was still standing in front of her.

"Sorry, I just wasn't sure what it was," Talia apologised.

"I'm sorry I didn't include a menu," the brother said sarcastically.

He dropped the water to the floor. "It's beef stir-fry, don't you eat that in the city?"

Talia saw a change in his eyes; his anger was growing. For a second, she was expecting the back of his hand, but no slap came.

"Thank you," Talia said, trying to defuse the situation before he erupted. "Why are you keeping me here? Why don't you just let me go?"

"You came here asking what happened to the other girls, so we'll show you," he said flatly.

Talia didn't respond. She didn't know what his answer meant, but she knew it wouldn't be pleasant.

He closed the door behind him and began reapplying the locks.

As soon as he closed the door, Talia hit her stop-watch and left it running until she heard the sound she thought was a gate latch. Twenty-three seconds total.

She would note the time that it took and test him again in the morning.

The food didn't taste as bad as it looked. Even though he'd called it a stir-fry, it was more meat and gravy on rice. There was very little in the way of vegetables; a couple of pieces of capsicum and two sprigs of broccoli, but that was it.

It didn't matter at this point; she was so hungry.

While eating, Talia sat staring at the bucket, the final destination for the food she was putting into her mouth. Suddenly, she came up with her escape plan.

Chapter 30

Picton December 2016

Jake had managed to get hold of Megan Lupia. He had dealt with mediums before. His thoughts on them had changed; he had gone from sceptic to true believer. Beliefs change when they save your life, he thought.

They met at Picton Café. It was a busy establishment, yet it retained the feel of a relaxed country café. The walls were a lemony yellow, and the floors were old polished hardwood. The tables and chairs were made of a light-coloured timber, with yellow cushions. Each table had a silver triangle in one corner which displayed the table number.

Jake ordered a coffee for himself and a chai for Megan.

"Mr Miller, you said on the phone you think Lucas is missing?" she said.

"Yes. Well, I'm not sure, but I can't get in contact with him. He told me you had lunch together yesterday. I'm trying to find out what happened after that which led to him checking out," Jake answered.

"Well, I don't know how much help I'll be, Mr Miller," Megan said.

"Please, call me, Jake."

She nodded.

"How did Lucas seem at lunch?" Jake asked.

"He was very distracted, and I know he was worried about Talia. We were supposed to all meet for lunch, but she didn't show," Megan answered.

"When did you last see Talia?" Jake asked.

"The night before at the tunnel. She was really shaken up by what she had seen in the tunnel. In fact, they both were, so Lucas drove her back to her motel. When we made the date, it was meant to be a morning coffee to catch up, but she said she had an appointment, so we made it lunch. I'll be honest with you, after Lucas left me yesterday, I rang Talia's motel. I thought for a second he might have done something to her. After all, he was the one who drove her back to the motel."

She paused, then continued, "I know most of the townsfolk, so I rang her motel and asked if they had seen her since last night. They said they had seen her in the restaurant for breakfast, and she'd headed out straight after that, so I knew she was alive and well in the morning."

Megan had finished her tea, so Jake offered her another. She declined at first, but Jake suggested joining him in some scones as well. She smiled and accepted.

"So, where do you think she went?" Jake asked.

"Maybe after the appointment she just left town. She had a hell of fright in the tunnel the night before. Over the years, I've seen a lot of people suffer all kinds of scares here in Picton and leave because of them. This place isn't for those who are afraid of the next world and whatever lies beyond," Megan said.

Jake made a note of the time of Talia's last sighting. "Lucas told me that Talia was here following up four missing girls and numerous bizarre deaths. Do you know about any of those cases?" Jake asked.

"I can't explain the four missing girls, except to say they didn't disappear from here. As for the unexplained deaths, they are what they are, some suicides, some accidents, and some…" she paused as if to change what she was about to say, "some more paranormal," she finished.

"What do you mean; more paranormal?"

"Picton is a beautiful country town and most people will come here for a few days, see the graveyard and go on a ghost tour and never see anything scary. They go home happy and they tell their family, oh, it was a bit eerie, but that's the extent of their thoughts on Picton. Others pass through not noticing anything different about Picton than any other small town across Australia.

"Then, there are the few, like me, who have what my mum used to call 'the power'. The people with the power can see the dead. Those who haven't moved on, haven't crossed. Some of these people have seen the town's ghosts walking in the cemetery, standing in the hotel window and even the girl who tried to out-run the train in the tunnel."

"I don't see how the paranormal could have anything to do with these deaths."

"People have reported they have felt an entity trying to strangle them in their sleep by a ghost that walks the hotel. Some have seen and been chased by the lady in the tunnel. Some think the ghosts are evil."

"You think these evil ghosts actually kill people?" Jake questioned.

"No, Mr Miller. I think it's possible that the ghosts feed off the person's insecurities, their past fears, and maybe by the time the ghosts are done, the people no longer want to live. If they survive, they leave, and that's what I suspect happened to the girl and your friend. They both escaped from here while they still could."

Megan picked a warm scone from the plate and began to pile on the jam, followed by the freshly whipped cream.

Jake asked, "What did they say they saw in the tunnel that had you so interested?"

"When they came out, they both claimed to have encountered the 'Hat Man'. The way they described it, it seems they had met a demonic spirit. Something that wanted to hurt them," Megan mumbled, as she finished her scone.

"Hat Man?" Jake questioned. He recalled Lucas mentioning it briefly over the phone at some point.

"I used to think Hat Man was a myth, something the crazy old Pastor Elijah Dwyer made up. Until some people on another tour saw him," Megan said.

All this talk of demonic spirits, ghosts strangling people and crazy priests was getting a bit much for Jake. But he had to find out what the hell was going on in this town.

Ignoring his better judgement, Jake asked the question he'd rather have left unsaid. "Where do I find this pastor?"

"He lives in the chapel next to the graveyard, with his granddaughter. I wouldn't bother trying to visit, they're hermits."

Jake frowned, imagining a big fat priest eating pizza while lying on a bed watching daytime TV. All hermits he had heard about were hugely obese.

Jake knew he needed to speak to this pastor.

Megan checked her watch.

"I'll be able to find the pastor on my own, so if you need to get going, please feel free," Jake said.

"Thank you, I have to prepare for my next tour. Maybe you'd like to come along?" Megan asked.

"I'll keep it in mind. See how the investigation goes."

"You're always welcome. Please keep me up to date on the investigation. If I hear anything around the traps, I'll give you a call."

Jake watched as Megan exited the café. As soon as she stepped out the door, the sunglasses went on and her sunhat followed. It was as if Megan had celebrity status. Maybe in this town, the lady who could see ghosts was the closest thing the town had to a celebrity.

Jake paid the bill and headed out. The worry about Lucas continued. Where was he?

Jake walked down the street, heading towards the cemetery. He guessed it was the only one in town.

He slowed from a brisk walk to a stroll as he approached the sign which read 'St Mark's'. As he walked along the fence-line that abutted the footpath, he could see a girl sitting at a red and yellow plastic table. She had some paper in front of her, and a cup of crayons to her right. She looked about six years old and had beautiful blonde hair, with a pink ribbon tied in a bow on each pigtail.

From where he was standing he couldn't see what she was drawing. As he moved closer, like a teacher looking over his students' shoulders, he saw the girl had drawn a moon on the left corner of the page. On the ground were rocks of some sort. The top of the page and around the moon had been coloured in a dark grey, or black, Jake assumed to reflect the darkness of night.

Jake stepped a little closer. Due to his height advantage he could see the right side of the page, where three people were drawn, the largest wearing a wide-brimmed hat and standing on the other side of the fence.

Jake leant on the fence as he watched the girl draw, not hearing a man approach until he spoke. "Are you one of those lolly guys?" the old man asked.

Jake turned, unsure if the comment was directed at him.

"I'm looking for the pastor who used to live here."

"Seems to me you were stalking the girl," the man said.

Jake now understood the lolly comment. "Not at all. I'm a detective." Jake pulled out his private detective identification. "I'm here to speak to the pastor."

"I'm afraid he no longer lives here. This is a private residence. The church no longer owns the chapel. It's my house now," the old man said. He turned to the child. "Olly— inside."

The girl with the ribbons in her blonde hair quickly packed up her drawing materials and headed inside. She didn't turn to look at either the old man or Jake.

"Are you the pastor?" Jake persisted.

"The pastor is dead. I'm afraid he died long ago."

The old man moved away from the fence and followed the girl into the chapel.

"You can't just ignore me," Jake called as the man neared the entrance. "I'm a private detective."

"I don't care. Get a warrant," the old man snapped back.

Jake stood on the path wondering what the old man had to hide. He watched as the man disappeared inside and the old wooden door slammed shut.

Chapter 31

Picton February 1944

Elijah laid the bible softly on the pew. He walked a few paces and laid another at the other end of the pew. He zig-zagged between rows from the front of the church to the back and then he did the opposite on the other side.

He met his father who was preparing the altar at the front. He had filled the tray of little cups with wine. The bread was cut up and placed on a second tray.

There was always the same number of bread pieces and a large chalice that his father would later fill with wine to serve his parishioners.

Tommy bustled in through the front door of St Mark's Church.

"Pa, can I go fishing with Adam at Stonequarry Creek this afternoon?" he asked enthusiastically.

Tommy, who had turned twelve in the winter, was Pastor Joseph Dwyer's elder son. There were only two years between Elijah and Tommy, but the boys were very different. Though they were both good boys, they liked very different things. Elijah was an inside boy, a reader, who loved to help his father at church. Occasionally, Joseph would find Elijah in his room wearing his collar, holding the bible and giving a sermon to his three stuffed toy bears. Tommy, on the other hand, was always outside either fishing, climbing trees or building a fort. He was always respectful and behaved himself in church, but he wasn't as religious as his brother.

"Sure, as long as you're back and cleaned up into your Sunday best before the evening service starts," Joseph said.

Elijah, who was busy arranging the candles, didn't see the nod of suggestion his dad gave Tommy or the sour pout on Tommy's face when he realised his dad expected him to take his younger brother with him.

Tommy's pout evaporated as he asked his brother if he would like to join him. "Hey Elijah, would you like to come down to the lake with me and Adam?"

"Adam and me," his father corrected him.

"Would you like to come down to the creek with Adam and me this afternoon to do some fishing?" Tommy asked.

"No thanks," Elijah said, too busy with the candles to even face his brother.

Tommy shrugged to his father, as if to say, 'I tried.' He turned to leave.

His father held up his palm. "Son, I think you should go. I can finish up here."

Elijah looked up at his smiling dad, who had placed his hand on his shoulder.

"Are you sure?" Elijah asked.

"Go," his father insisted. As the boys turned to leave, he added, "Boys, no roughhousing. No mischief; you hear?"

"Yes, Pa," Elijah answered immediately.

Tommy remained quiet.

"Did you hear me, Tommy?"

"Yes Pa. Sorry," he added, as an afterthought.

"Boys, don't go playing in that tunnel, or on the old disused pile of sleepers."

This time they both answered. They also knew the reason their pa had banned them from entering the tunnel. Townsfolk considered it cursed. Both boys had heard the stories at school. Neither was game to find out for themselves.

Tommy and Elijah called in at home so Tommy could collect his fishing rods and bait. He had spent some of Saturday morning digging up the back yard, gathering fresh worms in an old jam jar ready for the fishing trip. Elijah, who wasn't that keen on fishing, decided to take a book. There was nothing better than sitting under the shade of a tree and reading. He picked up his copy of *The Hobbit*, not a new release, but new to him. While he was waiting for Tommy, he quickly made some sandwiches. His mum even gave him some slices of lemon cake, wrapped inside a tea towel. Lemon cake was rare with the war still going on. Finally, Elijah filled their canteens with water and they were ready to go.

The boys headed off with the morning sun at their backs. It was about half an hour's walk to the lake, but the spot that Tommy had in mind was a little further.

"Are we there yet?" Elijah asked.

"It's just a little further," Tommy said.

"Why can't we fish here?"

"Because we're meeting Adam and his sister Becca under the bridge."

"Dad said not to go to the tunnel."

"We aren't, we're going to the creek under the bridge."

Elijah knew his dad wouldn't be happy had he known they were going to be fishing this close to the tunnel. Elijah also knew why Tommy hadn't said anything to Pa about Becca. He was smitten with her; had been since the fifth grade. Now they were both in high school and Becca had begun to blossom. He was sure his brother had taken note.

Elijah could see the two figures in the distance.

Both were wearing hats. Adam's was a straw hat similar to the ones the brothers were wearing. Becca had on a girl's sun hat with a floppy brim. Adam was wearing shorts, shirt and boots while Becca was dressed in a light blue knee-length summer dress with a white blouse underneath, and black summer sandals on her feet. Adam was a year older than Tommy, while Becca was younger by a few months.

Adam had already cast his line and was sitting on the bank with his feet dangling in the water. His boots and socks sat next to a knapsack behind him. He too had a jar of worms at his side.

"You caught anything yet?" Tommy asked.

"Nah," Adam said.

The spot they had chosen was flat, lightly grassed, and the bridge above provided enough shade from the summer sun. At the rear of the grassed area stood two silver birch trees.

Elijah quietly made his way to one of those trees and found himself a comfortable nook. He undid the strap of his knapsack and removed his book. He had never heard of hobbits or read about wizards before. As he turned the cover and began to read, he wondered if his dad would approve.

Tommy had forgotten his brother was even there. All his attention was on Becca. Even though he was making idle chatter with Adam and baiting his rod, his focus was on Becca. He studied everything she did, how she played and pulled the grass beside her, how her lips looked when she pursed them to blow the pollen off the wild fairy flowers.

Tommy glanced over to her again as he threw his first line into the water.

She smiled at him, blushing a little. Tommy loved her smile, as it revealed her dimples. A gust of wind blew across the creek sending Becca's hair across her face. She simply flicked her head in the opposite direction and her blonde hair went back into place.

Nothing flustered her, Tommy thought.

"Do you want to have a go?" Tommy asked her.

She smiled, revealing dimples again. "You'll need to show me how," she said softly.

Her hair blew over her face again, and this time she gave a little giggle. It was a giggle that Tommy immediately loved.

Tommy passed her the rod. At first, she held it incorrectly.

Adam laughed. Her face blushed with embarrassment.

"You're such a dunce." Her brother chuckled.

Tommy took hold of her hand. A spark ran up his arm as his fingers touched hers. He moved her hands to the correct position, placing her right index finger under the rod, ensuring it rested against the line. The touch of her skin sent his heart racing.

His eyes met hers. He could have looked at those eyes for hours if he had the chance. They were ocean blue and mesmerising. She softly licked her lips.

Maybe she wanted to kiss him. He had thought about kissing her many times; maybe now was the right time.

"You fishing, or just going to stand there looking at each other all day?" her brother mocked.

"Thanks, I have it now," Becca said, pulling her hands away.

Tommy dragged a spare handline out of his gear and baited the hook, which he had brought in case Elijah wanted to fish.

Tommy cast his line into the water, sat on a small grass patch on the bank, looked over to Becca and smiled.

She smiled back.

Fishing was slow. No one was catching anything. Tommy and Becca remained on the bank chatting about general stuff that kids their age talked about. There was only one thing they never discussed and that was the war. Their talking was full of the usual awkward pauses when teens sometimes don't know what to say.

"What do you want to do when you're older?" Becca asked.

"A detective," Tommy said swiftly. "You?"

"A teacher," she said, smiling.

Her answer sent Tommy's thoughts to something completely unexpected— the tunnel. Were the rumours true?

He turned his head. High on the hill in the distance the tunnel's dark mouth over his left shoulder stared back, as if it were alive and somehow calling him, whispering in his ear, "Come to me." A shiver ran through him.

Tommy recalled the day he had first heard the myth about the creature they called the Hat Man. It had become folklore amongst the students of Picton Primary. The myth had only grown over the last twenty-five years. By the time it reached Tommy's impressionable ears, the Hat Man had been responsible for Anne's death and her friends' as well. According to classmate Mark McGuire, Hat Man was able to breath fire from his mouth and put you in a trance with his eyes, and he was still haunting the tunnel.

Tommy, curious about Mark's Hat Man story, had raced straight to the church after school to see if it was true. His dad refused to discuss the validity of the story except to say it was based on a normal person who had done bad things. "Lost his way and now he is in jail paying for his sins."

Tommy was mesmerised by the darkness of the tunnel, still wondering if the Hat Man stories that Mark had told were true.

"Do you think he's real?" Becca asked. She must have noticed the direction of his gaze.

Tommy didn't answer. He was still deep in thought.

"Tommy?" Becca asked again.

"Huh?" he said, coming out of his trance.

"The Hat Man creature, do you think he's real?"

"Pa says it was just some guy who lost his way and now he's in jail," Tommy answered.

"Well, here's your chance to be a detective. We could go look and see for ourselves," Becca said excitedly.

She placed her rod on the bank and took Tommy by the hand, as a girlfriend would do. Sparks ran up his arm. Feelings of excitement and fear conflicted within his body.

"I don't think we should. Pa said to stay away," Tommy said.

"I thought you wanted to be a detective?" Becca questioned.

"Yeah, but Pa said we shouldn't go near the tunnel."

Becca ignored his pleas, pulling him up the hill by the hand.

He passed Elijah still nestled under his tree, his head in his book.

"Where you going?" Elijah asked.

"Up to the tunnel," Becca answered for Tommy.

"But Pa said—" Elijah was cut off mid-sentence by his brother.

"Don't be a baby. We'll be back soon," Tommy said, with an attitude Elijah didn't recognise.

Stunned, Elijah watched as Tommy and Becca walked hand in hand towards the tunnel.

They stood holding hands under the shadow of the tunnel's entrance. The heat had given way to a cool, if not cold, breeze from within the tunnel. Tommy noticed their arms had erupted in goose bumps.

Becca took the first steps inside the tunnel, but Tommy remained flatfooted on the outside. She pulled on his hand several times, yet he didn't budge.

"You, coming?" Becca asked with a smile that made the world disappear.

Tommy answered with his feet, stepping inside the darkness.

They walked deeper into the chill towards the alcove.

"This is where he pushed her," Tommy said.

"Well, he's not here anymore," Becca replied.

Tommy was busy scanning the tunnel for any sign of this mysterious Hat Man.

Becca placed her hand on his face. "It's okay. He's not here. We're alone. Do you like me, Tommy?" She stepped closer.

"Ye-ye-yes. Of course." He croaked and stuttered his answer.

"No one can see us here, Tommy. You can kiss me if you like." Becca smiled her world-stopping smile. He could only just see it in the dim light.

Tommy put his nerves aside, closed his eyes and leant in. The kiss was amazing, and like nothing he had ever experienced. He instantly wanted more. Her lips were soft and damp and tasted like strawberries. Her hair brushed against his face. He had never known feelings as wonderful as these before.

As he opened his eyes, his thoughts were instantly replaced by fear. Towering over Becca stood a faceless, shadowy man wearing a wide-brimmed hat and with eyes of blazing red.

Tommy screamed. Becca joined him seconds later. Her scream was so loud, it ricocheted off the tunnel walls and out into the open air. It reached both Elijah and Adam clearly.

Adam dropped his rod and ran towards the tunnel. Elijah stood up from his reading spot, dropping his book in the dirt, losing his place as it landed.

He stood motionless at the tree as he saw Adam run and then disappear into the tunnel.

Adam arrived in the tunnel to find both Becca and Tommy suspended in mid-air, three feet off the ground. Suspended in time and space—they were in a trance. Their eyes were wide open, fear on their faces, their hands still interlocked.

A thin, bony creature wearing a long coat and a hat stood behind them, transfixed, letting out a grumble, like a hungry dog.

Adam picked up several rocks that lay just inside the entrance, hurling them at the thing in the hat. The first rock flew high and to the left. The second one hit it right in the head, sending it backwards and Tommy and Becca sprawling to the ground.

Adam threw a third rock, this one bigger than the last two. It hit the 'man' in the right shoulder as it regained its balance. Hat Man shrugged and flew across the tunnel floor. Hovering inches above the ground, Hat Man was just feet from Adam's face. Adam wanted to back-pedal, but his feet refused to obey. Like Tommy and Becca, he was frozen to the spot.

Hat Man stood, eyes blazing. The two little holes that Adam thought was its nose flared and retracted every few seconds. Then as Hat Man grinned, yellow, jagged teeth appeared. A wretched smell came from its mouth. It was unfamiliar to Adam, but it was the worst thing he had ever smelt.

Hat Man raised his right hand, lifting it from down beside his leg, moving it into a throwing position. His arm was locked and loaded as if he was about to fling something at Adam, except his hand was empty. Behind him, a rock rose from the ground. It was bigger than all three of the rocks Adam had thrown. Hat Man swung his arm like a baseball pitcher. The rock flew through the air. It swung around Hat Man's shoulder. That was when Adam realised it was heading straight for him. His initial reaction was to try to duck and dive to the ground. Yet he couldn't move, no matter how hard he tried. The rock hit his forehead. Before he could react, he was sent flying backwards.

As he landed, he felt blood pour down his face. Through the dripping blood he watched as Tommy and Becca struggled to get up as if the spell over them had been broken.

"Run!" Adam screamed.

He repeated his instructions several times in the following seconds as he staggered out of the tunnel.

Hat Man followed him out into the sunlight.

He's coming for me, Adam thought, trying to run. His legs were not cooperating. They couldn't hold his weight and as his vision blurred with concussion and cascading blood, he couldn't seem to maintain his balance. Nothing was working. He dropped to the ground.

Adam wiped the blood from his face only to see Hat Man standing over him. Behind him he could see Becca and Tommy fleeing the tunnel. They veered towards the pile of sleepers stacked on the ridge.

Hide, Adam thought.

Hat Man's shadow was long and thin, just like the bony fingers that suddenly appeared out from under the coat. Adam was pulled up by the throat. He could feel the bones shifting against the side of his neck. The knuckles cracked and creaked as they moved.

Tommy and Becca scurried towards the sleepers, but Adam was no longer aware of where they were. His face remained inches from Hat Man's plain featureless face. Its snake-like nostrils continued to flare as if smelling the fear oozing out of Adam.

Adam felt as if he was about to be devoured.

He didn't realise until he felt the warm liquid against his leg, but he had begun to piss himself.

Bruises appeared under Hat Man's bony thumbs. Hat Man snarled again, displaying his horrible teeth. Adam felt his whole body shudder with fear.

Hat Man drew a deep breath, sucking up all the fear. When satisfied it had taken all Adam had to give, Hat Man squeezed its thin claws until Adam's neck snapped under the pressure. From his place near the sleepers, Tommy gasped as he heard Adam's neck crack. He could see Adam's head drop to one side, his eyes still wide open, his mouth agape as if about to speak.

Hat Man dropped Adam's body onto the dusty dry ground.

Tommy was ready to run again, but for some reason he needed to know what this thing, this Hat Man, was doing. It remained in the same spot staring at Adam's lifeless carcass; admiring its handiwork perhaps.

Before Tommy could work out what Hat Man was waiting for, it happened. Adam's soul rose, like the last smoke of an extinguished fire.

Adam clearly hadn't realised he was dead. He doesn't know what's happened, Tommy thought.

A bright beam of light appeared midway between Adam and the stack of sleepers where Tommy and Becca were crouched. The beam was brighter than any sunlight Tommy had ever witnessed.

Maybe it was the shock or the dry summer's day, or a combination of the two, but Tommy couldn't generate enough base in his voice to shout, so what should have been his call to run came out only as 'n' followed by a dry coughing fit.

Tommy's eyes captured the horror of Adam's soul fighting to reach the light.

Adam's soul had either reacted to his cry or was automatically drawn to the beam of light; either way it began to move. Hat Man reacted to the soul's movement, its bony claws leaping into action, slamming into the sides of Adam's soul somehow, disappearing into the translucent figure that was now Adam.

Once the claws were inserted, Adam's momentum towards the light ceased. Despite his struggling, he wasn't breaking free of Hat Man's hold. The light began to fade as quickly as it had arrived, then it vanished.

What Tommy saw next made him want his father and more importantly God's protection that he'd often spoken of. He tried to remember his prayers but they too, like his voice, had deserted him when he needed them most.

Hat Man lifted Adam's soul up and towards his mouth, then swallowed it.

"We need to run. Don't stop until we're clear of this place," Tommy told Becca.

She only nodded in agreement, still holding Tommy's hand.

They turned and sprinted down the bank, with the sleeper stack providing perfect cover. Elijah hadn't followed Adam. He'd chosen to stay behind and look after their belongings. At least that's what's he would tell Tommy when asked. The truth of it was that the scream that had sent Adam running to his sister's aid had the opposite effect on Elijah. Instead of filling him with adrenaline to run to battle, it had paralysed him with fear. He had interpreted the scream as not one of *help*, but as a warning to stay away.

Stay away he did. He remained under the shade of his reading tree, eyes transfixed on the hill in the distance. There was no sign of anyone since Adam had disappeared beyond its crest.

Elijah had been staring so long his eyes had begun to water.

Finally, movement came. It was Tommy and Becca running out from behind the sleeper pile back towards where they had been fishing. A huge rumble sounded behind them, which Becca first mistook for thunder. Tommy saw it first, tumbling behind him, chasing him. Somehow, the whole pile of sleepers had broken free and were hurtling towards them.

Tommy pulled Becca by the hand, and they darted to the left. The sleepers followed. One bounced behind them before lifting and hurling itself over their heads. Had it not been for Tommy's peripheral vision and exquisite timing in ducking, both would have been decapitated. Another sleeper rolled, edge to edge, accelerating along the ground as it chased the pair. Tommy expected the sleeper to bounce and fly through the air. Unfortunately for both of them he was wrong; it dived, staying just inches off the ground, taking their legs from under them.

As Tommy flew backwards through the air, he caught a glimpse of several other sleepers changing direction. It appeared as if they were alive. How could that be, Tommy thought.

He landed hard. With the fall, his connection to Becca was lost. Their hands separated for the first time since they had touched.

Tommy didn't see the second sleeper land on Becca, crushing her chest and killing her instantly, until he had stopped tumbling.

He sat there in disbelief, stunned. Time had stopped. All he could see was Becca's lifeless body crushed, almost split in two. The green grass on which she lay was covered in a widening pool of crimson.

Transfixed on Becca's now lifeless body, Tommy lost his desire for self-preservation. His fate had been sealed when Becca was hit; Tommy just didn't know it. Sleepers hurtled past him. One clipped his shoulder, another just missed his head, creating a swift gust of wind as it passed. Finally, a sleeper collected him. It struck him on the back of the head. There was nothing else for Tommy, until he rose.

Elijah had watched both Becca and his brother die. He stayed hidden behind the tree as the sleepers made their assault down the hill towards the creek bank. Only one sleeper gathered enough speed to reach the water itself. It was the first one that Tommy had managed to duck under.

With only one eye peering out from behind the tree trunk, Elijah saw something he would never forget. Two spirits rose as if called by Jesus himself. Becca was first, followed a few seconds later by Tommy. Both just hovered there looking at their own bodies.

A man stood at the top of the hill. He was tall, thin and wore a hat. Elijah thought about calling to him for help, but his gut told him to stay hidden.

The man didn't walk down the hill; instead, he glided. Elijah gasped, before clasping a hand over his mouth to stifle the scream and cowering back behind the tree's thick trunk.

Only managing a brief glance now and then, he saw what appeared to be the ghost of Tommy join that of Becca. Together, they ran off in the distance towards the creek. A bright light had appeared on the riverbank, brighter than any light Elijah had ever seen. He could even feel its heat from where he was standing. At first, he thought it was where Tommy and Becca were heading but they chose to ignore the light, instead continuing towards town.

By the time the light disappeared, the ghosts of Tommy and Becca were barely visible. Elijah remained hidden behind the tree. With the light gone, the heat had disappeared also. Suddenly Elijah felt very cold.

The tall man in the hat stopped the pursuit of Tommy and Becca once they had reached the bank. Now it was just standing there. Elijah hugged the tree, making sure every part of him was hidden.

When he dared to look from behind tree, the riverbank was empty. He scanned the hill for the man, but all that remained were the fallen sleepers and the crushed bodies of Tommy and Becca.

Elijah sprinted frantically back towards town, leaving the fishing gear where it lay and his book still at the base of the tree, pages fluttering in the wind.

When Elijah returned home, his face was ashen, sickly and drawn.

His mother immediately ran to his aid. "Elijah what's wrong? You look like death warmed up."

Elijah fell into her arms, mumbling incoherently. After realising Tommy wasn't in tow, she asked the whereabouts of his elder brother. His pa came running into the front yard at the cries of his wife. Elijah managed to tell his parents all he knew, including the mysterious 'man' he had seen after the sleeper collapse. The only part he omitted was the souls rising; that was just too bizarre.

"Where is Tommy?" his mum continued to ask.

"I think he's dead," Elijah replied.

His mum screamed. His pa comforted her in his arms. "Let's not jump to conclusions. I'll take the sergeant and we'll go and look," he said in a calm, forthright manner.

"Elijah says he's dead," she repeated.

"I'm sure he's mistaken, he's probably just injured," Pa said. "I told you boys to stay away from those sleepers because they're dangerous."

When Pa arrived back in the late afternoon, he too was ashen. Elijah stood at the window watching his dad tell his mother what he had known all along. Tommy was dead.

His mother fell to the ground. Her screams filled the afternoon air. That terrible sound was now etched in Elijah's memory.

His pa knelt beside her. Elijah and his parents were never the same after that horrendous day.

Chapter 32

Picton December 2016

Jake arrived back at his hotel after spending the afternoon driving around the town. He had been to all the places he knew Lucas had been; the wreckers and the Redbank Range Tunnel…only he hadn't stepped foot past the green gate. That whole place freaked him out for some reason.

He also walked amongst the tombstones, next to the chapel. It was quiet and peaceful. Nothing about it made him feel uneasy. He felt no evil presence amongst the dead, that was for sure.

It was nearing dinner when he walked up the steps of the hotel entrance to be greeted again by Isabella. Jake wondered if she had any other staff, or if she did everything herself.

"Any news?" Isabella asked.

Jake stopped at the foot of the stairs to answer her. He didn't want to come across as rude. "No, I'm afraid not."

"Well, let me know if there's anything you need."

"Will do. While I'm here, were there any calls for me? My mobile doesn't get any service around town."

"It's a bit of a dead spot for reception, this place. Let me check." Isabella shuffled through some papers on her desk, and about twenty seconds later was able to answer his question. "Yes, a Monique called," she said, holding a yellow Post-It note.

So that was the high-tech system run here in Picton. Yellow Post-It notes.

Jake doubted if everyone got their messages. He took his out of politeness and began to head for his room.

"Is Monique your girlfriend?" Isabella asked.

Jake again stopped mid-step. "No, she's a work colleague."

"Does she have any information on your missing friend?"

"I'll ring her and find out," Jake said, ending the conversation regardless of Isabella's intentions.

After speaking to Monique, the only new information Jake had to go on was about Lucas's phone. According to Monique's search, the last time his phone had pinged was off the same tower that Talia's phone had last registered.

It was a coincidence Jake couldn't ignore. What had they stumbled upon?

Whatever Talia had found, Jake now thought it was highly likely that Lucas had found it too.

Although hungry, Jake decided dinner would wait. He needed to go to the phone tower and see what he could find.

Isabella was still at the desk as he left the hotel.

"What did you find out?" she called.

Ignoring her, Jake continued on his way.

Upon his arrival at the tower, located at the corner of Old Hume Highway and Mount Hercules Road, Jake expected to find something; a broken-down car perhaps. There was nothing. Nothing but open spaces, bare paddocks and old farmhouses with the occasional shed.

He stood beside his car and looked across the wide-open fields abutting the highway. A house set approximately two hundred metres down from the corner was visible. Up the side road he could just make out another farmhouse, high on the hill, with the sun setting behind it. On the other side of the side street, perhaps a little closer to him, was a third farmhouse.

On the lower side of the highway were two long driveways, side by side. The only thing separating them was a pair of mailboxes. One read *Marsh*, the other *Forrest*. The driveways veered off in different directions. Jake could see the Forrest farmhouse down deep in the gully on his right.

Jake looked for the farmhouse on the left, but it was hidden from the road. As it was meal time it was likely the owners would be home.

Jake enquired, but neither the Forrests nor the Marshes had seen anything suspicious. No broken-down cars. Neither of them had seen Talia or Lucas either.

Jake headed over to the other side of the highway. He started with the house just down from the corner, followed by the one up the hill on the left. Again, neither of the owners had seen anything, or anyone.

So far, he had door-knocked the immediate area, without a single lead. The only remaining house was the one on the hill. After that he would have to door-knock along the highway until he reached the next tower.

Out of all the farms he had visited so far, this was by far the biggest. It had large sheds and a large barn, although the house was relatively small. Jake could see a large tractor sitting on the hilltop.

Jake made his way up the dusty drive and headed over to the house on his left. The steps were half rotten and a little dangerous, so Jake side-stepped those spots. The front door was made of timber; the house was weatherboard with paint peeling off, obviously affected by the sun.

Jake felt the floor shake as someone approached to answer his knock. The door swung open and Jake was staring at the neck of a hulking man in overalls. The overalls were covered in blood, the sight of which shook Jake a little.

The man seemed to realise his appearance had shocked his visitor. "I'm sorry about the blood; I had to butcher a lamb today. Gives us meat for a month. I haven't had time to clean up yet."

Jake introduced himself and showed his badge, as he had done at the four previous homes. The big guy introduced himself as Dave Brown. The name sounded familiar, but he couldn't quite place it yet.

Jake shook his hand and even though Jake was strong, he felt this guy was about to crush every bone in his hand.

Jake asked the same questions as at the other four residences. "Have you seen this woman or this man around here in the last couple of days?" Jake showed pictures on his phone of Lucas and Talia.

Dave said he hadn't seen either of them. Then he frowned. "Wait a minute, show me a photo of that guy again."

Jake swiped back through his phone.

"Yeah, I saw that guy. He was talking to my brother in the pub. He wanted to know about that girl who killed herself. Then he was asking about the ghost tours."

"When was that?" Jake asked.

"About two or three nights ago, I think. But I'd have to check with my brother."

"Is he home?"

"No, sorry; he's gone to the market. He'll be back tomorrow night."

"You sure you haven't seen these two around here?"

"Positive."

Jake described their vehicles to Dave. "Have you seen either of these?"

"No. Sorry." He grinned. "Maybe he got scared of the ghosts and left town. It happens a lot around here."

"What do you know about the ghosts?"

"They're a crock of shit, spread about by that crazy lady who runs the tour company. She makes hundreds of thousands a year from telling people about ghosts," Dave said dismissively.

"What do you know about the Hat Man?" Jake asked.

"That's just hearsay. Apparently, a hundred years ago this town had three freak deaths. Two of them ended up being identified as murders by a man who worked in the hospital. He killed a nurse, if I recall. Anyway, it turned out he'd been stalking other townspeople in a long coat and a big hat. I believe that's the legend of the Hat Man. The rest is embellishment by that tour lady."

"Megan?" Jake confirmed.

"Yep, that's her. Would you like to come in? I'm cooking some of the lamb now, and there's plenty to go around."

Although Jake loved lamb, the sight of a blood-soaked Dave put him off. The man should have cleaned up before preparing food. "I'd better get going, thanks. More houses to visit. Please call me when your brother gets back." Jake handed Dave his card.

Jake headed north up the highway. It was about three kilometres before he saw another tower. There were eight houses on the high side and nine on the low. Jake door-knocked every house; all but three occupants were home. None had seen anything of Lucas or Talia or their vehicles.

It was dead-ends all round.

By the time Jake arrived back at the hotel, it was 9 and he was past hungry. He would settle for something small, maybe just some hot chips; definitely not meat, not tonight.

Jake rang reception to see if he could order some chips. Isabella was still on duty. She advised him room service ran until 10. He was in luck. He placed his order.

"Do you want a burger with that?" she asked.

"No thank you," Jake responded quickly.

"Be about ten minutes," Isabella finished, before hanging up.

The chips were beer-battered, thick-cut and came with tubs of herb mayo and tomato sauce. They were delightful.

Jake had an accompanying Coke and rang Hayley while he finished off the last few chips.

Indiana was well and truly asleep, and Hayley was spending the night reading. Since Indiana's birth, she hadn't had a lot of time for it. The older Indiana became, the more time she seemed to gain.

Jake told her of his dead-end with Lucas, and Hayley provided a listening ear as she always did but offered no solution in this case.

Jake watched TV for an hour or so, trying to clear his mind.

Sleep took him before he could think any more about the case.

*

He woke suddenly to the sound of running water. Where the hell was he? Where was the noise coming from?

From the bathroom, his mind acknowledged. The rushing water sound had now changed to a slow drip.

Switching on the light, Jake noticed steam rising from under the bathroom door as if someone was having a hot shower or running a bath.

Jake got up abruptly. The bedside drawers had been opened. The cabinet drawers under the TV were also open. The steam had reached his bed. Jake could even feel the dampness of the steam against his arms.

Someone was in his room. Jake reached for his gun, a Glock that lay on the bedside table. The feel of the metal gun in his hand made him feel safer, yet the steam and the dripping sound terrified him. He looked over at the alarm clock to gauge the time. The clock was flashing midnight. He glanced at the wall clock; it also showed midnight. This didn't seem real. It seemed much later.

He stood barefoot on the carpet, his feet by now covered by the steam. With his gun by his side, he headed towards the steam and whoever was in the bathroom. The carpet felt damper the closer he got to the bathroom. As he reached the door, the carpet became wet; he could feel the water flow between his toes.

Jake thought about giving a verbal warning to whoever was on the other side of the door, as he would have done in his days on the force. Yet he thought it better to have the advantage of surprise.

The door was slightly ajar, so Jake flung it open to reveal the intruder.

He stood back from the door, his gun positioned by his cheek, both hands clasped around the grip, finger on the trigger, always ready for what he might encounter.

He stepped into the bathroom, arms now extended, gun at the ready. Jake fully expected to find someone, but the room was empty.

Water washed over his feet, overflowing from the bath, yet the taps were turned off. His immediate thoughts reverted to the ghost stories Megan had told him in the diner.

'A nurse is thought to haunt the hotel,' he remembered her saying. Jake made his way over to the bath, ready to release the water. He placed his Glock on the sink and leant over the bath. The water was hot, steam rising from the top.

Could this be the work of the ghost he'd been warned about? Before he knew it, Jake was overpowered and forced into the hot water by the body of a dead girl. Its flesh was blue and rotting. Arms came flailing up from under the water and dragged him under. Chunks of her slimy flesh fell off in the struggle.

Quickly and forcefully, Jake ripped himself free and scrambled to his feet. His gun was back in his hand ready to fire at whatever had grabbed him. Instantly the girl was gone. Had the girl in the tub been Gemma Bassil?

How was that possible? She was dead.

Had he just seen the ghost of the person they were investigating?

Jake double-checked the bath. Not only was the girl gone, the water had also vanished. The steam had dissipated. Jake triple-checked the bath. The corpse was gone. Everything was as it had been hours earlier. The bathroom floor was no longer wet. The carpet was now bone dry!

Had he imagined the whole thing? Was the vision of Gemma just a figment of his tired and overworked imagination?

Jake didn't know any longer. What he experienced had felt real enough – but was it?

Jake sat on his bed, every light in the room on. TV on. His knees were bent up, folded in. He crossed his arms and rested his head on them, with his Glock still gripped firmly in his right hand.

His body so badly wanted sleep, and it took all of his will to stay awake. He tried watching the TV just to keep himself alert. Only infomercials were showing, and the demonstration of a magical non-stick pot provided no help with his battle to stay awake.

Jake's eyes closed briefly before he forced them open again.

His eyes were back on the TV. He looked up at the wall clock. It still said midnight, although it must have been at least twenty minutes since he'd first looked at it.

The clock radio still flashed 12.00. Jake hadn't bothered to reset it and he wasn't going to.

The lady demonstrating a magic pot on the commercial showed the finished product of the scrambled eggs she had baked. "Light fluffy and delicious," she said. They looked delicious, Jake thought. He wondered if Hayley would have liked a magic pot, maybe. Jake even considered buying one, then realised that was exactly what the infomercial was hoping for, tired people like himself giving in when they weren't thinking straight.

Jake's eyes closed again. This time he succumbed to the need for sleep. He had lost his battle to stay awake.

Jake dreamt of a door, a bright, white door, shaking on its hinges. He and the door were surrounded by darkness. The floor began to vibrate. The whistle of a train sounded to his left, deep in the darkness. The floor beneath his feet began to rock and shake, and the train whistle sounded again. It was much closer this time.

A strong beam of light broke the darkness. At first, Jake thought it was a lighthouse beam. The light hit the side of his face, instantly blinding him. Jake stood back from the shaking door, shielded his eyes with his palm and looked directly into the light. It was a train and it was coming straight for him. The blackness around him gave up its secret. He was in a tunnel and Jake suspected which one. The only way to avoid being hit by the train was to go through the shaking white door. Jake dived for the handle as fast as his reflexes would allow. He pulled hard, but the door remained closed. He pulled again. The train was gaining ground quickly. Still nothing. Jake pushed and then pulled. The train was now almost upon him. From the corner of his eye he saw an alcove off the side of the tracks. Jake dived into the alcove expecting the train to whistle past soon after. Yet it was still in the distance.

Jake gathered himself.

The first thing Jake saw were two flaming red circles. They moved in unison towards him. Jake reached for his gun, whipping it from his belt and gripping it firmly by his side.

"Freeze!" Jake called.

The fiery dots continued to advance upon him.

Jake repeated his call, yet it went unheeded.

The tall man stepped forward, with eyes ablaze. Jake looked at his face yet couldn't see his mouth or nose. The man was wearing a wide-brimmed hat and a long jacket.

Out of the jacket appeared long bony hands, which pushed Jake in the chest, sending him flying backwards.

Jake fired his gun as his feet left the ground. "Soon," the Hat Man called, as Jake flew back into the path of the train.

Jake braced for impact, but nothing happened.

Suddenly he woke. He lurched his head up from his folded arms. The reflex action sent a sharp pain down the back of his neck and into his spine. Jake was breathing frantically, deep heavy breaths, his whole chest heaving. Sweat soaked his back.

The room was in complete darkness.

Power must have gone out, was Jake's immediate thought. He looked to where the clock radio usually sat but there was nothing. Jake was surprised there was no flashing lights; maybe the battery backup was faulty, he guessed.

Jake stretched out with his left hand and fumbled about the top of the bedside table trying to locate his mobile. His palm and fingertips padded the top of the table. He reached for his clock radio, but the tabletop was empty. Jake continued to pad down the table and finally the tips of his fingers touched the protective rubber casing of his phone. He clasped it and dragged it towards him.

Jake couldn't hear or see anything, but he could feel a presence. It was as if someone was watching him. His nose twitched. A foul smell hit him. It was a smell he had smelt once before. It was burning flesh.

Jake flicked the torch on his iPhone on. It lit up the bedside table. His clock radio was gone. He shone his phone around the room from the front door back towards his bed. There was nothing visible at first until it revealed a girl who was standing at the foot of his bed.

It was Gemma, naked and soaking, and staring at Jake, the light from his phone revealing her face. It had no expression. She closed her eyes, turned and walked away.

Jake watched her disappear into the bathroom.

Subconsciously, Jake had been holding his breath. Finally, he took a breath.

His heart was beating rapidly. It was going so fast he could hardly breathe. He sucked in air through his nose.

Jake crept to his feet, desperately trying not to make a sound. Unfortunately, his body was too big for that to be a possibility. When he stood up, the bed let out a creak that was only amplified by the still of the night.

Jake made his way quietly to the edge of the bathroom door. His feet standing on wet carpet for the second time tonight, Jake peered into the bathroom. Gemma's decomposing corpse was sitting quietly in the bath. She placed a washcloth over her face.

Music began to play on the clock radio that had relocated itself to the side of the vanity. It was resting delicately on the side. Jake noted it wasn't even plugged in. Jake didn't recognise the song playing immediately, but he was sure it was one of Katy Perry's hits.

A dark figure brushed past Jake. It was moving slowly. Jake tried to make out what or who it was but all he could be sure of, was that it was a human shape. Jake held his breath as the dark shape paused in the bathroom looking over the bath. The radio played on.

Without warning, the black shape threw the radio into the bath where Gemma was lying. Gemma's body shook, twitching and convulsing violently. Her legs buckled. Her body fell silent, motionless. The dark thing that had thrown the radio turned and left the room.

Jake was trying to process what he had just witnessed when the lights and the TV returned to life. The room was suddenly bright again. The clock radio had reset and was now showing 5.30 am.

Jake wondered who or what the other ghost was.

What was this whole night about?

Who was the dark figure? Was it the man from his dream?

Jake was totally confused.

Sleep for him was out of the question. There was no way he could sleep now after what he had just seen.

Chapter 33

Picton December 2016

Overnight, the container had cooled considerably. The humidity that had made the box nearly unbearable during the day was replaced by cold night air. It had cooled so much that Talia was shivering. The skimpy blanket was totally inadequate.

Talia had been woken by movement and talking outside her box about 6 am. It was the brothers. Their voices were unmistakable.

Breakfast was due in half an hour, if yesterday's schedule was anything to go by. Considering they ran a farm, Talia expected they would remain true to their schedule.

She lay there listening to them talking, trying to make out individual words, yet it all came through muffled. She could hear them moving around outside and listened patiently for that gate latch. As soon as she heard it, the count began. *One cat and dog, two cat and dog.* By the time she got to *twenty-four cat and dog*, the door opened.

The timing was within one second of yesterday's count.

Now she could plan.

Talia was sitting on her mattress like a good little girl waiting to be fed her breakfast.

This time it was the shorter and older brother who brought in the food. He'd been in the fields on the tractor when the younger brother had kidnapped her. He didn't seem to object to his brother's decision.

He placed a tray of food along with a fresh bottle of water on the floor of the shipping container and left without saying a word.

Talia looked at the plate. Vegemite on toast. She was starving, and she doubted two small pieces of toast would do much to ease her rumbling stomach.

Talia kept looking at the ceiling grates, but they were too high up. Even if she stood on the upturned bucket, she wouldn't reach them. She would be short by at least half a metre. There had to be another way to escape this prison.

Then the idea came to her.

Next time one of them came, she would be ready with the bucket in hand.

She thought her best chance would be to empty the contents of the now nearly full bucket, her toilet, on whichever brother came in next. While he was turning away from the flying crap (as anyone would do) she would then turn her bucket into a weapon, striking him repeatedly on the head.

It was hard metal, and swung with enough power it could do serious damage to someone's head.

Talia still had no idea why they had taken her or the other girls. To be sold as sex slaves, or tortured, or worse? She wasn't going to wait to find out. At the next opportunity she would have to make a run for it.

Where would she go? She couldn't just run without purpose or without any idea about where she was running.

She needed to see outside just to get her bearings.

Her toast was cold, and too thick with Vegemite for her liking, yet this wasn't the time to be picky about her food.

The water was cold and refreshing, yet it would only stay that way for a short time before the container heated up again in the summer sun.

Chapter 34

Picton December 2016

Jake didn't care that it was only 7.45 am. He had been up for hours and he was done waiting.

He dialled Megan's number. The phone rang a few times before switching over to voicemail. Jake clicked the receiver and dialled again. It rang a few times before switching over to voicemail once more.

"Fuck!" Jake screamed.

Megan was probably still asleep. Maybe she'd had a late night showing more ghosts on the tour.

He dialled again, and it rang twice before an angry and tired Megan answered.

"Hello?" she slurred.

"Megan, it's Jake. We need to talk."

"What's this about?"

"I'll tell you when I see you. Too much to get into over the phone," Jake replied.

"Give me thirty. I'll meet you at the coffee shop."

"Okay, thanks." Jake hung up and headed to the coffee shop immediately. He wanted to be waiting there when Megan arrived.

Jake waved her over as Megan entered the coffee shop.

"Sorry about my appearance. I rushed out." Megan sounded anxious.

Jake, who couldn't care less about appearance, especially his own during a criminal investigation, answered quickly and professionally, "You look great. I think I saw her," he added.

"Saw who?"

"Gemma Bassil," Jake answered. "Well, her ghost at least."

"What do you mean? What happened?"

Jake went through the details of the night before, from start to finish. "Why do think she visited me?"

"I think she was trying to communicate with you," Megan replied.

"Okay. But who do you think the other ghost was?"

"The one that pushed the radio into the bath?"

"Yes. Who was that?"

"I think it was Gemma too. She was trying to show you what happened."

"What do you mean...*Gemma too*?"

"Spirits are not like humans. They can do many things. I think she was showing you how she died. You said the clock radio was suddenly in the bathroom, she was in the bath and music was playing. I think she was showing you exactly what happened."

"If she was showing me her murder, why wouldn't she show me who it was?" Jake asked.

"Maybe she doesn't know who it was, only that it happened," Megan offered.

"Sounds crazy."

"Well, does what happened last night look like the crime scene photos?" Megan asked.

"I haven't seen them."

"I suggest you go and find out. Then you'll know. Spirits don't tend to visit people for fun. Usually they have a reason."

"Why don't spirits go to heaven?" Jake asked, looking away.

"You're not a spiritual man, are you, Jake?" Megan guessed.

"No, I've seen too much evil to believe in God."

"In my opinion, some spirits get stuck between their life on earth and wherever they're going. Until they can find peace, they're stuck here. That's why Gemma still haunts that room. Once she comes to terms with her death, she will move on. That's my theory anyhow. Oh, and I do believe good people go to heaven." She got up. "I have to go, but let me know how you fare with the crime scene photos."

She put on her yellow woollen cardigan which she had hung over the back of the chair.

Jake reached out and took her hand. "Wait, I have something else."

"Mr Miller, I really need to be going."

"I saw the Hat Man. He came to me in a dream."

"I really don't have time to listen to your dreams. Maybe we could catch up later."

"I don't think it was a real dream. I have marks; three lines like burns, where he touched me in my dream." He sat looking up at Megan's face. She had instantly become pale and she reached for her chair and sank into it.

"Did you speak to the pastor?" she asked.

"No, the old guy I spoke to said the pastor had moved out."

"The old guy *is* the pastor," Megan replied. "You need to speak to him."

"Why? What does he know about Hat Man?"

"He thinks Hat Man is the devil and killed his whole family. Speak to him." She sighed. "I really can't help you when it comes to Hat Man. A couple of people on my tours, along with your friend and Talia, are the only ones I know who have ever seen him. The rest is a myth that has been around this town for a hundred years." Megan stood for a second time. "I really have to go. I'm late for an appointment. Speak to the pastor and look at the crime scene photos and we can chat again."

Jake nodded and watched her leave. Then he jumped on his phone.

No service. He would have to go back to the hotel.

*

Jake returned to find the hotel reception unattended.

By the time he reached the top of the stairs, Isabella was just leaving his room.

"Just making up your room. Is there anything I can get for you?" she asked.

"No, I'm fine, thank you," Jake replied.

The room looked clean. The bed was made, and there were fresh towels in the bathroom, but one thing puzzled Jake. She had no cleaning equipment, and no trolley full of dirty linen with her. Oh well, maybe she'd already done that and had just come back to finish off a few things.

He headed for the phone sitting on the desk at the end of the bed and dialled Monique. While he waited for the phone to connect, he pulled up the chair that sat at the desk. The phone connected to an automated receptionist. "If you know the extension number, please enter it now, otherwise hold for reception," the robotic voice stated.

Jake entered Monique's four-digit number and waited again. He picked up the pen sitting on the pad to his right. That was when he noticed it. At first it was almost invisible, but the harder he looked the clearer it became. There were indentations on the notepad. Someone, maybe Lucas, had written himself a note.

All Jake needed was a pencil to bring it to life. He searched the desk drawer. There were 'with compliments' slips, local restaurant menus, some promotional matches, and resting against the back of the drawer, a grey lead pencil.

Jake glided the edge of the pencil across the indented words. Three lines appeared.

Red Truck F100?

Gemma's Friday afternoon?

Talia?

"Hello?" a voice from the phone said. "Is anyone there?"

Jake stopped staring at the inscribed page. "Monique, it's Jake," he mumbled, still trying to think what the note meant.

"I was about to have this call traced, Jake," Monique said.

"Having stalker issues again?"

"No more than usual," Monique said.

Jake wondered how many crazies the top cop would attract. He had attracted a few in his time and he was only a detective.

"Monique, could I bother you with a few requests?" He'd originally rung wanting help with the crime scene photos, but since he'd discovered the note he had two other searches to be done.

"What do you need?" she said.

"Who do I speak to about getting a hold of the crime scene photos for Gemma Bassil's death?"

"Inspector Mike Connolly. He's based in Thirlmere, just outside Picton. Tell him you worked for me. He'll give you whatever you need."

"Will do, thanks," Jake said.

"What else do you need?"

"Could you find out if any calls were made from this room on Friday the 14th of August 2014?" Jake reeled off the direct line of the room. He waited while Monique scribbled it down at the other end. "Finally, I need to know if there are any red Ford F100s registered around here."

"Okay. But that could take some time. I'll get back to you as soon as I can," Monique said.

Jake was desperate to look at the photos of a deceased Gemma, before the images of the night before faded from his memory. It would be first on his 'to do' list.

But the leads Lucas was following up had also piqued his curiosity. Lucas had said the phone he had found at the wreckers had a photo of a red Ford F100. Had he subsequently located it?

*

Thirlmere December 2016

Jake arrived in Thirlmere just before 1 pm. He walked up the steps leading to the police station as if he owned it. In some ways he still felt a part of the police force, even though he had left months ago.

"Inspector Connolly?" Jake asked the officer at the counter.

"You are?" the officer queried.

"Det—" Jake, stopped himself. "Jake Miller. I'm a private detective."

"Is it regarding something in particular, Mr Miller?"

"Gemma Bassil."

"One moment." The officer disappeared through a door behind the counter.

Jake turned to sit on a bench, before realising there was a guy sleeping across it.

Jake had seen it many times before; guys would usually hide out in the police foyer when they had someone chasing them, wanting to do them harm. Usually it was someone who had slept with someone they shouldn't have.

Jake stood against the wall, folded his arms and waited.

The officer returned. "The inspector will be with you shortly."

"Thank you." Jake waved an arm in appreciation.

The man on the bench suddenly sat upright. He looked around, got his bearings and then gave a sigh of relief when he saw the officer behind the desk.

Jake assumed he'd had a bad dream, or his situation had hit him when he'd woken. "Can I please speak to the detective?" the man asked.

"Sir, you have been told to go home," the officer said calmly.

"But he said he'd kill me! Why won't you help me?" the man asked.

Jake had noticed him looking over his shoulder several times since approaching the desk. Whoever had scared him had done a good job.

"Sir, we've spoken to the man in question. He denies ever threatening you. Unfortunately, our hands are tied until he does something, or threatens you in front of witnesses."

"So, he has to kill me before you will do something?" The man was now terrified and agitated.

"We need him to break the law, or to have proof of him breaking the law. As the detective said, go to the courthouse and apply for an intervention order."

The man thought about his options, took another quick glance over his shoulder and headed out of the police station.

Jake watched as the man paused on the steps outside the station, looked both ways and then sprinted off towards the parking lot.

"Mr Miller!" a male voice called.

Jake returned his attention to the counter.

The inspector stood in the doorway, his wide, stocky body blocking the entrance.

"Did Mrs Bassil hire a whole team of detectives?" he asked.

"Why do you ask that?" Jake said.

"I spoke to a PI about Gemma only a couple of days ago, or maybe you're his replacement? The other guy didn't seem to have much of a clue."

"Lucas is part of my team," Jake said, ignoring his dig at Lucas's ability.

"So how can I help you?" the inspector asked.

"I'd like to see the crime scene photos, please."

"Can't Lucas guide you on that? After all, he's seen them."

Jake didn't want to tell him Lucas was missing as well. At least not until he had heard back from Monique. "Lucas could have taken photos of the crime scene with his phone, but he didn't. He did the right thing. Just one quick look and then I'm out of your hair," Jake offered.

Inspector Connolly knew Jake was right. Lucas could have taken copies of the crime scene; obviously he hadn't. "Come through," the inspector motioned, waving Jake towards him.

The inspector took Jake to the same room he had taken Lucas. He placed the large file on the desk. "Just let me know when you're done."

"Thanks."

Jake was surprised at how helpful the inspector was being. Maybe that was the difference between country police and city police. City police were often more guarded and less friendly. He wondered what Lucas's impressions of the inspector were. He had dealt with the country police more often, and maybe he saw them differently.

Jake sifted through the file, report after report. The police pathologist's initial report was followed by a second and independent pathologist's report.

He flicked through all the statements and the list of the deceased's belongings.

Then he came across the photos. The first was of Gemma in the bath. Exactly as in his dream, the room was steamy, and the radio was at the bottom of the bath. The body was in the same position as the ghost of Gemma had displayed.

Megan was right. It was a re-enactment. This meant one thing. She hadn't killed herself. Based on his vision, she had been murdered. Someone had thrown the radio into the bath. But who? Why?

Jake wondered if she'd met someone while she was in Picton with Paige. A relationship that had gone bad, maybe?

It was a line of enquiry he would need to follow up further.

Jake left the file on the desk. On his way out, he thanked Inspector Connolly for his assistance.

Driving back, those two questions occupied his thoughts. Who? Why?

Jake knew the answer lay in 'why'. If he found out why she was murdered, he would find out who had killed her.

*

Isabella greeted him at hotel reception as usual. "I have some messages for you, Mr Miller," she said, waving more yellow Post-It notes above her head. "A lady named Monique called. She's rung twice. She's not very patient. Seems bossy."

Even if Jake wanted to answer there wasn't a break in Isabella's one-way conversation. "It's as if she didn't think I had given you the message. I told her you were out."

"She's bossy, all right," Jake answered.

He went to retrieve the messages, but Isabella wasn't ready to part with them quite yet.

"It's a good thing you didn't get tangled up with her. You would regret it for the rest of your life. Believe me," Isabella said. Her expression went from one of happiness to one of anger and spite, as if she had once been told she was impatient and overbearing herself. "She wouldn't even tell me what it was about. I think she assumed I must be Picton's Queen of Gossip."

"She's a police officer. She wouldn't be able to tell you. It would be confidential," Jake said.

"Don't you think I can keep confidential information?"

Jake didn't want to get into the whole meaning of that with Isabella because he knew it would be futile. Instead, he humoured her, just to end the conversation. "I'm sure you can. I'll let her know."

Jake didn't even close the door to his room. The urgency to speak to

Monique was buzzing through his body. She had called twice; she must have something of interest.

He looked at his mobile. It showed no missed calls or messages, yet he was sure she had tried his mobile. How did people in this town survive without mobile coverage?

The phone rang only once before Monique answered.

"Hi Jake, I found some interesting stuff."

"Go on."

"We traced the phone from the hotel. There was a call on the Friday afternoon which, from what we can gather, was only minutes after Gemma checked in."

"Who did she call?" Jake asked.

"Inspector Connolly."

"The police department, do you mean?"

"No, Inspector Connolly on his direct number."

"Why would she call him?" Jake asked, frowning.

"No idea, but I think you need to find out."

"I agree."

"In regard to the red F100, I found four registered to addresses in the Picton area," Monique continued.

"How many actually in Picton?" Jake asked.

"Just the one. Registered to a Mr Brown, last registered in 2012. Hasn't been registered since."

Brown? Suddenly, Jake remembered the name. Lucas had mentioned he had spoken to the Brown boys.

"It's registered to an address at 12-16 Mount Hercules Road," Monique said.

Jake knew that was where they lived, right next to the tower...the tower where both Lucas's and Talia's phones had last registered. It was a coincidence too big to ignore, and a great place to start.

Jake decided to keep his revelation to himself, for now anyway. "I'm going to check out that address. It's just near the tower. If that's a dead-end, then I'll try the others," Jake said.

"Do you want me to call for backup?" Monique asked.

"No, I'll be fine. I'm going to wait until later tonight."

"You always did like doing things under the cover of darkness." Monique laughed.

"You still know me," Jake joked. "How long was Gemma's call to Connolly, by the way?"

"Brief, one minute and forty-two seconds."

"Enough time to make an appointment or maybe ask a question or two but nothing of substance."

"Sounds about right."

Jake thought of telling Monique about the dream but dismissed the idea almost instantly. He trusted Monique, but trust only gave you so much credit. He didn't have enough credit for such a crazy story.

"I have a meeting I need to get to. Now, promise me you won't go doing anything stupid?"

"I promise," Jake said.

It was a promise he couldn't guarantee he'd keep. He had done some crazy things before.

Chapter 35

Picton December 2016

Talia had pissed and shat everything she had in her into that disgusting metal bucket. She had even vomited because of the smell. The only bad thing was, she had vomited away from the bucket and not into it.

Now all she had to do was wait. Lunch had come and gone. It was getting late in the afternoon; the prison box had even begun to cool down.

Talia had moved her bedding from the usual spot in the top right corner to just in front of the door. She was hoping it would disorient him, just briefly—a second or two was all she needed.

She had gone over the plan in her head a thousand times, and it seemed like each time a new 'what if' arose.

What if she dumped the bucket on him, and couldn't get past the door?

What if the gate he came through locked automatically each time? She would be trapped.

What if she got past the gate and sprinted off the farm and couldn't find anyone to help her? Then she would be recaptured.

The 'what ifs' stopped running through her head when she heard the gate opening.

She started counting *one cat and dog, two cat and dog*. She knew she was behind by one or two seconds. She tried to keep counting steadily in her head while she positioned herself to the right of the door, bucket in hand.

Talia had reached twenty-one in her head when the younger brother stepped inside.

Her plan of disorienting the man by moving the bed had seemed to work. As soon as he entered, he stopped. He stood with her meal in one hand, two fresh bottles of water in the other, staring at the empty bed lying in front of him instead of the far-right corner, as he was used to.

Talia wasted no time in throwing the contents of the bucket over her stationary target.

Poo and piss flew from the bucket, hitting him in the face. Her aim couldn't have been better if she had rehearsed it. Large chunks hit him in the face; Talia swore she saw a piece of crap hit him right in the eye.

Talia charged at the burly man, swinging the bucket as he tried to shield his face.

Instinctively, he dropped what he was carrying, and raised his hands to his face, leaving her dinner to fall to the floor amongst the remains of the bucket.

The bucket connected with the back of the man's skull. Dave staggered a little and the bucket flew out of her hands as it collected him on the right side of his head.

The momentum sent Talia sprawling out through the door.

She landed firmly and unceremoniously in the dirt. She fought the pain that shot through her ankles and hips and got to her feet swiftly. Her right knee caved in a little and sent a sharp pain up her leg when she took her first step.

Talia saw her captor lying face down in the excrement, motionless, and assumed he was knocked out, not dead. She also knew he wouldn't stay that way for long.

A padlock hung from the open door.

Talia frantically removed the padlock and flung the door shut. As it was closing, she could see the brother stirring.

He was coming to.

She hurried to thread the padlock back through the handle. In her panic, she fumbled with it and it fell from her grasp to the ground.

She could hear the brother try and get to his feet. He moaned loudly, probably still unsure what had happened.

Talia quickly swept her fingers over the dirt, looping the fumbled lock with one of her fingers. There was a loud thud followed by another "Arrgh." She assumed he had fallen to his knees or his belly, unable to stand due to his concussion and still unsteady on his feet.

She took the metal lock and threaded it through the loop under the handle, then pressed her fingers and thumb together hard. The click that followed was the most fantastic sound she had ever heard. The man now locked inside the box began to hammer on the door with his fists.

Talia's adrenaline took over. She bolted through the gate.

It was freedom or nothing!

Without looking back, Talia could hear the metal door of the container being bashed behind her. The gate led her to a dusty path covered by a few loose stones. She had arrived at the back of the farmhouse.

She knew instantly she was still on the farm where she'd been captured.

She could see the garage to the right and beyond it, a driveway to the road, directly in front of her.

Her car was nowhere to be seen—not that she had the keys anyway.

She poked her head out and looked down the drive. She couldn't see the other brother.

She looked to her right. Over her shoulder, high on the horizon, a tractor was working in the fields. It was the other brother. She could see his big frame sitting in the cabin. She doubted he could see her. If she could make it to the garage, it would provide cover for her dash to the road.

Wasting no time, Talia took a deep breath and darted out from behind the house. She ran as fast as she could.

She felt exposed the whole time before reaching the garage where she dived for cover. Once hidden by the garage, she stopped to regain her breath. She needed to prepare herself for another sprint, a longer one out in the open with nowhere to hide until she reached the shrubbery of the neighbour's driveway.

She peeked out from behind the garage to get a fix on the tractor. It was still sitting on the horizon. The brother was still there. He was looking down at something in the cabin.

Anthony Brown couldn't hear anything over the noise of his tractor, but he had seen everything. He saw movement from the back of the house as the girl sprinted across the dusty drive and hid behind the garage.

How had she escaped?

Where the fuck was Dave?

He had to get her back before she made it to the neighbour's place.

He climbed down from the tractor, picking the rifle up from the floor. It would be a tough shot from here but one he would have to make. He couldn't kill her either; that would defeat the whole purpose of taking her in the first place.

He loaded his .308 magazine. It held four cartridges, and he had to slide the bolt in between shots, so for tasks like this it proved cumbersome. At this distance it would test his accuracy.

He clicked the magazine into the bottom of the rifle, lifted and slid the bolt back, and watched as the first bullet loaded into the chamber.

Anthony tucked the butt of the gun firmly under his chin and looked through the scope.

As she neared the letterbox, she would be fully exposed. It would be his best chance to make the shot. Every step she took after that would make his shot harder.

In the right-hand corner of the scope was his letterbox. In the middle sitting right between the cross hairs was the space between the gates. She would soon be on target.

Talia sprinted as fast as she could go. The first run had tired her. Consequently, her second run wasn't as quick as she had hoped. She saw the gate directly in front of her. It was open, and the green letterbox sat atop the right-hand fence post.

She passed the letterbox and, in an instant, was running along the road itself. The surface was loose, the gravel uneven and slippery, and if she wasn't careful she could lose her footing. Before she had time to tell herself not to jinx herself, she was sprawled out on the road, face and palms in the dirt. She got up and as she did so, an excruciating pain shot up her left leg. She noticed blood pouring down her jeans, too much blood for a scraped knee, she thought.

Still deeply concerned the brothers weren't far behind, she quickly raised the leg of her jeans to discover a wound, in fact a hole. She had been shot in the calf. Panicking, she looked around, but couldn't see either brother. How had she been shot? She had heard no sound other than the tractor.

Frantically she sought out the tractor. It appeared empty. The driver was gone. She quickly scanned the horizon, and a loud bang echoed nearby. A puff of dust hit the ground beside her.

She couldn't tell where the shots were coming from, but someone was shooting at her. Must be Anthony.

It didn't matter, she thought. If she stayed a moment longer, he would hit her again. She had heard once that if you were being shot at, to run in a diagonal pattern. It made it harder for the shooter to aim than if you were running in a straight line.

She stood up. The pain in her calf was horrendous. She took a deep breath and ran as best she could. Even though it was more like a hobble she was at least moving, and she made sure to change directions, although her injured leg prevented her from making much progress.

Anthony was now standing leaning on the fence post, cigarette in mouth, rifle in hand.

"You going to give up now? Or do I have to kill you where you stand?" Anthony asked.

Talia turned and looked how far she had to go to reach the neighbours. She began to cry. She felt utterly defeated.

"Just leave me alone," she sobbed.

"I can't do that, I'm afraid. You know too much," Anthony replied.

"Then just kill me!" Talia screamed.

"We will, soon enough."

Talia had asked for it, but when she heard his words, fear overpowered her body and she began to shake.

Without a word, Anthony approached her, picked her up one-handed and hauled her over his shoulder, and headed back to the farmhouse.

"You know how hard that shot was?" Anthony asked as he walked.

Chapter 36

Picton December 2016

Jake had so far done as he had promised Monique, which was to wait for dark.

As much as he wanted to go to the Browns' farm and keep them under surveillance, he knew sitting in front of their house in broad daylight would be indiscreet. Jake also knew if they had the slightest inclination that they were under surveillance, they would go to ground and if anything was happening, it would stop and possibly never be uncovered.

Darkness was his only option.

In the meantime, he had decided to keep an eye on the church. Dining across the road from it was the perfect cover.

Jake sat down at a table near the window.

The waitress came to offer Jake some bread and take his drinks order. As usual he didn't order any alcohol, only a ginger ale.

"That looks like a beautiful building. Is it still used as a church?" Jake asked the waitress.

"No, unfortunately, it's such a shame."

"Who lives there now?" Jake enquired.

"The same pastor who used to preach there. He bought the house and the church from the ministry after a family tragedy. He has basically been a shut-in ever since."

"That sounds horrible. I thought I saw him there with a young girl the other day?"

"Yes, That's his granddaughter, Olly, poor thing. Never knew her parents. They were killed in a horrific accident on the outskirts of Picton when she was born after her mum had died." She no longer looked cheery.

"Sorry, I shouldn't have asked."

"No, it's okay. Just one of the sad events in Picton's history."

She left to get his ginger ale and returned ready to take his main order.

"I don't want to upset you any further, but do you know why he became a hermit?" Jake asked.

"It's no problem," she said, placing a glass with three ice cubes in front of him and an open bottle of ginger ale on the table. "He's…how would you say…a self-imposed shut-in. I guess."

"Self-imposed?"

"Ever since the accident, he believes the devil is out to get him. He has lost any faith he had. It's so sad."

Jake half smiled, a sad smile, unsure what to say.

"Now, what can I get you?" the waitress asked. She had purposely changed the subject. It was obviously upsetting her.

"I can't decide between the roast and the fettuccine. What would you recommend?"

"I'd go with the roast lamb. It's fresh off the farm, local too."

Jake remembered the brother at the farm covered in lamb's blood. It instantly put him off the roast.

"I think I'll go the pasta. Maybe I'll get the roast next time."

She took the order and left Jake to finish his bread.

Jake hoped he hadn't upset her by not accepting her recommendation, yet he feared he had. Can't please everyone, he thought.

No one entered or left the church the whole time Jake was sitting eating.

In fact, there looked to be no movement at all.

I need to talk to this pastor again, Jake decided.

Chapter 37

Picton December 2016

They had never come to check on her at this time of night. Usually, 6 o'clock dinner time was the last visit for the day. Something was going on.

Both brothers were standing in the doorway, one behind the other.

When the brother had carried her back to the box, he had checked the injury to her leg. She was lucky it had only put a gash at the edge of her calf. Anthony stitched up the wound as best he could. There was no pain relief for Talia. She had passed out. When she came around, she noticed Anthony had wrapped her leg in a fresh bandage. She couldn't understand why he had gone to the effort to stitch and dress the wound when they clearly said their plan was to kill her.

"Get up!" the bigger brother said.

Dave looked as if he had copped the worst of the bucket. He had a large patch across his forehead. She assumed he too had needed stitches. She hoped it was the case anyhow.

Both the brothers had gloves on. That's not a good sign, Talia thought.

"Follow us," the brother commanded.

She did as she was asked. She walked slowly through the gate she had earlier sprinted through. She stepped off the gravelled dirt path and followed them onto the porch of the house. It felt as if every board was rotten underfoot and could give way at any time. The house looked old and dishevelled. She couldn't decide if it needed a paint or a bulldozer. She was leaning towards bulldozer.

One brother walked in front of her while the other followed, to prevent her escape.

Her car was waiting for her, yet she had no idea where she was going. Were they letting her go?

Talia stood on the cracked porch steps that seemed in far worse condition than the porch boards themselves. The middle step had given way altogether.

In front of her car was a white ute. It wasn't the red F100 she had come to the farm asking about.

"Get in the driver's seat of your car." The smaller brother pulled the gun from his waistband and waved it at her vehicle. "I'll be sitting in the back. You will do exactly as you're told, do you understand?"

Talia knew that the consequences of not doing as she was told would be a bullet in her back. She had begun to think the brothers were not going to kill her. Instead, she felt it was likely she would be sold into a prostitution slave house, hidden somewhere nearby. She suspected that all the deaths she had been investigating were elaborate cover-ups for killings when the slave house had no further use for the victims.

It was the only thing that made sense to her. What else could they be doing? Why keep her for days only to kill her? What purpose did that serve?

The country road was dark, other than her headlights. The taillights of the younger brother's old ute in front of her was the only other light she could see. The brothers made sure to take back roads, anything to avoid the main roads. When the ute braked, Talia had no idea where on earth she was, and she guessed that was the way the brothers wanted it.

"Get out," the voice behind her said.

She stepped out. She was in a turning circle, one that looked as if it had been made by occasional use, rather than design. As dark as it was, she could tell she was in in the middle of bushland somewhere. She began to rethink her whole prostitution theory. This was how Ivan Milat had killed. Panic shot through her body.

He stood behind her, gun pointed at her back. "Open the boot," he ordered.

She complied.

"Take the rope."

She scanned the floor of the boot. She didn't recall carrying any rope. The spare wheel was there, and her bag, but that was all. Then she looked to the left and saw a bundle of rope on the floor. The brothers had placed it there. The rope had a noose tied in one end. They were going to hang her; make it look like another suicide, she thought.

Dave had joined them at the back of her vehicle. "Follow him," Anthony said.

Dave led the way. He walked off into the darkness, with only his dimly lit torch beam to guide him.

Despite the lack of light, Talia recognised where she was. She was standing on the far side of the Redbank Range Tunnel. They had parked on the overgrown disused railway tracks on the other side of the tunnel. She looked down and could see the dense gully below, about a twenty-metre drop. Was this where they were going to hang her—leave her dangling from the track over Stonequarry Creek?

"Take her into the tunnel. He'll come for her," Anthony said.

Dave continued to lead the way.

He entered the Redbank Range Tunnel.

Talia stopped, paralysed in fear. Anthony must have kept walking because suddenly she felt the gun press into the small of her back.

"I can't go in. Please don't make me," she whined, shaking her head.

"Keep going," Anthony replied, jabbing her with the gun and pushing her towards the tunnel.

Talia shuffled slowly forward. Anthony could see her delaying tactics and shoved her forward violently. Talia fell to her knees. She could see the overgrown sleepers and caught a glimpse of the creek below.

Jump for it, a voice in her head called. Although it would mean certain death.

But at least it would be at your own hands, not due to these scum. You would control your fate…

Yes! Talia agreed. Why give them the satisfaction? If I'm going to go, I'll go out my way.

She took a deep breath and prepared to jump to her death.

Do it, do it now.

She had taken two steps towards the edge and was about to push off when she realised the voice she was hearing was not her own. She didn't know whose it was, but she was suddenly sure she didn't want to die tonight.

A hand grabbed her sweater before her brain had corrected her course. "Don't even think about it," Dave said.

The tunnel towered over her head like the giant clown-mouth at Luna Park. She was pushed through the entrance by the constant prodding of the gun in her back. She went from being pushed to being dragged by her shirt. She could feel her heels digging in the dirt.

The tunnel felt as if it had closed behind her. The temperature dropped, and the night sounds were instantly silenced. Talia felt an unwelcome presence; the same one she had experienced last time she was in the tunnel.

On that occasion she had come in contact with Hat Man.

A jolt of fear shot up her spine. Her body was sending off signals every way it knew how. Sweat poured from her forehead, her hands trembled, the hairs on her arms stood up. Alarm bells were ringing.

Talia knew she was in trouble.

"Scat!" Anthony called out from behind her.

"We have one for you," Dave, the brother in front, added.

From the alcove on the right, the faceless being she had seen a few nights before glided out into the tunnel. Its coat was hovering just above the ground. It made no sound as it glided to a halt.

It stood there silently, with burning, fiery-red eyes staring at them.

Chapter 38

Picton December 2016

With his car hidden behind a windbreak of pine trees in a far back paddock, Jake entered the Browns' farm property from the back. It had become a habit, perhaps a bad one.

Jake wanted to see if the red F100 was here and if it was operational.

The cows in the back paddock were quiet, hardly stirring as Jake crept past. The house was in darkness except for a small glimmer of light shining from the front. Jake assumed it was the porch light.

There was a large shipping container at the back of the property. Jake guessed the owners were using it to store farming equipment or stock feed. He was surprised to find it had a small door, just big enough for a person to enter.

The door was damaged and buckled as though it had come in contact with an angry bull, and a big one at that. Jake stepped over the twisted metal door that lay half off its hinges. He noted several unlocked padlocks on the ground, as well as one still bolted to the middle lock. This was definitely not a storage shed. Jake knew the second he stepped inside that it had been used to keep someone captive, and whoever it was, appeared to have broken out. Lucas, he thought. He would be strong enough to get out of here. By the look of the door, it had been bent and kicked in until he got free. Jake noticed blood on the floor and then a trail to a bucket. Maybe Lucas had ambushed his captor.

Jake couldn't be sure. He didn't have time to investigate the scene further now. He needed to find the F100 if it was here, before the brothers returned home. Jake headed out from the container and into a large storage shed, one of several he had seen on the property.

A large tractor and a plough were stored there. Behind were hay bales stacked from the floor to the rafters. At the rear of the shed, Jake could see a large mezzanine area.

There appeared to be car-like shapes stored under tarps. Jake manoeuvred his way through the machinery and headed towards the tarps. He lifted the cover off the first vehicle. He could tell by the shape it was too small to be a F100, but curiosity got the better of him. It was a dark blue Toyota RAV4. A 'P' plate stared back at him from the back window. Jake pressed his face up against the window. Inside was clean except for a few scraps of paper. Looked like a girl's car, Jake thought. This car had been here a while, judging from the flat tyres.

Jake replaced the tarp and wiped the dust from his face and hands. He removed the tarp from the second car. This one, a Mazda, had been reversed in and the plates had been removed. The tarp had very little dust on it compared to the RAV4. Jake again tried to look in through the window. This car was a mess. There were folders and notes thrown all over the place. Someone had been rummaging through it.

Jake opened the car door and was greeted by a chiming sound and a bright interior light. The car battery was still functioning. This car hadn't been here long at all.

Jake scooped up the papers and sat on the seat, closing the door to silence the annoying chime.

After flicking through several pieces of paper, he came across something he recognised, a brochure detailing *Ghost Tours in Picton*. It had Megan's company logo. Whoever owned this car had met Megan, as her card was attached.

Jake opened the glove box. He was hoping to find some registration papers or owner's manual; something that would identify the owner of the vehicle.

He found the manual resting under some papers. The name on the inside cover stopped Jake in his tracks.

Mr L. Taylor. Lucas's car.

Where the hell was Lucas?

Jake searched the rest of the car and found a loaded Beretta under the passenger seat. Lucas had obviously thought he wasn't in any danger if he had left his gun in the car.

Jake placed the Beretta back under the seat, deciding it was best not to remove evidence from the crime scene.

Jake had to see if Lucas was here also.

There was another shed at the front of the driveway and Jake headed there next. He paused at the corner of the tractor shed and double-checked if the house was still in darkness. It was.

He made his way down the driveway towards the front of the house. His search had taken him in a wide arc, from the storage container up to the large shed and now back down to a second garage. If the F100 wasn't here, the only other place it could be was in the shed in the lower paddock at the front of the property. That was unless the owners were out driving it.

Jake arrived at the front of the garage. The door was closed. It was a large heavy sliding door, padlocked and chained. He wasted no time in deciding what to do, simply pulling out his Glock and shooting at the padlock. The bullet almost ricocheted back at him. Luckily, it didn't hit him. Jake dragged the chain off the door and pushed the door slowly ajar, just enough to slip through.

This shed was pitch black. There were no gaps in the roof to allow the moonlight to filter through. Here, he would need his torch.

Jake grabbed for his phone and even though he had no service the torch function still worked.

There were more cars in this garage, including the mysterious red Ford F100.

Now Jake needed to see if this thing was still in working condition.

Chapter 39

Picton December 2016

Talia was so fixated on the burning eyes of Hat Man, she didn't notice Anthony slip the rope over her head. The eyes of the beast kept her mesmerised even as the noose tightened. It wasn't until she began to gasp for air that she finally realised what was happening to her.

A smirk began to appear on Hat Man's face where previously it had been expressionless. Talia thought she even captured a glimpse of some teeth but couldn't be sure in the darkness without her glasses.

The rope tightened against her throat. Talia clawed at it, desperately trying to get her fingers between the rope and her throat, anything to gain oxygen. It was no use. There was no way to create some space. The air supply in her lungs was quickly running out and the more she struggled to breathe, the more she panicked and the more she panicked, the faster the air was depleted.

Talia pushed back against her attacker, slamming her head back into his chest.

Anthony, who had hold of the rope, hadn't expected this much fight out of such a little package. The force on the back of her head almost sent him stumbling backwards, but Talia was no match for someone with such a large frame and solid legs.

Before she could muster a second push, she was shoved forward, with what felt like a boot to her lower back. The rope cut into her throat.

Talia suffered a quick secondary push to her left knee. She again figured it

215

was his boot doing the damage. This time she fell to the ground, her knees grinding into the gravel as she landed, tearing away both material and flesh. The rope burnt and cut into her neck once more, cutting the final air from her windpipe. Her vision went hazy before she blacked out.

The rope then loosened, and a sudden rush of oxygen brought her back to consciousness in a spluttering gasping mess. When her vision returned she could see Hat Man was now closer.

Once more, the rope was pulled tight and the foot pushed against her back.

Her vision began to fade again as the choking continued.

The last thing Talia saw before blacking out again was Hat Man calmly approaching, his fiery-red eyes glowing in the dark.

Talia didn't realise she had died until she was standing over her own body.

Her body was slumped in the tunnel, the noose around her neck. Anthony was holding the other end of the rope. He had removed his foot from her back.

Talia stepped away and stood against the inside wall of the tunnel, watching the brothers haul her body along the ground with her heels dragging in the gravel.

After a few metres, Dave scooped her up and placed her limp body over his shoulder.

She screamed but nothing came out.

Hat Man stood staring at her not more than two metres away. He was grinning at her; she could see his jagged yellow teeth.

"Come," he called, his voice dark and hollow.

"He will come for you if you don't go. You don't have a choice; you're his now," Dave said as he turned to exit the tunnel, still carrying her body over his shoulder.

"What does he want with me?" Talia asked.

"He wants your soul. He collects them," Dave replied.

Anthony came up and grabbed Dave by the shirt. "Come on, we have to leave. We can't be here," Anthony said, dragging him towards the exit as he spoke.

"Go to him. It will be easier that way," Dave added as they left the tunnel.

Talia stood against the wall staring as the red-eyed monster approached. Its arms were outstretched, its fingers, bony and thin, protruded from the long jacket.

Talia tried to back away but there was nowhere to go. She was trapped.

The men had left the tunnel, although she could still feel their presence outside. Hat Man moved metres in an instant by floating across the ground. This thing was no 'man'; Talia was sure of that. A smell of sulphur floated with him. It was strong and overpowering. His breath was rancid. Even though she was dead, Talia still had her senses.

"What do you want with me?" Talia asked.

"Your soul," Hat Man replied.

His bony fingers clawed down on her shoulders. She turned away, desperately trying to remove herself from his grasp. She kicked him, but her leg appeared to go through him. How could that be? How could he hold her if when she touched him, she went through him?

Hat Man opened his mouth wide, and his jaw appeared to dislocate like that of an anaconda. The rancid smell escaped from it and a strong wind rushed in from behind Talia, as if an invisible train was bearing down on them both.

Hat Man's mouth was like a vacuum and Talia could feel herself being sucked into it. She was being eaten. Her hair was being sucked into his mouth, then her eyes, into the dark abyss. After that, everything went numb for Talia.

*

The brothers had hung Talia's body from the old disused railway tracks, dangled at the end of the rope between the tracks and the bottom of the ravine.

Her vehicle lay abandoned not far away.

They piled into their white ute and were ready to leave, when Dave froze with the keys in his fingers. As he fumbled to place them in the ignition, they slipped from his grasp and fell to the floor.

Anthony, who was also frozen in fear, slapped his brother. "Hurry up.

Let's get out of here," he pleaded.

"I'm trying," Dave replied. His big hands and thumbs suddenly seemed way too cumbersome to handle and operate the delicate keys quickly and with any precision.

After more fumbling, Dave managed to start the engine. "Do I run him over?" Dave yelled.

"Go straight over him, if you have to," Anthony replied.

"We took too long in the tunnel," Dave shrieked.

Dave shifted into gear and dropped the clutch. The wheels spun on the loose gravel and the old metal rail, before gaining some traction on a sleeper. The ute went sideways first, before sling-shotting forward and fishtailing as it approached Hat Man.

The ute went straight through Hat Man. He passed through the ute as if he was smoke, arms stretched out, his hands clawing both the brothers across the chest as he went.

"Soon," Hat Man said in a cold, rough voice.

Dave looked in the rear-vision mirror and Anthony turned to see Hat Man standing behind the ute.

"Is he still standing there?" Dave whispered.

"Yep. It's like we didn't even hit him," Anthony replied.

Anthony returned his gaze to meet his brother's. Dave's eyes darted back to the track in front of him.

"Your shoulder looks burnt," Anthony said.

Dave quickly looked down, taking his eyes off the road momentarily to see his shirt had been burnt in three horizontal lines. He assumed his skin had suffered the same fate.

"You've been burnt too," Dave pointed out, returning his eyes to the road.

Anthony looked at his own chest. He had the three same horizontal burns as his brother.

"What do you think he meant by 'soon?'" Dave asked.

"Maybe he wants to be fed again, soon."

"Maybe he's becoming hungrier?" Dave offered.

"Maybe he wants to eat us next," Anthony wailed.

"Why would he, when we're supplying him with innocent souls for him to devour?" Dave questioned.

"I don't know. He's the devil. How do I know how his mind works? If we just keep doing what we're doing, we'll be okay. I'm sure of it." Anthony tried to sound convincing.

Dave gave a final glance in the rear-view mirror. Hat Man was still there, his fiery-red eyes looking back at the ute as it drove away.

Talia's lifeless body swung in the mild night breeze, halfway between the bottom of the creek and the tracks.

Hat Man's appetite satisfied, he returned to the tunnel.

Chapter 40

I stood in the in-between looking down at my lifeless body and the white door at my back. The door had been shaking more and more over the past few days, as if it was calling me. Maybe I had overstayed my welcome in the in-between; maybe it was my time to move on.

It shook violently behind me once more and this time I didn't think it was ever going to stop.

Whether the door led to Heaven or hell, I had resigned myself to my fate. Whatever was beyond the door I was ready to accept.

I summoned up enough courage just to touch the silver knob, but I doubted I would be able to convince myself to turn it. The knob shook in my hand and the quiver went through my palm and travelled up my arm and into my shoulder.

I took a deep breath and turned the knob. The shaking instantly stopped. The door swung away from my hand, opening inwards. Only darkness greeted me.

"Hello?" I called. I had no idea what I was doing.

No answer came. No sound of any kind.

"I was told you wanted to see me? Hello?" I repeated.

"You need to help Jake," a soft female voice replied.

I couldn't see who had spoken. I only knew the voice had come from within the darkness.

"Why, what will happen?" I asked cautiously.

"Go to him, before it's too late."

I stepped into the darkness of the room. A young lady greeted me. Her face was disfigured. Her long brown hair was torn from the right side of her face. Her right eyeball was missing; the cheek below was torn away. Four of her teeth were showing through the gaping hole.

"Your friend is in danger. Only you, with faith, can save him," she said.

"In danger from whom?" I asked.

"I cannot speak his name here."

"Who are you?" I asked.

"I am Paige," she replied.

It dawned on me it really was Paige. The same girl who had died in the car accident, related to the suicide case that Jake was investigating.

"I don't understand. Why is Jake in danger?"

"The whole town is in danger. He comes for them all."

"Who? Who is coming?" I asked.

The disfigured woman moved closer and took both my hands in hers.

A vision of a tall man in a hat with fiery-red eyes stood before me. I could smell him. He had no face, no nose, no mouth. He was just red eyes with a blank face.

"Who is it?" I asked.

"The locals call him Hat Man," Paige answered.

"Why don't you stop him?" I asked.

"I have already crossed, and this is as far as I can come. Once you cross, you can't go back."

"How did you get here?" I asked.

Once again, she took my hands and a vision came into my head. While I saw the pictures, I could also hear her talking to me as if she was narrating the scene for me.

"We were at the Redbank Range Tunnel looking for ghosts. We had decided to go by ourselves. We thought we would have a better chance of a sighting without the tour crowd," she began, and as she spoke, I could see Paige and another girl, whom Paige had told me was her best friend, Gemma.

They were strolling through a dark tunnel, late at night. They seemed to be in the middle of nowhere. I couldn't see a road or any signs.

"Where are you?" I wondered aloud.

"Picton New South Wales," Paige answered.

I had heard of it before. As the vision continued, Hat Man appeared from nowhere. I watched as the girls ran in terror, desperately trying to escape the tunnel. The Hat Man chasing them didn't seem to change speed and didn't seem to care if he didn't catch them. He chased them anyway.

I watched as the women ran. They sprinted for several hundred metres. I could see they were clearly exhausted and running on adrenaline. By the time they reached their blue Ford, Gemma was gasping for air.

Paige got in and started the car. Hat Man had reached the end of the tunnel where the darkness finished and the outside world began. He stepped out and continued after them.

Gemma was busy trying to get service on her phone without any luck. Paige threw the car into drive and jumped on the pedal. The wheels spun before gaining traction and they rocketed down the dirt track. They would have only been two hundred metres down the road when they saw a Ford F100 parked on the opposite side of the road.

Paige pulled over. "Quick, take a photo," she told Gemma.

"Why?"

"Maybe it's the creep's car; quick, get the number plate," Paige urged.

"Move up a little. I can't quite get it."

I saw Gemma click away. I was so immersed in what was happening with the girls I had almost forgotten where I was. It was strange watching these two girls having a conversation. They appeared so full of life, yet now they were both dead.

As Paige jerked the car forward she screamed, and Gemma dropped the phone in fright. It tumbled down the driver's side seat and disappeared.

"Shit!" Gemma cried.

Paige hit the accelerator hard. The car was moving again.

"Did you see those guys?" she asked Gemma.

Gemma nodded. "Yeah, I saw them."

"They were dragging a woman into the scrub. Maybe a kidnapping!" Paige yelled, amazed her friend had missed it.

By this time, Paige had swerved, and the back tyres sent the car drifting across the loose dirt that had built up on the edge of the road. Instantly, the car jerked and whipped back in a sideways drift. Paige tried furiously to correct it, but it only made matters worse.

The car slammed into a large gum tree, crushing the driver's side, sending shattered glass flying over Paige. Her head hit the tree, killing her instantly, then it bounced off the steering wheel and was whipped wildly back and forth into the broken window, glass fragments tearing at her face each time. Finally, when she landed, her head was mangled and torn, resting on her shoulder.

Gemma's head jerked forward, only restricted by her belt, which burnt into her chest. The force of the impact fractured three of her ribs, and broke her collarbone and her right arm and leg.

Even though Paige was dead, I could still see everything that was happening. It was as if I was Paige's spirit, watching over the crash site.

Gemma's breathing was shallow.

A pair of boots appeared at Gemma's upside-down window. A large hand reached in and cut the belt holding Gemma.

"Dave, someone's coming. We can't take her," a voice from the scrub called.

The boots vanished.

Doors slammed further up the road. "There's a car down there," a middle-aged man called out.

Paige let go of my hands and the vision fell away.

"You need to go back," Paige said.

"How do I get back? I'm stuck here."

"You haven't crossed yet. You're not like me. Let me help you." Paige placed her hands on my chest. Immediately, I felt an electric current through her palms; her hands were like resuscitation paddles. I felt every inch of the shock. Every kilowatt ran around my body and ended up in my back teeth.

I was jolted back to life and opened my eyes. I was no longer in the in-between. I was back in my body and it hurt like a motherfucker.

Chapter 41

Picton December 2016

The F100 was unlocked, and Jake lifted the hood.

He was no expert on cars, but he could tell this car wasn't operational. No motor, no go. There were several different makes and models of cars in the shed. Jake counted five others, none of them particularly valuable or rare.

Jake shone his phone torch around, checking the rego labels. Some were current, some missing.

Maybe the Brown boys were making money on the side from stolen vehicles. They wouldn't be the first farmers who were habitual car thieves. At the far end of the shed was an office door, more like one in a panelbeater's workshop than in a farmer's shed.

He tried the doorknob. The door was locked.

Jake took a step back and kicked the door in. The lock shattered. Pieces flew off into the darkness. The door swung back hard, tearing off the top hinge as the momentum carried it back.

Jake entered the room and tried to scan the contents. He realised he hadn't stepped into a thieves' workshop but had stumbled upon something far worse.

The shipping container now made sense. He had found a pair of potential killers; not only were they very active, but also extremely experienced.

The wall of the room displayed drivers' licences, locks of hair, and polaroid photos of girls taken captive. There was a collection of earrings, necklaces, hair ties, and other personal belongings. Trophies, Jake thought.

There were even mobile phones sitting on a wooden shelf.

Jake looked at them and imagined the girls in their last desperate moments at the hands of these men.

Trophies.

Reminders of their dominance and control.

Trophies, to relive their experiences.

Jake had no idea how many girls they had captured or killed, but he guessed up to seven based on the number of cars. He was sure that given enough time, these cars would be linked to victims. After seeing Lucas's car, Jake realised the likelihood was that he too had come off second best, had fallen victim to the brothers.

If he was still alive, he may have been kept in the container. But that was damaged and empty. If he wasn't there, where would he be?

Where did serial killers usually keep their victims? Jake reflected on past cases. Some had kept their captives in boxes, sheds and even underground huts, but the ones who held their victims for a while generally kept them in their home somewhere.

Perhaps they had lured Lucas into the house and jumped him?

Maybe he was still there?

Now was as good a time as any to check it out.

Jake made his way back through the cars and headed out into the night. The moon was now providing enough light, so Jake didn't need his phone torch to make out where he was going.

He leant against the shed door and tried to close it, but it had come off its track. He left it slightly ajar. The chain remained on the ground, the padlock dangling from the handle.

Heading for the house, Jake crossed the dirt driveway and walked cautiously to the house. He stepped onto the veranda and tried the front door, but it was locked. It took him a few seconds to pick it and gain entry.

The front door opened directly into the lounge and the first thing that greeted Jake was the glass-eyed stuffed deer's head, mounted on the far wall above the fireplace. It had an expression of innocence about it.

On each side of the fireplace were wall-mounted bookshelves that went from the floor almost to the celling. They held an assortment of books, magazines and some old thick encyclopaedias.

To the left was a kitchen with an open sitting area. There was no sign of Lucas. Jake was about to head through the lounge when a horrible thought crossed his mind. That day he had met the brother covered in blood…what if it had been Lucas's blood, not a lamb's at all?

Jake almost vomited at the thought.

He didn't want his mind to think its next thought, but it was too late. The thought had already formed in his mind.

What if Lucas was cut up and in the freezer?

It was a thought he didn't want but one he couldn't ignore, considering what else he'd found so far.

The kitchen resembled something you would expect to find in an abandoned house. The tiles were falling from the wall in rows, the floor lino was ripped, and the oven was rusted and missing the door.

There were two freezers in the kitchen. One was the fridge freezer, the other was a large chest freezer. Big enough to store a dismembered body, Jake assessed.

Jake opened the fridge freezer first. He was surprised to find just two food items, a cheap brand of frozen pizza, and some choc-chip ice cream.

His stomach lurched as he placed his hands on the lid of the chest freezer. Lifting the lid, he envisaged finding Lucas's severed head with dismembered body parts underneath.

He hadn't seen Lucas in a few years, and this was not how he wanted their reunion to be.

His heart was racing.

A puff of chilled air rose as Jake lifted the freezer lid up above his head. He shivered.

At first, all he could see were red lumps in bags, covered with shaved ice. Clumps of ice were wedged in the corners. It looked as if the freezer had never been defrosted.

Jake removed his pistol and started digging through the ice with the barrel.

It was hard to make out what kind of meat was in the bags as they were all covered in ice, frozen solid and stuck to one another.

He couldn't immediately retrieve any single bags to make a closer inspection.

All the while, at the back of his mind, Jake wondered when the owners would return home. Would he hear them if they did? He hoped so.

Finally, Jake managed to scrape away enough of the ice covering to get a good look at one of the bags. It was chicken. He could tell by the colour of the meat. He scraped and dug at the ice at the other end of the chest. He tugged at a bag wedged in the far corner. After a few minutes of digging and rocking it back and forth it came loose, bringing the bag below with it. The top bag could have been meat, although Jake couldn't be sure exactly what cut. His guess was some type of lamb and by the shape of the bone, he thought it was probably chops.

The bag below clearly contained human remains; bright-red, polished nails were visible through the plastic. Jake could count five fingers.

Jake gasped, almost dropping the bag. Whoever the hand belonged to had been in there for some time. Lucas had been missing only a few days, so he might still be alive.

Another horrific thought ran though Jake's mind. What if Lucas wasn't in the freezer, because he was still being dismembered in the bathroom? That was usually where it happened, in the tub. The blood was easy to contain and easier to drain away, but most of all, it was easiest to clean up.

The floorboards groaned as Jake made his way through the lounge, peering out of the dust-covered window for any signs of a car or the boys.

Nothing, only darkness.

Jake continued his way past the bookcase, and down the narrow hall. The bathroom was much like the kitchen, falling apart, with tiles missing. One of the vanity cupboard doors had fallen off while the other had a hinge missing, leaving it hanging at right angles.

A shower curtain was drawn across the bath. It was a combo bath-shower, like the ones in cheap by-the-hour motels whose main clients were whores and johns.

Jake didn't hesitate in swiping the curtain aside, revealing only a few shampoo bottles and white tiles. Yet the emptiness didn't answer the question of Lucas's whereabouts.

Jake knelt and shone his torch in the bottom of the tub. The drain looked clean; no signs of dried blood. He scanned the wall tiles; nothing.

The tiles on the floor beside the tub, however, appeared to have specks of red. It was dried blood, Jake thought. They had been cleaned but as with many killers, their cleaning of the grout lacked diligence.

His battery was running low, so he tapped on the power save mode and turned off his flashlight. He noticed he had one bar of service. It was the only time, apart from when he'd been standing directly under the tower on the main road, that he'd had any service.

He needed to call for backup, before the boys returned.

Jake removed Inspector Connolly's card while he still had battery, to tell him what was going on.

The connection was choppy. It was breaking up, as Jake listened to the ringing on the other end.

The line cleared.

"Inspector Connolly."

Jake spoke quickly while the line was clear, being careful not to move at all.

"It's Jake Miller here. I've found signs of serial murders at the Browns' farm in Picton." Jake waited for a response.

Nothing came.

"Inspector Connolly, are you there?"

"Sorry, the phone dropped out, I only heard you say signs of murder," came the reply.

Jake wasn't sure if this phone connection was strong enough to get the information across. He repeated himself.

"I know of the Brown boys, Jake. Don't go anywhere. Stay there. I'm on my way."

"I need you and your guys to put out an arrest warrant on the two boys. I think they've been working together. Get your forensics here to process the crime scene. There is evidence all over the place, cars, victims' trophies, body parts, blood," Jake said.

"Of course. Where are the Brown boys now?" Inspector Connolly asked.

The phone crackled a little as the inspector spoke, but Jake managed to make out what was being said.

"They're out, I have no idea where they are."

"Jake, are you armed? Can you defend yourself if they return?"

"I have my Glock on me, and my shotgun in the boot of my car, at the rear of the property."

"Just stay hidden. I'll be there within fifteen minutes."

Jake was about to thank him, but the line disconnected.

Jake's battery had five per cent remaining now. The service bar of a few seconds ago was gone.

He thought it best to hide in one of the sheds until the inspector arrived.

He was on his way back past the bookcase in the lounge when something familiar caught his eye. It was two thin gold-spined books, the same gold spines he had seen in Gemma's room. Jake tugged one of the books out. The gold binding led to a diamond black and white front. It was exactly the same as Gemma's diary.

Turning the cover, he recognised the writing. It was another volume of Gemma's diary. There was no doubt about it.

Thursday 3th August.

Dear Dad

I hope I'm doing the right thing? I've decided to go back to Picton and make a statement to the police about what I saw just before the accident.

I know what I saw was real, both with the man in the hat and the men dragging the girl into the bushes. The doctors have said I suffered severe head trauma and the memories may not be real. I have been told it could be a movie I saw once and now my mind is replaying it as if it happened to me.

It feels real. I remember seeing Paige, next to me driving. I remember seeing the red ute and trying to take a photo of it. It must be real. I don't have my phone anymore, so I can't check.

I remember seeing Paige lying there next to me, her face torn, blood everywhere. All those things are real so why would the girl being dragged be any different?

I am so confused Dad.

I wish you were here to help me.

I wonder every day what happened to that girl?

Is she dead?

If I give my statement, then they can at least investigate it and maybe they'll find out what happened.

I gave my statement to a police station. Apparently, they sent it on.

You always told me to do the right thing. I am sure this is the right thing.

Jake flicked the page.

Friday August 14th

Dear Dad

Coming back here brought so many memories; well at least I think they are mine.

I'm staying in the same room that Paige and I stayed in a few months ago. It's a bit creepy being back here, but not because of the so-called ghosts. I think that's just a way for the town to make money.

I rang Inspector Connolly. He is coming tomorrow morning to take my statement. He said he never received my statement from the Victorian office.

I have just had dinner in the bistro. It wasn't very good either I might add.

It's been a long drive, so I am quite tired and my back is hurting from the long drive, so I am going to take a bath and get an early night.

Really glad I'm doing this; it will put my conscience to rest.

As always lots of love

Gemma xxxx

To end up here, there was only one way that could have happened. Somehow, between that entry and the one the next morning, one or both of the Brown boys had been in her hotel room.

One or both of them had probably killed her and made it look like a suicide. They'd done a pretty good job of it too.

But now their secret was about to come out and soon they would face justice.

Jake only had one question.

Why had Inspector Connolly never mentioned the planned meeting with Gemma for the following morning?

Considering Gemma was found dead in the bathtub the following morning, it was probably just an oversight.

Jake placed the gold-bound diary down the back of his pants and added the other one from the shelf. This was one lot of evidence he was taking with him.

No sooner had he tucked his shirt back into his pants than lights flashed across the front of the house.

Too soon to be the inspector, Jake thought.

He crept to the window and peered out.

He heard a vehicle pull up. Doors opening and closing.

Fuck, it was the brothers! Jake could hear them talking but couldn't hear the exact words. He thought he made out the word 'shed'.

The taller of the two headed towards the house while the smaller one ran towards the garage. He had met the taller one previously. Dave, if he remembered correctly.

The other man was standing at the front of that steel sliding door holding the chain with the open padlock dangling from it.

"Fuck, fuck, fuck!" Jake swore under his breath. He knew his mistake instantly. The door being left open had set off alarm bells with the brothers.

Next thing Jake knew, the house shook as the large brother ran up onto the porch. Jake ducked down under the windowsill. The only cover he had was some dusty old La-Z-Boy recliner which barely covered him. Better than nothing, Jake thought.

He'd removed his Glock without even realising. If this was going to turn into a gun fight, he was ready.

Jake was sitting on the floor, his back up against the wall and his knees drawn up so none of his body protruded from behind the recliner. He listened for the door.

He had to wait. Surprise was his only advantage and considering there were two of them, he needed every advantage he could get.

The door opened. Jake felt the cool night air across the top of his head.

Then he clearly heard, "Dave, come here!" from across the drive.

Jake heard Dave sigh heavily and close the door behind him.

The house shook again as Dave leapt off the porch and headed towards his brother.

The room fell silent.

Jake waited five, maybe ten seconds, before he dared to peek out the window again.

He saw the brothers both standing at the front of the steel door, looking at the chain. One had a torch trained on the garage. They both walked inside.

Jake thought through his options. The first was to run for his car, but he didn't want the inspector getting ambushed.

He peeked again. They were back now in front of the garage. Both men were looking for the intruder. Jake knew he had to move from the lounge before one, or both, of them returned to the house. He was a sitting duck if he stayed here.

He moved as quietly as he could, staying low and heading back towards the bedrooms, worried that the house groaning and creaking would give up his presence. He was only halfway down the hall when he heard the front door open for a second time.

Instantly he slowed his movement, trying desperately not to make a sound. He wasn't where he wanted to be. He had hoped to be hiding in one of the bedrooms by now.

Their voices were loud.

"Someone's been here," one of the brothers said. Jake thought it must be the other brother.

"We have to find them," Dave replied angrily.

"Dad will be pissed if he finds out we haven't dumped the belongings," the other replied.

"We won't tell him. Will we?" Dave suggested.

Silence.

"Anthony, we won't tell him, will we?" Dave repeated emphatically.

Anthony only grunted in agreement.

So, they are both here, Jake thought. Anthony and Dave Brown, the serial killing brothers.

"You check the house. I'll check the other shed. Whoever it is, kill them. They already know too much," Anthony said.

Jake heard drawers open and the unmistakable sound of weapons being loaded. He peeked out the bedroom window, and while his view of the drive and the gate wasn't as clear as from the lounge room, any car lights should light up the night and the house.

There was nothing, only darkness.

Jake twisted his head, trying to get a view of the main road. He couldn't see much and more importantly he couldn't see lights.

"Fucking hurry up!" Jake muttered.

He could hear Dave searching the house from room to room, switching lights on as he entered, followed by the opening of wardrobe doors. Jake even thought he heard him getting down on all fours; probably checking under the beds.

Jake had made it all the way to the last bedroom on the right. He hadn't counted how many rooms were bedrooms, only that he had passed three other doors before he'd reached the room where he had taken refuge. The window was located at the far side of the room. The door to this room opened against the foot of the bed. Opposite the bed was a double wardrobe with timber doors. On each side of the bed was a two-drawer bedside table. The one on the near side had a lamp sitting on top.

The first thing Jake needed to do was remove the globe. He needed to stay in the darkness. Every advantage was critical.

Dave's search had moved to a room two down from where Jake was. He was getting closer. Jake had to move now. He pulled himself out from between the bed and the window. There was only just enough room, so he didn't hit the wall or move the bed. The light globe was screwed into an open opaque glass fitting, decorated with butterflies and birds. Luckily for Jake he could access the globe without removing the fitting. It was a simple and quick job.

Jake knelt on the bed and reached up so his fingers touched the bulb. The bed sighed as he stretched to grasp it. Jake froze, listening for sounds of Dave suddenly stopping his search and heading towards him.

Dave hadn't heard the bed. Had he been a room closer Jake doubted he would have been as lucky.

The bulb came out with a slight push and half a turn, and the bed creaked again when Jake removed his knee.

This time Jake heard Dave's footsteps stop instantly.

Jake rolled across to the other side of the bed towards the bedroom door and braced himself for a soft landing. He backed up against the wall behind the door. When the door opened it would help conceal him. Jake placed the bulb on the floor just inside the door, hoping Dave would kick it or better still, step on it. He just wanted Dave to be looking down when he entered, if only for an instant. It would give Jake enough time to strike.

Jake stilled his breathing and flipped his gun around so he was holding his Glock in the reverse position, butt up. His eyes were intent on the door handle, watching for the slightest movement.

The handle jiggled before turning and the door suddenly swung in on Jake. He waited, frozen, breathless, calm. Dave's large frame appeared, and he scanned the room for what had caused the noise earlier. Jake watched as a big hand curled around the door, and he knew the man was ready to check behind it. Jake heard him as he took another step forward. His step was heavy on the wonky timber floor beneath the threadbare carpet.

Crunch. The globe shattered under his hefty weight.

Jake knew that was his time to strike.

Jake knew the human mind well. Dave did what any person does when they step on something that breaks; they immediately look to investigate what they have just broken.

Looking down exposed Dave's cerebellum. Jake aimed for the middle of the back of his head and whipped the butt of his pistol down hard. He hoped the hard whack would disrupt his balance and movement long enough to bring Dave down quietly.

The hit was hard enough to cause big Dave to stumble forward before he fell to the floor. Jake was surprised at how quickly he'd fallen for such a big guy. His body thudded face first into the carpet. Jake watched as Dave tried to steady himself before succumbing to the effects of the blow and losing consciousness.

He wouldn't be out for long. Jake now needed something to tie him up with before he regained consciousness. He no longer owned handcuffs, as he had handed them in with his badge and gun. Jake was going to cut the cord of the lamp but decided to check the bedside drawer first. The top drawer only held some pornographic tapes and a few loose condoms.

Jake riffled through the second drawer. It resembled his kitchen drawer at home, containing AA batteries, rubber bands, a pencil, and some packing tape. Jake grabbed the tape. He wasted no time in binding Dave, taping his feet and his wrists, and tying his wrists together with the cord from the lamp. Lastly Jake taped his mouth, not just across the face but right around his head, three times.

Jake dragged his hostage back to the lounge, ready for Anthony.

Dave moaned before he woke. His head was hurting, and he didn't remember what had happened exactly. His breathing was laboured. He couldn't move his hands or his feet.

It took him a minute to realise he was lying in his own lounge room, flat on his stomach facing the front door. He could see the beam from his brother's torch bobbing about outside, as he went to and fro across the front of the house. Finally, he watched the torch jump around as his brother took the stairs to the front porch, before switching it off as he entered the house.

"Dave, what the ... Who the hell are you?" Anthony asked, pointing his pistol straight at Jake.

Chapter 42

Melbourne December 2016

I didn't know what day it was, or even what year. I had no clue how long I had lain in that hospital bed. My body was considerably thinner. Any previous muscle definition had wasted away, and I could tell I had severe muscle atrophy as soon as I tried to lift my hand. My arm felt as if it weighed a ton. There was no way I would be able to help Jake in this condition. I thought about trying to stand but gave up on that idea when I couldn't even raise my right foot off the bed.

"I can't help you or Jake like this. What do you expect me to do?" I asked the empty room.

Without warning, a sharp pain drove through me, from the soles of my feet to the tips my ears. I couldn't see anything, but it felt like electricity flowing through my body.

I tried to lift my foot again and this time, it cleared the bed easily and I had the strength to hold it elevated in mid-air.

Had Paige somehow fixed me?

Possibly.

I tried to stand up. My legs were still a little like spaghetti, but I managed to stand after about ten minutes of trying. Mind you, I was exhausted already, and I hadn't gone anywhere. Once I was standing, I walked, holding onto the bed. Pain shot up my leg. This pain was different from the electricity that had flowed through my body earlier. With my limited medical knowledge, I thought it was most likely to be the beginning of a blood clot and I worried it would eventually travel from my leg to my brain and I would die where I stood. I had heard many stories about people who had gone on long-haul flights and five minutes after disembarking at their destination, they had died in the terminal. This was caused by the clot forming on the flight with such little movement of the legs, and then shifting as soon as movement resumed. Sometimes the clot went to the brain, sometimes to the heart. Both were likely to be fatal.

It took about thirty minutes of stumbling and near falls before I felt half comfortable on my feet. The whole time I was worried a nurse would walk in and try to stop me.

If what Paige had shown me was real, Jake was in danger. He was in NSW in a place called Picton. It rang a bell, deep in the back of my mind, yet I didn't know why. I had a vague recollection that I had discussed it with Jake at some point, but I couldn't remember any more than that. I looked in my side table. In the bottom cupboard was a blue bag with my belongings; wallet, shoes and some clothes. I rifled through the bag. My suit pants and shoes were there, but my jacket and shirt were missing.

I remembered being shot in the chest as I was running to the mansion. I looked down at my chest. The wound had now healed but the scar was still prominent. The blood-soaked shirt and jacket I had been wearing had probably been tossed out when I'd arrived in the ER.

I put my pants and shoes on, although they looked stupid without socks. I left the hospital gown on and tucked it into my pants. I imagined it looked rather odd, but my appearance was my last concern. I placed the wallet in my back pocket and headed out of the room.

The nurses' station on my ward was empty, luckily. The last thing I wanted was people knowing I was up and about. They would never let me leave. I scooted past the desk and headed down the hall and out of the ward.

The halls on the ground floor were all green, making me feel I was still in my dream. I followed all the exit signs.

By the time I was halfway down the third corridor, my walking had improved although there was pain in both my calves. As I passed a sign saying,

'Lung Function Centre', a nurse stopped me.

"Are you all right, sir?" she asked me.

She must have noticed my strange gait, and the hospital gown tucked into my pants.

"Just going outside for a smoke," I replied.

"You will have to go out through that door. The main doors are locked. You do realise it's past 11 pm, don't you?"

I tried to pretend I did. It explained why the place was almost empty.

Her helpful look turned to disgust and with a frown, she snapped, "You're in a hospital. Don't you think it's time to give up the smokes?" and she stormed off.

I must have looked like a stroke patient. Hell, I felt like one with only half my body working properly.

The night air was still warm so I assumed it was summer, but I didn't know if it was the same year. Had I missed Christmas? Part of me remembered seeing people from above, but was that real? Paige was real, I was sure of that, wasn't I?

I wasn't sure of anything. Everything seemed so scrambled.

What if I headed to Picton for no reason? What would I do then, drive back home?

I supposed so. I couldn't risk Jake being in trouble and me not going. I had to find out.

I headed for the car park, all four storeys of it. I needed a to steal a car; preferably an older one. The newer ones had too many security devices; older ones were easier to enter and easier to hot-wire.

On the third level I found a Holden Commodore. I looked around and found I was alone. In the middle pillar of the car park was a fire extinguisher cabinet. I thought about breaking the car window with my elbow, but the notion was followed by a vision of me bleeding to death on the way to Picton. I opened the cabinet. Just what I needed, an extinguisher. I took it back to the Commodore and rammed it into the back window. The glass shattered. The car had no alarm.

Nothing sounded my entry.

I opened the glove box and released the boot. I needed tools.

In the boot next to the spare tyre was a red toolbox. I flicked the lid, and there were several screwdrivers, pliers, spanners, some electrical tape, and a flare.

I took the whole box with me and sat in the driver's seat. I was hoping I could just break the ignition with the screwdriver. Usually, the lock had to be drilled out first. I hit the spanner against the end of the screwdriver, hearing the pins and springs break. Like magic, it started.

Maybe I should have been a car thief.

I didn't bother stopping at the boom gates. I was sure by the morning they would realise someone had broken out.

I had no GPS, no phone and absolutely no idea how to get to Picton.

The only thing I did know was that NSW was north of Melbourne and the best way to get there was by following the Hume Highway.

It was a good place to start.

I headed on the western ring-road towards the airport. By the time I reached the Hume Highway, a fuel light had flashed up on the dash. The car I had stolen was running low on fuel.

I had my wallet, but I had no idea if any of the cards in there were still valid. If I'd been in a coma for years, they might have expired. I searched my wallet for cash. I found a hundred tucked away behind my badge insert. I remembered always hiding one there for emergencies. If this wasn't an emergency, nothing was. It was enough to get to Picton. I hoped.

I stopped at the next service station. Everything looked the same, so perhaps I hadn't been out of action that long at all.

I went to fill the car only to realise I had to pay first. (After 11 pm they didn't allow people to gas up without first paying.)

I walked in and paid for $50 worth of petrol.

The pain in my leg seemed worse.

I began to fill my tank.

A red Toyota with two blonde girls in it pulled up. Both looked dressed for a night out. Ready to party.

They took one look at me and started giggling. One girl filled up while the other talked to her through the passenger window, taking selfies at the same time.

"I'm going in to get some smokes; do you want anything?" the blonde girl in the dark blue dress asked.

"No, I'm fine," the girl in the passenger seat replied. Then she took a second look at me and decided it was best to go with her friend.

"Wait— I'll get a drink," she called out.

The girl in blue replaced the pump back in the bowser and they both walked inside.

I noticed a phone sitting on the middle console of the girls' car. I looked up. The girls were still in the shop, walking between aisles. They were now getting more than smokes and a drink.

I pulled on the door handle of their Toyota, opened it, and took the phone and the charger attached.

I now had a GPS.

The first thing I noticed when I thumbed through the phone to find the GPS was the date. I had been in a coma for eleven months. A year of my life gone, vanished. The time in the in-between had seemed only hours. I had done some long stints in hospital before, but this was a record.

I placed the stolen phone in the centre console of my stolen car, so I could see the screen while I drove. Before today, I had never stolen anything in my life. Now I had become a serial offender.

Chapter 43

Picton December 2016

"I'm Detective Miller and you're both under arrest. Put your gun down," Jake ordered.

Jake had his Glock pointed at Anthony while he had Dave's gun pointed straight at the back of Dave's head.

"How do you figure that? I don't put my gun down for anyone," Anthony replied.

Anthony's demeanour was extremely calm, totally unflustered. He didn't seem to care that his brother was being held hostage or that they had been caught.

This really concerned Jake.

"The police are on their way," Jake said. "Put your gun down!"

"I could legally kill you now. You're in my house, you have a gun to my brother's head and a gun on me. Nothing stops me from ending you right here," Anthony said.

"I suppose you're used to killing people, aren't you? I know about the girls," Jake replied.

"Killing people is no different from killing a pig or a lamb; just different-tasting meat," Anthony said.

Where the fuck's the backup? Jake thought.

Dave began to muffle a scream, so Jake dug his boot toe into his back to quieten him.

"What did you do with my partner?" Jake asked.

"Don't know who you're talking about."

"You have his car in your shed. Where is he?"

"My brother took care of him. Turned him into pig food, I think." Anthony smirked.

Jake had met some callous killers before, but this guy was clearly disturbed.

"Maybe take the tape off my brother's mouth and you can ask him yourself?" Anthony suggested.

"I doubt that's going to happen."

Jake wondered if he would have to fire first to get out of this. "Why did you kill the girl in the bathtub?" he asked.

"We didn't."

"Don't lie to me."

"There's so much going on here. You're out of your depth, copper," Anthony said. "You'll be dead soon, so it won't matter, but I'll make sure you meet him before you go."

"Meet who?" Jake questioned.

"You'll find out, very soon."

Jake wondered why Anthony would deny killing Gemma when he was so quick to admit his brother had done something to Lucas. It was something that Jake couldn't answer yet, but he was sure when the police arrived he would find the evidence.

Dave tried to get up. Jake again dug him in the back with the toe of his boot.

Out of the corner of his eye, he saw headlights and heard the cop's cruiser pull to a stop.

Connolly walked up the stairs calling out to Jake. Then he walked in, fist over fist, one hand holding his torch, the other holding his gun.

"All right son. Put your gun down!" he said to Anthony.

Anthony placed it on the floor next to him.

Connolly put his torch away and pushed Anthony against the wall before collecting his gun from the floor.

"Stay there," he instructed Anthony. He turned to Jake. "What's going on here?"

"They've been killing girls, and I think they killed my partner. Go look in the shed; there are cars and trophies from the victims everywhere. There's even a hand in the freezer." Jake was controlled, firm and emotionless in stating the case to Connolly.

Connolly flicked the light in the lounge on.

Jake kept his eyes on Anthony who was now leaning against the wall with his palms pressed against the plaster.

Jake's eyes had trouble adjusting to the light after spending so long sitting in the dark.

Items that had only been shadowy objects previously now came to life. The fireplace showed its character. The books now had identities. Stephen King novels were there, as were some by Lee Child. There were even some books on Ted Bundy that Jake remembered Brodie having read.

Jake looked back from the bookcase to Anthony and Connolly.

Then Jake saw it, sitting on the far wall to the left of the bookcase. Suddenly his stomach churned, and terror gripped him. He realised he was in big trouble.

Jake just hoped Connolly hadn't caught him looking.

"You search the house, Jake?" Connolly asked.

"Only the freezer and the outside sheds." He indicated Anthony. "Aren't you going to cuff him?"

"He isn't going anywhere," Connolly said calmly. "I'll call the office for backup. You can get going. I'll handle it from here."

"I'm not going anywhere, until the homicide department arrives," Jake said.

"You're no longer a cop, Jake, you can't call the shots."

"Sorry, can't do it. I'm not going anywhere until they're locked up," Jake said firmly.

He stood, his left foot still firmly resting against Dave's back. "Cuff him."

Connolly sighed, then walked over to the wall where Anthony was leaning. He tapped Anthony on the back. As Anthony turned, Connolly handed him back his gun.

"It's a shame, Jake, I genuinely liked you, but you just couldn't keep your nose out of our business." He nodded to Anthony. "Kill him."

Anthony stepped forward, gun at the ready.

Jake had dragged Dave to his knees and was crouched behind him.

Dave was his shield.

Jake had nowhere to go. It was either make a stand here or die. He pressed his gun hard against Dave's head. "I'll kill him, I swear."

Connolly didn't seem fazed by Jake's threat. "I'll save you the trouble, Jake." He drew his own gun and fired three shots into Dave, instantly ending any leverage Jake might have had.

Jake waited to feel the bullets enter him after they had passed through Dave. None did. His shield was too thick-set. After all, he was the size of a tree. Probably grew up on a diet of meat and potatoes.

Jake wasted no time. Immediately he returned fire. His first shot was aimed at Anthony. It clipped his arm before straying wide, hitting the wall that Anthony had been leaning against minutes earlier. The second of his shots was dead on target, hitting Connolly just under his police name badge.

In the academy, they called that shot centre mass. It was where Jake had aimed, and it was where he'd hit.

"He'll come for all of us now," Connolly spluttered.

Jake didn't understand what that meant. He didn't give the comment the attention it deserved.

Anthony didn't hang around long enough to see Connolly hit the floor and gargle his last breath. Instead he decided his best course of action would be to hightail it out the back door.

Jake had no idea where Anthony had gone, only that it was out the back and into the darkness.

He ducked down behind the kitchen bench to try and establish a visual on Anthony, but in the pitch black with the lights on behind him, it was impossible.

The lights began to flicker before going out. At first Jake's immediate thought was that Anthony had cut off the power, until he heard the scream behind him.

He would have sworn under oath that the scream belonged to a dead man.

It was Dave's voice. Jake swung around, startled, finger on the trigger. He was on his haunches with his back against the kitchen cupboards looking into the lounge room.

Jake could see Dave's body was still lying there motionless. How could it be him? But it was. He was sure of it.

A silhouetted figure appeared out of thin air as if it had arisen from the body.

It's Dave, Jake thought in bewilderment, but it wasn't, not really. It was more like a transparent aura. A ghost.

Whatever it was, it just stood there staring down at the body. It then took three big steps back from the corner of the room.

It saw Jake staring at it, but it seemed more concerned with something else. It turned back towards the corner of the room, before moving away again. It stepped further back towards Jake.

Jake smelt it before he saw it. Its eyes were transfixing, but it was the hat that he noticed first.

It appeared out of the dark corner of the room. Jake stood to get a better look.

Whatever it was, it wore a wide-brimmed hat and had fiery-red eyes. It frightened Jake more than anything had ever scared him before.

Jake didn't think the thing had noticed him.

It seemed focused on the transparent Dave. Jake noticed its long arms that suddenly withdrew from its coat. Its hands were long and had thin fingers like rake forks.

Jake stood in dismay at what he was seeing. He watched the shadowy Hat Man insert his claw-like bony fingers into the silhouetted figure of Dave. Then its blank face, where nothing had been seconds earlier, opened up like an anaconda's mouth for a meal. But instead of swallowing what Jake now believed was Dave's soul, it inhaled him, head first.

Jake's trepidation escalated as he watched the big brother's soul get sucked into this Hat Man, before his very eyes. It was like watching a vacuum suck up dust.

Jake stepped back towards the rear door that Anthony had just used, being careful not to draw its attention. Yet it had hearing like a deer. Its head whipped around. Its eyes fixed on Jake. Jake noticed they looked even deeper, brighter. Whatever it was, it was feeding on the souls of the dead and feeding seemed to make it stronger.

The Hat thing rushed at Jake, and it was only metres away. Had Connolly's soul not risen at that instant, Jake was sure it would have come for him.

The second Connolly's spirit rose, it became transfixed on the silhouette that seemed to be frozen over his own corpse. Jake wondered if this was the soul realising that the body in which it was once housed was now dead.

Whatever it was, the silhouette seemed stunned. It just stood there. Connolly hadn't even registered Hat Man's presence.

Connolly's spirit turned to Jake. "When it comes for me, run."

Hat Man, as if being lured by Connolly's spirit, left Jake, floating instantly to Connolly.

"We don't get the light for what we have done," Connolly said, apparently resigned to his fate.

Jake didn't understand what he was talking about and he didn't want to stick around to find out.

Where had Anthony gone? His attention had been so taken by this thing that he'd briefly forgotten there was a killer on the loose.

Hat Man had no sooner put his claws straight into Connolly's throat than glass went shattering over Jake's back. Jake felt a bullet whiz past his cheek, yet he saw it as it hit the Hat Man. It glowed orange as it flew through his shadow and hit the wall on the far side of the lounge.

Hat Man turned and hissed at Jake like a tormented cat. Yellow jagged teeth appeared in a mouth that hadn't previously existed.

Jake wasn't sure who Anthony was shooting at, but he suspected it wasn't Hat Man. He decided to take Connolly's advice and sprint for the back door. Three more shots rang out. Glass smashed with each shot, and one of the shots even collected two cups that had been left on the sink. The shots followed Jake's path.

Anthony was aiming for him, all right. The shots seemed to be coming from behind the container at the rear. It sounded like rifle shots, rather than a handgun.

Jake dived out the back door, taking cover behind an old rusted water tank. He looked for the slightest movement but in the darkness, he could see very little, only outlines.

Jake heard the crunching of rock underfoot, followed by a flutter of steps, but the sound came and went so quickly it was hard to gauge exactly where it was coming from.

Off to his right, movement caught his eye, then more bullets thudded into the house behind him.

Jake crouched tighter into the curve of the tank to protect himself.

He knew where Anthony was heading; the barn where they had Lucas's car. Jake assumed he planned to hide amongst the farming machinery and the hay, waiting to cut him down. That was what Jake would do if the positions were reversed.

Jake ran to the barn and kicked the door ajar, holding it for a few seconds with his foot, keeping his body and head out of harm's way. Jake knew the tractor was to his right, Lucas's car was under cover in the middle and to his left was some type of cropping farming machinery. Jake tried to imagine where Anthony would hide. Between the cars, crouched in the darkness, or maybe up in the mezzanine, hiding in the hay, for height advantage.

Jake hoped Anthony would think the same. He was a killer and a good one at that, one with plenty of experience. An experienced killer would use the mezzanine, Jake confirmed with himself.

The barn was darker than outside. The glow of the moonlight was eclipsed by the barn roof. If he was in here, Anthony would have noticed the door open and the light enter.

Jake dived behind the grille of Lucas's covered Mazda. The barn door swung shut behind him, enclosing him in darkness. Flickers of light filtered in through gaps and cracks in the roof. They helped visibility slightly.

Jake closed his eyes, trying to help them adjust to the darkness. He closed one eye and lay on his belly. He slid under Lucas's car on elbow and knees like an army soldier.

The fit was tight. For a second, Jake wondered if he would get stuck. There was only about two centimetres' clearance.

He could see a pair of feet on the mezzanine floor, but he was too far under the car to see the mezzanine itself. Jake crawled forward. His head was close to the rear bumper, and the chrome almost grazed the back of his head as he lifted it to look up.

Now he could see the mezzanine floor, and it was covered in hay bales.

Jake cursed to himself.

Anthony was probably sitting on one of the bales, finger on the trigger, just waiting for a clean shot. The hay was stacked four bales wide, and there was a small space between each stack, easily wide enough to slide a rifle barrel into.

There was no way to tell where Anthony was. It was the perfect hiding spot. As soon as Jake got out from under this car, he would come under fire immediately.

Anthony had all the advantage, and Jake couldn't get to a position that would give him a shot. Then he thought maybe he could move Anthony.

Jake scooted backwards to the front of the car. He slid out. He was back behind the front bumper bar. He headed to the passenger side door, only because it was off centre from one of the four spaces between the hay bales, and it would make any shot more difficult than the driver's side, which was directly in front of one of the spaces between the bales. Jake opened the passenger door. Instantly, the chime sounded and a shot rang out.

A bullet shattered the door window, sending glass fragments flying in all directions. Jake felt bits hit him in the ear, nose and cheek. A second bullet grazed his right forearm. The force of the bullet flung his hand backwards, jarring his shoulder, at the same time sending his Glock flying off into the darkness.

He dived onto the car floor, keeping as low as possible, his legs hanging out the open door.

Jake expected to see the keys hanging from the steering column. There was nothing there. He noticed a button on the passenger side of the car. It had keyless entry; the only problem was that the keys needed to be in the car.

Jake remembered seeing a set of keys when he'd found the folder with Megan's contact details. He couldn't remember exactly where. He lifted the console as another bullet shattered the back window and thudded into the back of the passenger seat.

Jake put his head down under the dash. He saw the handle of Lucas's Beretta, then recalled that he'd seen the keys in the under-dash coin holder.

Jake retrieved the Beretta and crawled further into the vehicle, his arse now curled over the middle console.

Three more shots rang out. One flew high, skimming the dash, then piercing a hole in the front window. Jake felt the second one slam into the back of the driver's seat headrest. The third shot hit just above the glove box, causing the airbag to deploy. Jake pushed his hand down on the brake, using his other hand to push the button. The Mazda started instantly. The engine was quiet.

Jake slipped the car into reverse before removing his hand from the brake and exchanging it for the accelerator. He pushed hard. The car jerked at first before hurtling backwards.

Jake listened for the car hitting the beam; soon enough, the loud crack came. He expected the mezzanine to come crashing down with it. But it held steady, though it sagged a little when it lost its front support, and a few hay bales toppled off, landing on the bonnet of the Mazda.

Jake hit the brake and flicked the car back into drive. Pulling on the wheel, he turned it hard right. He needed to take out the other front support of the mezzanine. He pushed hard on the pedal, and the back wheels spun on what Jake suspected was loose hay, before they got traction and the car lurched forward. Using the reversing camera, Jake lined up the pole with the middle of the boot.

The upright snapped more easily than he'd expected, perhaps because it had been weakened by the loss of the other support, and the mezzanine came crashing down. Jake could see Anthony bounce off the boot and land hard on the hay-covered floor of the barn. Seconds later, a bale toppled on top of him. Jake wasted no time in putting the car back into reverse. He slammed the pedal down to the floor, and the car went straight back over Anthony as if he was a speed hump. The Mazda bounced up before it hit the ground.

For the first time, Jake lifted his head and looked out the front windshield.

He flicked on the headlights. Only the driver's side headlight worked; the other must have been damaged either by a bullet or by hitting the mezzanine. The light was enough for Jake to see Anthony, still alive, badly injured, but not yet dead.

Anthony got to his knees. His legs looked shattered, and his body resembled a large tree stump surrounded by hay. He pulled his rifle from the hay next to him and put it to his shoulder.

As Jake sat in the driver's seat, Anthony fired.

Jake ducked as two bullets pierced the windscreen.

He wanted to return fire, but his gun was in the hay somewhere, and the Beretta was sitting under the passenger seat out of reach..

Jake ducked his head as Anthony fired again. He pushed his foot down hard on the pedal. He didn't lift his head until he heard the car rattle over Anthony. Driving over Anthony's crushed body, he thought he deserved no less after what they had done to Lucas and all the others.

The brake lights provided enough light for Jake to see Anthony's spirit rise from his corpse, followed by the smell of sulphur. Then he saw Him stepping out of the shadows as if he had been there all along, watching the battle. Perhaps he had been.

The Hat Man with fiery-red eyes aglow swept past the cropping machine and floated through the front of the Mazda, pausing near Jake. Its head turned. A smile appeared on the previously blank face, now only centimetres from Jake's own face. Its teeth, jagged, sharp and yellow, were now visible.

"Soon," it said as a waft of foul odour floated into Jake's face. Then out of nowhere a bony hand with long claw-like nails dangling from the tips of the fingers appeared and swiped Jake's face though the shattered window.

Jake felt the nails on his cheek before he even saw the hand move.

This thing will kill me if I stay, Jake told himself. He needed to leave, yet he remained frozen in the seat.

Jake could see in the rear-vision mirror that Anthony's spirit had realised he was dead.

Hat Man, still grinning at Jake, turned its head. It had a choice either to feed or to go after Jake. It was one or the other.

It chose to go to feed. As it flew to Anthony, Jake reversed the car a little, before driving the battered vehicle straight though the barn doors, sending wood flying as he exited.

He sped back to town, away from that thing. Whatever it was, it was pure fucking evil.

Chapter 44

Victoria December 2016

I'd been travelling for just over an hour. My legs were cramping, and I had a nagging pain in my calves. Whatever was happening couldn't be normal.

I tried to ignore the strange sensation at the back of my mind and press on, but the pain nagged at me.

This isn't right, Brodie, you need medical attention, my mind persisted. "Yeah, yeah," I answered myself and continued, ignoring my own advice. Although I didn't want to admit it even to myself, I was worried.

I didn't understand how I could be tired, after all I had been asleep for eleven months. Yet after an hour's driving, I was close to exhaustion.

"You can rest soon," I said to myself. "Keep going."

My body didn't want to obey. My eyes were feeling heavier by the second. It was as if someone was hanging off them, trying to pull them down like window shutters.

White lines passed by swiftly, and the occasional set of headlights travelling in the opposite direction kept waking me, but then there were seconds of darkness. I was drifting off.

I put the driver's window down. The chill of the outside wind hit me in the face and refreshed me, but the effects didn't last long.

I needed to sleep, if only for a few minutes.

It had to be soon, before the car chose a tree to rest against.

'Maygar's Hill Winery 2k.'

A sign appeared off to my right. If I pulled off there, I could at least sleep in the car.

The winery was large, with hill upon hill of potentially award-winning vines waiting to be harvested at exactly the right time. Wineries meant years of hard work, money and sweat, all of it coming down to the day of picking which would spell either success or failure.

The homestead was small in comparison to several accommodation cottages scattered across the property, perhaps for weddings or special occasions.

I thought the cottages would suit wine drinkers who overindulged on sunny Saturday afternoons and decided to stay the night rather than driving intoxicated.

I parked the car just outside the entrance gates, turned off the lights and locked the doors. It was almost 1 am by this time.

Chapter 45

Picton December 2016

Jake had one more arrest to make before he left this God-forsaken place once and for all.

He parked Lucas's mangled car diagonally across the entrance of the hotel. The car moaned as he switched off the engine and climbed out.

Glass fell to the ground when he shut the door and headed into the hotel. The reception was unattended, which wasn't a surprise for that hour of the night.

With his bloodstained hand, Jake tapped the little bell on the counter three times. Isabella was nowhere to be seen. In his other hand, below the counter and resting against his leg, was Lucas's Beretta.

Jake suspected she had been tipped off. Maybe Connolly had warned her.

"Isabella!" Jake called out.

She poked out her head from her office door down the hall, past the reception area.

"Oh Detective, you woke me. What's wrong?" she asked.

Maybe she hadn't been tipped off after all. As Jake couldn't see her hands, he wondered if she might be armed, ready to open fire.

"Can you come out here? I have some news I really need to talk to you about," Jake said as calmly as possible.

"Can't you talk to me from there? I'm in my pyjamas."

She wasn't moving. As he still couldn't see her hands, the alarm bells rang.

Obviously having noticed Lucas's car parked across the entry to her hotel, Isabella asked, "What happened to your car?"

"Had an accident."

Jake knew she could see his blood-soaked hand, yet she didn't ask if he was okay.

She had been tipped off.

Jake drew his gun above the counter and aimed it straight at her. "Show me your hands."

At first, it appeared as if she was going to obey.

That was until she stepped out into the hall and flung open her pink polka-dot dressing gown, revealing her own gun. It was a shotgun and at this range, it would be devastating.

Jake reflexes were quicker, and he managed to get a shot off before she did, but it went high, sailing into the wall behind her.

"What did you do to my boys? You fucker!" Isabella called out before firing her shotgun. The shot tore apart half of her front counter, sending splinters of wood flying in all directions.

Jake, who had dived behind the wall, timed his return fire perfectly. As soon as the shot went off, he fired two more quick shots, knowing she would have to pump her gun to reload.

The first clipped her right hand (pure luck, Jake thought), while the second bullet hit her right shoulder. Her shotgun tumbled to the floor. Isabella staggered backwards. Jake took the opportunity to rush at her.

He took her like a rugby player making a try-saving tackle, hitting her hard and fast.

He heard a bone break beneath him, not his, maybe her hip or leg.

"You cocksucker!" she cried.

Jake stood up, dragging her by the gown as he kicked the shotgun away, sending it sliding back towards the entrance.

She spat at Jake as he dragged her up. Isabella stood with ease, and Jake wondered what he had heard break; something, he was sure of it.

He took the cord of her gown and bound her hands together. It would hold until he could find something more suitable. Isabella looked fine;

nothing broken apart from her hand and maybe her shoulder. Maybe she had a cracked rib?

Jake sat her down on the bottom step of her hotel stairs.

"You know, your boys and your husband are dead," Jake said without sympathy.

"He wasn't my husband."

"Boyfriend then? I saw the family photo at the boys' house."

Isabella nodded. "My house," she clarified.

"Well, either way, they're all dead."

Jake drew out from the back of his pants the journals he'd found at the house.

"Which one of them killed Gemma? I know one did, because I found these in the house."

"Neither of them," came the reply.

"So, it was Connolly then?

"No."

"Don't lie to me."

"I killed the slut. She was going to tell on my boys," she replied.

Jake realised she was telling the truth. She had no reason not to.

"What happened?"

"I told you, the slut was going to dob on my boys."

"I want to know everything," Jake said.

"When she and her slutty friend had the accident a few months earlier, she saw the boys heading into the tunnel with some food for Hat Man."

"By food, you mean a human?" Jake asked. "Hat Man, is that the thing that lives in the tunnel?"

She nodded. "If we fed him, he kept away from us. Sometimes we wouldn't see it for months."

"What happened when Gemma came back?" Jake asked.

"She made a call to Connolly, to tell him she had seen two boys chasing a girl the night of the accident. She named my sons. Apparently, the boys chasing the girl caused the accident. I had to get rid of her. Connolly was going to kill her the next day, but when I heard her having a bath in her room,

I let myself in. There she was, lying in the bath, face washer over her face and radio playing on the vanity. So, I pushed it. She didn't even know I was there. It was easy to cover up. It looked like an accident." Isabella grinned. "She still haunts this place, especially that room. I have lost a lot of business because of that bitch."

Jake just wanted to slap her smug, remorseless face. "The other night I saw her in the room."

"Most people do when they stay in there," Isabella replied.

"Why didn't the Hat Man take her, after you killed her? If she haunts here, then she didn't get eaten?" Jake asked.

"I don't know. My only guess is, it was feeding somewhere else. Look, I don't know all the ins and outs of that thing. The boys once told me sometimes when the Hat Man takes them, their soul splits. I guess a part of it is consumed and a part of it stays here." Isabella looked around as if Gemma's spirit was watching.

"I take it she didn't go towards the light either?" Jake said grimly.

"She didn't accept that she was dead. She just stood staring at herself in the bath."

"Why kill her? I'm sure Connolly could have covered it up."

"He'd dismissed her calls several times. She even made a statement to police in Victoria. It was sent to Connolly to investigate and he covered it up, yet she wouldn't let it go."

So, they had killed Gemma because she'd been rattling the wrong cage.

"What about Lucas, your boys kill him?" Jake asked.

"Yeah, he was nosey, like that reporter mole, come around here asking all sorts of fucking questions, wanting to examine this and that. Do fucking tests on the radio, like a dog with a bone he was. Well, he followed that bone all the way to his grave." She spat, as if spitting on his grave.

Jake stood stunned, trying to control his rage. "What happened to his stuff?"

"Took what was valuable, dumped the rest."

There was no empathy in her, no emotion, no soul, just evil, Jake thought.

"I'm taking you to Thirlmere Police Station," he stated. He walked her out to the car. Putting her in the back seat of a Mazda with her hands tied behind her back only with a dressing gown cord was not an ideal way to transport a criminal, but what other choice did he have?

He thought about ringing the station and getting them out here, but he didn't know who else she knew. People could disappear on the way back to the lockup, especially in a town like this. It would be a lot harder to cover up this crime once he was back at the station.

Jake headed off into the darkness, one headlight showing the way.

"Did he come for the boys?" Isabella asked from the back seat.

"Who?"

"You know who I'm talking about, the one that did that to your face."

Jake touched the side of his cheek, checking it in the mirror. The three horizontal scratches were still there. They were red and painful, just like a burn.

"Yes, he came for them, but I don't think he's a man," Jake replied.

"He is no man. This thing is the devil," Isabella snapped.

"There is no such thing."

"You saw him for yourself and you still doubt the devil exists? Did you see it feed?"

Jake nodded.

"That's not human. You're a marked man."

"What do you mean, 'marked'?" Jake asked.

"Those burns on your face are his mark. He'll come for you. When he comes for you, there's no escape." She laughed. "He's coming for you!" she repeated, laughing louder.

"Shut up!" Jake shouted.

Jake passed the sign, 'Thank you for visiting Picton', then passed the last petrol station in town.

Seconds later he saw a sign saying, 'Welcome to Picton Population 4721'.

Jake blinked twice. What the fuck just happened?

He looked over to the other side of the road. The service station he'd just passed on his right was now on his left. He was heading back into Picton. He'd been spun around. But how?

"I told you, you're marked. He won't let you leave," Isabella reiterated. "Let me out, he's coming for you. Let me out, you prick!" Isabella kicked the seat like a spoilt child.

"You're staying with me and if he comes for me then he will come for you too," Jake retorted.

He drove the car over the median strip and onto the other side of the road. The tyres squealed and screeched as he turned the car around again.

For the second time in a minute, he passed the sign and the service station. A thick white fog rolled in suddenly, out of nowhere. The only other time Jake had seen something as bizarre was in San Francisco near the Golden Gate Bridge. With one headlight out, his visibility was severely restricted.

Only fifty metres past the service station, Jake saw him. He was hovering in the middle of the road.

Part of Jake wanted to drive straight over him, but the marks on his face started burning a little more, as if to provide a warning.

Jake hit the brakes hard. He heard Isabella's forehead hit the back of the front passenger seat. The tyres gripped and then gave and gripped again. The car shuddered to a stop.

Jake sat there staring at Hat Man. Less than twenty metres away, it hovered against a backdrop of a thick blanket of white fog.

Jake had seen how fast Hat Man could move. He was getting out of here.

"I told you he was coming for you. There's no escape!" Isabella screamed. "Please let me out. He'll kill us both."

"I've already told you, you're staying with me. If he comes for me, then he'll come for you too," Jake promised.

"You bastard pig!" Isabella wailed in despair.

Jake took a side street and headed back into town. If this really was the devil, then there was only one person who could help him, and he was locked inside the church.

*

At the church, Jake dragged Isabella out of the car and knocked on the door. A light inside flickered on before a peephole opened. The elderly man's face appeared behind an iron grille of the church door.

"I told you to leave me alone," the old man said.

"I need your help, Father. I have seen him. Help me stop him," Jake begged. He looked over his shoulder, terrified that the Hat Man was standing behind him.

"You've been marked," Pastor Elijah Dwyer said, noticing Jake's red cheek.

Jake touched his cheek. It felt hotter than before.

"Who's she?" Pastor Dwyer asked, peering at Isabella.

"Isabella Brown."

Pastor Elijah Dwyer stood there looking at her, dissatisfied with Jake's response.

"She tried to kill me. Let us in, and I'll tell you the story," Jake said.

Pastor Dwyer closed the peep door. It felt like an eternity before the door swung open.

"Please keep your voices low; my granddaughter is asleep," Pastor Dwyer said.

He led them into a small chapel. There were disused pews stacked each side of what would have been the aisle, and at the end of the room was a raised area which Jake assumed would have once been the altar. Now the chapel was being used as a sitting room. There were two small couches on each side of the room, and a rug on the original timber floors. And the original altar had been converted into a makeshift play area for the girl.

The pastor offered Jake a rare smile.

"I heard you abandoned your religion?"

"People talk. I don't pay any attention to it," Pastor Dwyer replied.

"I didn't introduce myself. I'm Jake Miller. I'm a detective, I mean I was a detective," Jake corrected. He didn't believe in God, but he didn't want to begin a habit of lying in church. "I'm a private investigator now. Can you tell me about the Hat Man?"

"Well, firstly, its name is Scat. I believe it's a demon, summoned from hell. I don't necessarily think it has a gender," Father Dwyer explained.

"Summoned by whom? How did it get here?" Jake asked.

"A hundred years ago when my father, Pastor Joseph Dwyer, worked in this very church he was told by a nurse that she and her two friends had performed a séance, and soon after the Hat Man was seen around town. All three people who performed the séance died in unusual circumstances."

"What sort of circumstances?"

"The man shot himself, the nurse was crushed to death in the morgue by a cadaver's bed and the third was hit by a train in the Redbank Range Tunnel."

"They don't sound too unusual, apart from the morgue episode," Jake replied.

"The train wasn't even due. It arrived at the station forty minutes late."

Jake was unsure how to answer. In the end, he remained silent.

Pastor Dwyer continued, "People have disappeared from all over these parts, not just here in Picton but from neighbouring towns too. Sometimes there are two or three accidents and then nothing for years. Then in 1944, the Hat Man directly affected our family. My older brother Tommy was killed. I still remember it as if it was yesterday."

"You don't think it was an accident?" Jake questioned.

"It was no accident. I was there. I have seen the Hat Man myself."

"Did the Hat Man get Tommy?"

"No, he and Becca ran away. He saved their souls. I wish I could say the same for Becca's brother; he wasn't so lucky."

"Why didn't the Hat Man take you?"

"I hid behind a tree like a coward," Pastor Dwyer replied, looking at the floor in shame. "Some nights I see Tommy and Becca running through the tombstones," Pastor Dwyer added, diverting the subject from his cowardliness.

He shuffled in his seat, looking sore and uncomfortable.

"You, okay?" Jake asked.

"Just old. I am eighty-eight years old. My joints tend to freeze up if I sit still too long."

"What happened after Tommy died?" Jake asked.

"For the first few months, Homicide looked for the man in the hat, but no one was ever found. They thought it was a paedophile who had tried to abduct Tommy and Becca." Tears rolled down his face. Even though the memories were decades old, they were still raw to the pastor. "Life went on as normal for a few years, although nothing was normal any more. Pa lost some of his belief in God. Not that he said so, but I could see it in the way he conducted his Sunday sermons, the way he prepared for church. Then when Mum passed in 1953, Pa began to drink. He became an alcoholic. In 1961, he was found hanging off the Redbank Range Bridge."

Just past the tunnel, Jake thought.

Jake knew that it couldn't have been the brothers. It was before their time. He wondered if Hat Man had had something to do with it.

"Sounds to me like the Hat Man got inside his head!" Isabella chimed in.

Pastor Dwyer scowled at her.

"Do you think it was the Hat Man?"

"I think the grief my mother suffered caused the cancer that killed her. And I think he filled my father with enough darkness that his only option was at the end of a rope."

"So, is that why you don't go out into the town?" Jake asked.

"No, after Pa passed I ran the church here until November 2010. It's strange how the worst days of your life seem to present the most vivid memories. All you want to do is forget them, but somehow, they get burnt inside somewhere deep and they never leave.

"It was a cold morning, a lot of fog and mist around, and I was always nervous when my son drove long distances but that morning, I was exceptionally nervous. My son Richard and my daughter-in-law, Kate, were setting off to visit her family. She was eight months pregnant. It was a joyous time. Being so far away, she had missed out on all the little things that go with pregnancy, especially when it's the first grandchild for both families."

Pastor Dwyer closed his eyes and took a breath.

Jake could feel that what was coming next was hard for the pastor to say.

"Until, until…" His voice began to falter, as if a lump was forming in his throat. The pastor crossed himself and said some type of blessing or prayer in Latin that Jake was unfamiliar with.

Jake looked over at Isabella who had sat her frumpy frame down in the pew in the next aisle. Her look had gone from contempt to fear and panic. She must have known the story that was coming.

"Until the accident." Pastor Dwyer turned away from Jake as he spoke, instead choosing to look at the cross of Jesus hanging on the wall. Jake thought he was either seeking comfort or assigning blame.

"A truck careered onto the wrong side of the road, colliding with my family's car. All three of them were killed. The only survivor was Olivia, whom they managed to deliver after my daughter-in-law died. I have raised her since birth. I am all she has known: this place is all she has known."

"You think the Hat Man had something to do with that accident?" Jake questioned.

"After they left for their trip, I was walking in the grounds when I saw him standing at the other side of the river, mist at his feet. Those fiery-red eyes stared at me. When I looked again he was gone. Does that answer your question?"

Jake nodded, and the pastor shuffled in his seat again.

"How does being a shut-in help you?" Jake asked.

"This is a house of God, and the Hat Man or the demon or whatever he is, is prohibited from setting foot on this soil. It's holy."

"Can we defeat it?" Jake asked.

"I don't see how," Pastor Dwyer replied. "I hear that bullets go straight through it."

"I saw that happen tonight. They have no effect. I think when someone dies, and it feeds, it gets stronger," Jake replied. "What about some holy water and a crucifix, would they protect me?"

"Maybe a little." Pastor Dwyer sounded doubtful.

"If it was summoned here, could we perform an exorcism to kill it?"

"An exorcism is only if the demon has taken over someone's body. This demon is in its own form. We could try to cleanse the tunnel where it hides, but my faith isn't strong enough to cast out a demon. It has taken quite a battering over recent years. I can't help you any further; I'm sorry."

"Pastor, we need you. The town needs you."

"I'm sorry," he repeated.

Jake frowned. "Tell me, Pastor. How come the Hat Man never killed this evil bitch and her family?" he asked, turning towards Isabella.

Isabella answered with a one-finger salute, which Jake thought was inappropriate considering they were standing in a house of God. He turned his attention from her back to Pastor Dwyer, who didn't react at all.

"Evil doesn't kill evil, so while they were committing their evil acts, it left them alone. Once they were dead, their souls were food just like everyone else's," Father Dwyer said.

Jake examined the small, old church; the place the pastor had called home for the last six years. How could you live in such small confines without venturing outside?

His eyes took in the wooden cross below the three arched, stained-glass windows, and he said, "Pastor, come with me. We will defeat this thing together."

The pastor stepped away, distancing himself from Jake.

Jake shook his head in disappointment.

"I can't. I am sorry."

"Pastor, we need you. The town needs you. Is this how you want your granddaughter to live? Only going outside in the daytime and not leaving the grounds of the church?"

"If it stops her from being taken, then it's how it must be."

Jake removed Lucas's Beretta and began unloading the bullets. "Well, I'm not going to hide here. I would rather die on my feet than live the rest of my life on my knees like you. Hiding in a church is not living."

Pastor Dwyer looked at him and bowed his head, and Jake knew he was bowing it in shame.

Jake took the handful of shells from the magazine and began dipping them into the holy water in the font, ensuring that the firing pin end remained dry. The last thing he wanted was a misfire.

He took a blue Disney water bottle he had spotted earlier from one of the pews. It was clearly the granddaughter's. Bubbles reached the surface as Jake dunked the bottle in the font of holy water. It filled fast.

Holding the bottle in his left hand, Jake took the sacred cross from the wall below the stained-glass windows.

"You can't take those things; they are not yours," Pastor Dwyer said.

"I am taking them, Pastor. It's not open for discussion. I need a bible. Are you going to give me one, or do I have to steal that too?"

Without a word, the pastor handed him a bible.

Jake took the bible, nodded in appreciation and then grabbed Isabella by the wrist and yanked her down the aisle in front of him.

"A word of advice. He will be at his strongest at night, especially seeing he has just fed," the pastor's voice echoed down the aisle.

Jake stopped in his tracks. "Are you saying we should wait until morning?"

"I would, but I am not you. The Hat Man lives in the tunnel only because it's dark. Demons hide in the shadows during the day."

"Any other advice you might want to give me?" Jake said.

"Well, you look as if you're ready to hunt a vampire. Demons are different from vampires, you know. You can't just kill it by putting a wooden stake through its heart; you need to perform a cleansing ritual."

"Don't you have to be a priest to do that?" Jake enquired.

"No. Anyone can kill a demon. You must remember the demon is not a human spirit; it is a dark entity that shapes itself into human form to fit in. The Hat Man, as you call it, is from hell itself, and only belief in God and love of God can remove him. You show him fear, then he grows stronger. You show him you have faith, and you can banish him from earth."

"Sounds easy." Jake's only problem was, he didn't believe in God.

"He will eat you up," Isabella cackled.

Jake ignored her.

"We'll leave in the morning then," he instructed Isabella.

The pastor attended to Isabella's hand, applying a fresh bandage that covered all but her fingers. Jake tied her feet to take pressure off her hand.

While Isabella slept on one of the couches, Jake sat opposite, waiting for the night to end.

Chapter 46

Melbourne December 2016

I don't know whether it was the pain in my legs or the stranger bashing on my window with his flashlight that woke me.

"You can't stay here!" he shouted into the glass.

I waved and nodded and started the car with my screwdriver. My left leg had been stretched over the passenger seat. It was protesting loudly in pain. I raised the pants leg.

Tender, hot, red, and pulsating. Most likely, clot-ridden.

Soon the clots would likely travel north to my brain and either give me a stroke or kill me.

"Just a few more hours and you can do what you want with me," I told my leg.

My attention returned to Jake.

I didn't know how he needed my help, only that he did.

The vision I had been shown was clear. Jake was trapped in a tunnel, with a man, a thing, a man in a hat—something from another dimension, something from hell.

After re-entering the highway, I continued north, north towards Jake, towards trouble; perhaps, towards my death.

The drive was quiet, the low hum of the motor broken only by the occasional road train.

A word came into my head. "Soon," spoken by a low, gruff voice I didn't recognise. The voice was how I imagined a troll under a bridge would sound.

It sounded mean, mad, evil.

Chapter 47

Picton December 2016

Jake had spent the hours between 12 am and 2 am hovering over a candle, reading bible scriptures, looking for anything that might be helpful. Nothing stood out. He wasn't expecting a chapter on how to banish a demon, but he was hoping for something.

He was about to turn in himself, when he caught Olly peeking out from the side of the altar. Quietly Jake moved towards her. She was hugging a stuffed faded bear.

"What's your bear's name?" Jake whispered.

"Teddy," she mumbled.

"He's beautiful."

She held the bear out. "Cuddle you," she said.

Jake took Teddy and gave him a hug. At that moment, he realised how lucky he was.

"Let's get you back to bed." Jake picked her up and she held the bear tightly.

He walked down a hall past the altar and through a small kitchen, behind which were two small rooms.

The girl's name was written on her bedroom door in colourful wooden letters. Jake pushed open the door that was slightly ajar. Her room had just a few toys, a bed and a lamp. Her walls were covered with her own drawings. Every drawing depicted the Hat Man. She must have seen him. Jake was about to ask her more when he realised she had fallen asleep on his shoulder.

He tucked her into bed with Teddy wedged tightly under her chin.

"Everything all right?" a voice from the door said.

"She came out. I just put her back to bed; didn't think you were awake."

"I'm a light sleeper. You are good with her."

"I take it she has seen the Hat Man?" Jake whispered, eyes fixed on Olly's wall.

"Unfortunately, she has."

Jake could see the sorrow in the pastor's eyes as he left the room.

"You have children?" Pastor Dwyer asked

"A baby girl," Jake replied. "What do I say to get rid of him?" Jake asked humbly.

"Just keep it simple. Something like, 'in the name of the Father, the Son and the Holy Spirit, I banish you from this earth," Pastor Dwyer offered.

Jake turned back towards the lounge. He needed sleep before the morning.

"Most importantly, Jake, you need to believe in what you're saying."

Jake paused a moment, before continuing without a reply.

As dawn finally broke, a dense, ominous fog began rolling into town like a billion cotton balls.

Isabella remained asleep. She had snored the whole night. Jake decided not to wake her until he was ready to leave. The less he had to deal with her the better.

Normally, as it rose in the sky, the sun burnt off the fog yet half an hour later, it lingered, appearing thicker, denser, even more ominous than before.

Jake suspected today wasn't going to be any ordinary day.

He woke Isabella. Pastor Dwyer let them freshen up in his residence at the back of the church. Jake only saw the kitchen and the bathroom, both of which were small but neat. The pastor provided toast and juice for breakfast. Jake sat opposite Isabella as she ate, after which he decided to re-tie her hands but untied her feet so she would be able to walk. This time, he used some rope the pastor had lying around. He checked that she was secure and that her circulation wasn't restricted.

With holy water, cross and bible all stacked in a Dora the Explorer backpack, Jake and Isabella took their first steps outside the church in over twelve hours.

The air was crisp and clean, the wind warm. The fog swirled around Jake and Isabella's feet and seconds later, he couldn't see his shoes. By the time they reached the path, away from the sanctuary of the church, the outside world had vanished. Pausing at the gate, Jake looked both ways as if checking for traffic, except it wasn't cars he was afraid of, it was Hat Man.

"He could be waiting for us in the fog and we would never know," he mused aloud.

"You're going to kill us both," Isabella said.

His legs still trembling, Jake forced himself through the gate. Isabella kicked up a fuss, as he knew she would. He pulled hard on her tied hands, almost dragging her along.

Lucas's car was parked outside the front fence at a right angle, with the left tyre over the curb. The car seats were damp from the cool night air. As Jake sat down, he felt the wetness seep into his pants.

"Oh shit, me fucking pants are wet now," Isabella's obnoxious voice came from behind him.

He ignored her. He planned on ignoring her for the rest of her life. She was nothing but a low-life serial killer to him.

The hunk of damaged metal that once was Lucas's car started with the first push of the ignition button. The motor was still quiet, yet when the car moved it sounded as if every part of it was being tortured. If the car could speak, Jake had no doubt it would cry out in pain.

He headed south towards the end of town, turning right at a closed and now disused road. The fog was still thick, still eerie, making driving difficult.

When he arrived at the end of the road, Jake was confronted by a green gate blocking the road. The sign on it read: 'Road closed. Tunnel closed. Entry prohibited'.

The fog had cleared a little as if it was making a path for him.

Jake exited the car, a damp patch from the seat now evident on his pants. Gravel and dirt crunched beneath his shoes as he walked around the car.

He removed Isabella from the car. At first, she resisted, trying to hook her legs around the seat in front of her to avoid being dragged out.

Jake was strong; much too strong for Isabella. In the end she fell out of the car, landing her fat rear in the gravel.

"I am not going in there. No fucking way!"

The south side entrance to the tunnel stood a hundred metres away. Although it was just a structure, to Jake it seemed to have a personality, a demeanour, an attitude, a cold and unwelcoming presence.

Jake stared and gulped.

Isabella refused to walk forward.

Jake dragged her. Stones gouged her knees and she let out a cry of anguish. It took another few paces before her knees become so sore she gave up her fight and found her feet.

"You know he'll kill us both," Isabella murmured from behind.

"Shut up," Jake responded instantly.

He didn't want to hear her chatter, not now, not ever.

"He'll take our souls," she added. She dropped to her knees, begging for Jake to let her go.

Jake, ignoring her protests, only pulled on the rope harder. He could hear her dragging in the gravel for a few seconds, before she gathered her feet under her and decided to walk again.

They arrived at the entrance to the tunnel.

It was cold, almost icy, five to seven degrees less than the outside temperature. It was as if they were about to walk into a fridge.

Jake took a breath and stepped into the darkness.

His legs of jelly nearly failed him.

As he walked into the tunnel, the world outside began to disappear and when Jake looked back, the outside world shimmered and glistened as if it were a different dimension. Jake felt like an animal trapped inside a zoo enclosure; he could see the outside world but couldn't get there.

Jake and Isabella both moved forward with trepidation, Jake waiting for the second when the mysterious Hat Man would appear. He removed the bottle of holy water from the pack and began to splash it about. Sprinkles of it hit the walls, and the dirt floor in front of him. Jake was using it like weed-killer, yet they were alone.

"In the name of the Father, the Son and the Holy Spirit, I banish you," Jake repeated over and over, as they walked deeper into the tunnel.

Jake swirled the bottle. It was a little over half full as he approached the tunnel's alcove, midway along.

Jake sprayed each wall with it and repeated his cleansing speech, except this time he added a second line.

"In the name of Jesus Christ, I banish you."

Jake reached the end of the tunnel. He stepped out into the daylight and immediately felt warmer.

Isabella was walking so close behind, she trod on his heels a few times as they made their way through the tunnel.

"It's worked. He's gone. We can leave now," she said.

Jake paid little attention to her ramblings. His focus was on the car that was parked at the edge of the ravine.

Jake began his walk towards the vehicle, but before he could reach it, a dangling rope caught his attention in his peripheral vision.

It was tied to one of the disused tracks that led over the edge of the ravine.

Jake lay on his belly and looked over the precipice, his shirt and slacks becoming soiled.

Something was dangling at the end of the rope; a body, a girl's body.

Jake wondered if it was that of the reporter Lucas had spoken of.

The dead body was swinging in the breeze.

Jake thought about pulling her up but decided against it. Something about this whole place didn't seem right. He felt as if he was being watched.

Jake examined the vehicle without opening the door. He checked the seating position, which was in close to the wheel, far too close for one of the Brown brothers to have been driving, unless they'd readjusted it afterwards.

"Your boys do this?" Jake said to Isabella.

She didn't offer any excuse, just nodded in the affirmative.

Jake now knew where the Brown brothers had been last night; they were here, feeding him.

Jake headed back into the tunnel, pushing Isabella forward in front of him. At first, she resisted, until Jake threatened to use his gun by placing his hand on his holster inside his jacket.

Isabella begrudgingly entered the tunnel for the second time that morning. Jake followed closely.

Again, the sudden and dramatic drop in temperature was noticeable.

As they passed the alcove again, Jake noticed Isabella turned her head away.

Jake on the other hand, felt compelled to look in case he saw the mysterious Hat Man.

Instead, he saw empty space, nothing but darkness and shadows.

Jake stared at the shadows for a moment, looking for any movement.

Nothing.

He moved on.

He was three or four paces past the alcove when he first smelt it.

It was a faint, subtle smell at first, then stronger. The smell was unmistakeably that of sulphur.

A tidal wave of fear struck Jake, a sensation stronger than he had ever felt before. It was the fear of impending doom.

He was here. Somewhere in the darkness, Hat Man was here.

*

New South Wales December 2016

As the darkness made way for morning and the sun appeared on the horizon, the throbbing pain in my leg had become a strong constant ache. The pain suggested a possible deep-vein thrombosis. If that was the case, it would lead to a stroke and potentially to my death.

I even talked aloud to myself, so I could check my speech wasn't slurring. The last thing I wanted was to have a stroke while driving. I imagined myself having a head-on collision with a truck.

I didn't say anything in particular; just random words. Boot and shoe and tape and gun. Fucker and bitch usually came out when the pain in my leg flared.

I realised I should have stayed in hospital. Whatever was wrong with my leg would probably kill me if I didn't get medical attention soon.

I wondered why Paige would wake me from my coma and direct me to come here, only to let me die.

Why wouldn't she help me? I wondered.

I knew she was watching me from the in-between.

"Paige, help me," I called.

Of course, there was no answer.

Maybe she couldn't help me.

Maybe she could only watch.

I drove on.

*

Picton December 2016

Isabella got a whiff of the sulphur too. She screamed and began to sprint for the tunnel's entrance. She wanted out.

The fiery-red eyes of the Hat Man appeared before her and he stood blocking her path. To get out, Isabella would have to go through him. With her hands still tied, she ran, half-crouched over.

With her head down, she ran straight towards Hat Man and at the last second, she managed to avoid his outstretched arms.

Jake watched Isabella fly past Hat Man, then suddenly, he saw her levitating against the roof of the tunnel. With one wave of his arm, Hat Man dragged her along the roof and back towards Jake. She was only metres in front of him when Hat Man swung his arm in a downward direction.

Isabella went from floating against the roof to being slammed into the dirty, rocky ground.

Her crumpled, torn body lay slumped and bleeding on the tunnel floor.

Jake gasped at what he had just witnessed. The thing had moved her without even laying a finger on her. He had telekinetic powers.

Jake shuffled forward cautiously.

He aimed the bottle and squeezed it. Water spurted like a bullet. The water splashed onto Hat Man's chest. Steam rose in a puff. Jake expected to hear a scream or some form of anguish. Instead, there was nothing.

Just silence.

Jake took the cross and recited his banishing call.

"In the name of the Father, the Son and the Holy Spirit, I banish you from earth."

Hat Man stood motionless.

The words had no effect.

As Jake crept closer, a devious smile spread across Hat Man's face. His yellow teeth shone in the darkness. His fiery-red eyes narrowed and dimmed, as Jake stepped ever closer.

"Jesus Christ demands you exit this earth," Jake said, spraying more water from his bottle. It landed just in front of Hat Man's feet and evaporated into a small puff of steam.

As soon as the words 'Jesus Christ' left Jake's lips, Hat Man hissed and growled.

The Lord's name in combination with the water had an effect.

"Jesus Christ banishes you from this earth," Jake repeated.

Hat Man hissed and reared, arms and long bony hands poised as if readying himself for battle.

Jake squirted more water. It was running low now, with only a quarter of the bottle left. Shouldn't have wasted it in the entrance, he thought.

He stepped closer. Jake was doing all the moving. Hat Man was just hovering. Jake began to feel he was walking into a trap.

They stood about five metres apart, like duelling gunslingers from the Wild West.

Jake stared.

Hat Man stared back.

Jake was set upon. He was so transfixed by Hat Man he failed to notice Isabella.

She came at him hard and before he knew it, her arms were wrapped around his neck and her fingers were scratching and clawing at his face.

The first thing Jake noticed were that her eyes had rolled back so all he could see were the whites. Her face was criss-crossed in cuts from being dragged across the tunnel roof.

He struggled to keep her off him, with a cross in one hand and the bottle of holy water in the other. Jake raised his forearm to try and fend her off, but she had gained strength.

She was stronger than she had ever been. She was chanting continuously in a dull monotone.

"*Satanas qui laetificat juventutem meam. Veni, omnipotens aeterne diabolus! Diabolus, custodiam!*"

Jake had no idea what she was saying although he recognised 'Diabolus' as the word for devil. He also recognised '*Veni- omnipotens*' as come almighty was aeterne eternal Jake couldn't be one hundred percent sure, but he thought his translation was close. It would mean she was chanting '*come almighty eternal devil.*' Jake knew then and there, he was in a situation he might not get out of.

Jake fell backwards under Isabella's immense force. She swiped at his face. Jake held up the cross, pressing it against her forehead. Smoke poured out, flesh burnt, yet she did not let up. She swung again wildly, this time collecting both the cross and the bottle of water, sending them flying off into the darkness of the tunnel.

The chanting didn't stop. She repeated the same words over and over again.

And she kept scratching, clawing, biting. It was as if she had turned into a zombie from some post-apocalyptic movie. With his free hand, Jake tried to fend her off again. With one arm under her throat and the other on her forehead, he could feel the heat where the cross had burnt her forehead radiate into his palm.

Her hands wrapped around his throat and began to squeeze. Jake still couldn't push her back. She was too strong. He was losing this battle fast.

He had to do something quickly before she killed him.

Jake kneed her in the crotch. She didn't even flinch.

He used his forearm to clip Isabella in the chin again, but it had no effect. He did it several times. Nothing.

Jake thought if he had hit anyone else like that, he would have knocked them out, but not this bitch. Apart from a bloody mouth, she was unrelenting.

Jake was really struggling to breathe. He could feel the oxygen being squeezed out of his body. He felt as if his eyeballs were about to pop out of his skull.

Bloody saliva from the bitch's mouth dripped on his face as she pushed down harder on his throat. The parts of the tunnel he could see went black as he faded in and out of consciousness. The more he struggled to breathe, the less oxygen he took in and the closer he came to suffocating.

Her chanting face faded into darkness and then a few seconds later it reappeared, eyes still all-white, mouth still moving to the chant, salivating.

As if in an entirely other world, Jake heard a distant voice. "In the name of the Father, the Son and the Holy Spirit and in the name of our Lord and Saviour, Jesus Christ, I condemn you back to hell!" the voice shouted.

Jake blacked out again.

When he woke, the thing on top of him that had been Isabella was smouldering from her back. Her grip had loosened. Jake gasped for air while he could.

Realising her grip had weakened, Jake took advantage of the opportunity and head-butted her strong and hard, hitting her flush on the nose.

For the first time, his attack had an impact on her.

Isabella rolled off him, and the chanting stopped.

Jake reached for his Beretta, aimed at her chest and fired.

He slowly regained his feet and stumbled on the rocky cobblestones of the tunnel's surface.

He could see Pastor Elijah Dwyer dousing Hat Man in holy water.

He had come. Maybe he still believed in his faith after all, Jake thought.

As he splashed water on the Hat Man, Isabella burnt. Jake realised Hat Man was controlling Isabella. When he burnt, she burnt.

Jake's eyes darted into the darkness, searching for his water bottle. He located it, but it was now empty.

The only holy water Jake had left was on the tips of eleven bullets remaining in his Beretta.

"Pastor, step away!" Jake yelled.

The instruction echoed through the tunnel and by the second echo, Jake had fired three shots at Hat Man's chest.

Jake saw a burst of steam explode where every bullet landed. Every explosion was followed by a high-pitched shriek.

He had hurt it.

Jake was sure it was working.

He fired again, another group of three.

Again, the puffs of steam rose, and the cries followed.

Hat Man turned to face Pastor Elijah Dwyer. It was the first time Jake had seen him move since he'd appeared.

He floated swiftly towards the pastor across the tunnel floor.

"Pastor, you don't have the faith to banish me. You wear the collar of faith, but it has left your soul. I can smell your fear!" Hat Man bellowed.

It was the first time Jake had heard Hat Man speak more than one word. His voice was gruff, almost monstrous.

Ignoring, Hat Man's words, Pastor Elijah continued his cleansing ritual, flicking more holy water towards the creature.

Despite smouldering from the holy water, Hat Man bore down on the pastor, hissing at him like a cobra about to strike.

"Where is your God now?" Hat Man growled.

Pastor Dwyer continued as if what Hat Man was saying had no effect on him. Raising the hand in which he held the cross, he pressed it hard into Hat Man's head, sending the wide-brimmed hat flying into the tunnel. The horns on Hat Man's head were now visible.

The cross burnt, and smoke poured from Hat Man's skin. But Hat Man was gripping the pastor around the throat. Although the pastor tried to back away, Hat Man's grip was too strong.

It spoke again, "Your God won't come. He won't save you. He didn't save your wife or your son. I have their souls, and they belong to me now."

The pastor squirted his remaining water all over the face of the now hatless demon. Its skin steamed before melting away like an ice cream left in the sun.

"In the name of…" the pastor began.

Hat Man struck in one quick motion, so fast the pastor didn't even see him move. His bony claws wrapped around the clergyman's throat, and the nails drew blood as they squeezed. Pastor Dwyer could feel his larynx being crushed so tightly he could neither speak nor breathe.

"See? No God," Hat Man boasted.

Pastor Dwyer pushed harder on the cross. Hat Man removed the cross from his head with his other claw. As it caught fire, he held it, crushing the flaming cross to dust.

A burnt outline remained imprinted on his forehead, but it seemed to have had little impact, Jake thought, as he watched them.

Isabella looked dead. Jake thought about checking for a pulse but decided against it. He thought she had probably been killed when Hat Man had thrown her to the ground.

Jake had five shots left. He hoped it would be enough, or he too would end up dead. Or worse, consumed by Hat Man.

Chapter 48

Picton December 2016

I had found some Panadol in the centre console. I took four, twice the recommended dose. The pain in my leg eased momentarily, but I knew the problem remained.

I passed a sign, on my left. It read 'Welcome to Picton'.

It was the sign Paige had shown me in the vision.

A thick fog descended the instant I entered the town, engulfing the car.

I slowed down. My radio went from having crystal-clear reception to static. I switched stations. All static.

I looked at the phone I had taken. The GPS had begun to lag, and the directions had stopped. The green line I was following had ended abruptly.

'No Service' showed in the top corner. That would explain the GPS also stopping.

Perhaps the phone's owner had contacted her service provider and reported it stolen, and it had been disconnected.

Surely if I headed into town, a local would be able to tell me where the tunnel was.

Had I not been driving so slowly, I would have missed it.

'Tunnel closed to Public. Do not Enter'.

I pulled the car into a gravel side road, which I followed for approximately a hundred metres before I spotted a car which was bullet-ridden, blood-smeared and heavily damaged.

I dragged myself out to inspect the abandoned vehicle. As soon as I applied any pressure, the pain instantly returned to my leg.

This place looked so familiar. This was it, I was sure of it.

I saw a wide, gravelled path from the car leading to a tunnel off in the distance. It looked like an old train line. Although I couldn't see any tracks, some of the old sleepers were still there.

Across the gravel walkway was a green gate. It reiterated the sign at the highway. I ignored it and dragged my throbbing, swollen leg over it. Pain shot through my body like a lightning bolt.

Fog lingered each side of the path, creating a runway to the tunnel. It was enticing me, encouraging me to enter.

I was only metres out from the entrance when I heard gunshots ring out from within, followed by muffled voices.

I headed cautiously into the darkness, leg throbbing, pain intensifying.

Jake was down to his remaining three bullets.

The pastor appeared to be losing the battle. His cross had been destroyed, his holy water was spent and the Hat Man, into whom Jake had unloaded several bullets laced with holy water, had only temporarily been halted before returning to full strength.

The cleansing wasn't working. Something was wrong.

Hat Man held Pastor Dwyer in one outstretched arm. "Did you ever wonder what happened to your father? Before you die, I think you should know," he said demonically.

His grip around the pastor's throat was so tight he couldn't even nod in response.

"I told him to hang himself from the bridge. He was so weak, so disappointed in your God, that he did as I said. Did your God come and save him? No. He just left him swinging at the end of the rope. What you don't know is, I killed your mother too. I put that cancer in her. Once she was gone, your father was easy to break. I'm sure he would have been asking where his precious God was. First his son, then his wife; his faith was shattered."

The pastor's eyes bulged; his face was red with anger. This thing had killed his whole family and now it was going to kill him.

"Don't worry, Pastor, your family is waiting for you. You will join them in my kingdom."

Without another word, Hat Man slit Pastor Dwyer's throat with one of his long nails. Blood sprayed all over Hat Man. The pastor collapsed to the floor, desperately trying to cover his throat with his hands, but it was to no avail. He couldn't stem the tide of blood.

"I missed your brother all those years ago, but I won't miss you and I won't miss Olly."

The pastor, who couldn't reply, lay slumped on the ground staring at him, his eyes full of fear.

His body began to convulse. It twitched two or three times, then went still.

Now he will come for me, Jake expected. His hand gripped the gun even tighter. Three shots left, he reminded himself. If I get down to one and I'm still no closer to ending this thing, then I'll bite it myself. There is no way I am letting this thing end me.

Hat Man stood over the body…

Waiting.

Then Jake realised he was waiting to feed.

The apparition of Pastor Elijah Dwyer rose. As it did so, a blinding, white light appeared between Jake and the pastor's body. Jake shielded his eyes. He could just make out the pastor's spirit travelling towards the light. Then he saw Hat Man stick its bony claws into the spirit, preventing it from moving forward.

Hat Man's mouth opened like an anaconda's and began to suck in the pastor's spirit. Jake had seen this before, at the Browns' house, and it wasn't something he wanted to witness again, but he was transfixed, unable to look away. He stood immobilised, fixated on this thing from another world.

Then Jake heard his name being called in the distance.

*

As I made my way deeper into the tunnel, I could make out what appeared to be a tall man eating the feet of a second man. It was bizarre. Beyond, I could see an extremely bright beam stretching from the tunnel celling to the floor. There stood Jake, transfixed by the shadowy figures.

"Jake!" I called again.

He was in a trance, staring out into the tunnel, at the horned man and what appeared to be a disappearing shadow or apparition.

I repeated the call for Jake three times. No response.

By the time I had approached the horned man, he had finished digesting whatever it was he was eating. Whatever this thing was, it scared me just to look at it. A feeling of dread came over my body.

This must be the evil that Paige had told me about. The thing looked like the devil itself.

It turned its head. Its eyes of bright blazing red bore down on me. It was as if they had direct access into my soul. I felt he knew everything about me just by looking at me.

A sudden fear raced through my body, a fear I hadn't experienced in a long time. It was the same fear I'd felt when I'd had my heart operation at the age of eight.

It was a horrible feeling, one I didn't want to experience again.

As I cautiously approached the horned man, it fled, or so I thought. When I looked again to see where it had gone, it was over standing in front of Jake.

It had travelled ten metres in a second.

It now had Jake by the throat, its long bony hands holding him tight, squeezing.

It pulled Jake in close. His feet were swinging in mid-air. The thing drew in a breath as if it was trying to smell his soul.

Nostril-like holes had appeared on the creature's face. In and out they moved as it sniffed.

How strong this thing must be to be holding Jake off the ground with one hand!

As I passed the lifeless pastor, I saw a small bible had fallen from his pocket. I collected it, though bending down sent bolts of pain firing up my leg. On the cover was a cross.

Jake was doing his best to fight off the thing.

"God didn't save the pastor. God won't save you. Your soul will be mine!" the demon bellowed.

Its breath smelt of death, a smell I knew Jake also recognised immediately. It was rancid.

I took the bible and slammed it into the shadowy horned man's back and pushed as hard as my body would allow.

The horned man hissed and snarled, trying to reach behind him.

Fire erupted where the bible touched. Smoke poured from him.

Then it happened. First, I felt my vision go blurry. Not now! I thought. Please, just give me a few more minutes.

I tried to talk but no sound came out. I felt my face droop; I had no control over my mouth.

I was having a stroke. The clot had finally reached my brain.

Then my legs went.

Down I went. I had instantly become a sprawling useless heap.

I was paralysed down my right-hand side. The stroke had hit hard. Although I could see and hear, I couldn't move.

I was about to die, and the last thing I would see was this devil-like creature killing my best friend.

The horned man had transformed from a human shape to a half-snake half-human creature. It had hands, a torso and a head, yet its legs had transformed into a serpent-like tail.

It turned and faced me. Its snake tail coiled around my motionless body and it began to squeeze. I felt my ribs crush. I felt my clotted leg burst and break.

I heard Jake scream in the background. My eyes shifted from the hovering serpent devil to Jake. A woman, fat and ugly and covered in blood, was on his back and she was clawing at his face.

Jake was doing his best to fight her off.

The deceased pastor, who had been lifeless only moments ago, joined her in attacking Jake's face. His head was hanging backwards, eyes facing the ceiling. His head bounced so much as he moved that I was waiting for it to fall off.

The air was being choked out of me. Every time I tried to breathe, I could feel the serpent tighten its grip.

"How is the heart going, has God fixed that for you yet?" Its breath stank as the words came out of its mouth. "Look at what God gave you. You have never had any faith. God wrecked your life; you could have been anything, but you were given a raw deal."

I could see jagged yellow vampire teeth as it spoke. The thing smelt me with its flared nostrils.

"I had already killed you once. But I am happy to kill you again," the thing said viciously.

I had no time to consider what he was talking about.

It squeezed harder; I couldn't breathe. It was killing me.

I didn't realise immediately that I had died. I guessed that either it had choked the life out of me or a bigger clot had hit my heart. There was no real feeling. No pain. I just drifted away. I had always feared death, wondering how it would end. I was glad I was with Jake.

I only realised my fate when I saw my body lying on the tunnel floor. My eyes were wide open, fixed on Jake.

When my soul rose, the serpent-horned-man turned to face me, as if being called to me. Within seconds it had grabbed me, inserting a claw in each shoulder. This was the real demon, stripped away from its human form.

I grabbed at its claw with my right hand, trying to release the grip. Then I realised my sprit could move.

A bright light appeared off to my right. I knew the light was for me; a reward for being good on earth.

The serpent opened its mouth, ready to consume me.

"Jake, shoot it!" I called out.

My voice sounded soft. I was worried it didn't exist any longer, and Jake wouldn't hear it.

Jake had thrown the pastor against the tunnel wall. Freeing his gun hand, he raised his weapon and fired at the back of the serpent. The demon screamed and hissed, turning its head a full one hundred and eighty degrees, trying to see what had hurt it.

With it distracted, I pulled towards the light.

"You know…you're right, I never had faith. Faith is for those who haven't seen the afterlife. I have seen it twice now, and I know there is a God. I'll show you he exists."

I found strength I had never had as a human being and it felt good. I pulled the serpent closer and closer to the light. I was going to go into the light and it was coming with me.

The serpent's head spun back to me, its eyes burning through me. It hissed, unlocking its jaw, and its claws dug in deeper. The grip tightened.

"Again!" I called out.

Jake fired again.

The serpent reared in pain, hissed and spun its head back to Jake. After the shot rang out, the pastor and the woman increased their ferocity upon Jake.

Jake had blood pouring down his face from where they had clawed him. He looked as if he had been attacked by a wild bear or a large feral cat. The fat woman was now going for his eyes. She was on his back digging her thumbs into his eyes.

I pulled, fast and hard, digging my heels into the tunnel floor for leverage. I was now only two steps away from the beam of bright, golden light.

The serpent turned its attention back to me. I could smell the stench of death from its belly as the jaw opened over the top of my head.

It was wet and slimy, and smelt putrid.

"Again!" I cried out.

I couldn't see Jake anymore. The serpent's mouth was down over my eyes.

I could hear him slamming something against the wall of the tunnel. My guess was the lady who was on his back.

"It's my last shot!" Jake called out.

I felt the thing's mouth touch the tops of my ears, then go over the lobes. Everything was dark and muffled.

The deeper it took me, the louder the screaming was. At first, I thought it was coming from the outside, from Jake.

Then I realised it was coming from within. The screaming was all the past souls it had devoured. All were screaming in eternal hell and I was about to join them.

I could feel my feet begin to lift off the ground.

"Shoot!" I screamed.

I heard a distant gunshot that sounded a galaxy away, yet I knew it was only a few metres.

I slipped out of the serpent's mouth. Only its claws were hanging onto me.

I felt it rear up and whip around in pain, towards Jake.

I grabbed it around the waist and pulled one more time.

I could feel the warmth from the beam as I stepped closer to it.

I was closer now.

I pulled again as hard as I could manage.

Finally, I stepped into the light.

I heard an ear-piercing scream like I had never heard before. The serpent combusted, it seemed. Thousands of tiny ashes fell over my face, covering my spirit.

Hundreds of little glimmers of light shot up the beam. I guessed these were all the souls taken by the serpent.

Jake was watching me. Both the pastor and the woman had fallen silent the moment the serpent had turned to ash.

My body, lying in the corner, remained lifeless.

Surrounded by light, I waved to Jake.

He waved back.

Then I was gone.

*

Jake sat silently in the cold dark tunnel. He had just witnessed what appeared to be hundreds of stolen souls head into the light.

They were free.

Wiping the blood from his face, he got up and headed out of the tunnel. The sun was brighter than he had ever seen it, so bright it hurt his eyes. The sky was blue and cloudless.

Jake's phone sounded, indicating messages waiting in his voicemail. It was the first time since he had been at the Browns' farm that anything had come through. Jake removed it from his pocket; his service bar was full.

Jake rang the Thirlmere Police Department, followed by a call to Monique. He explained everything. He knew he sounded like a lunatic, but he told them the truth as he knew it.

Monique had called the Department of Social Services to attend the church and collect Olly until a foster home could be found for her.

Jake's wounds were only superficial; bruises plus a few claw marks where fingernails had dug in, the type you would expect from a brawl. Nothing more.

Two ambulances and four police patrol cars arrived. The paramedics requested Jake accompany them to the hospital. He refused. Instead, he insisted one of the uniformed officers take him to St Mark's Church.

He found Olly sitting on the altar step waiting for her grandfather to return. In her hands she was grasping a letter.

Jake knelt in front of her. "Hi Olly, do you remember me?"

She nodded but did not speak.

"Are you waiting for your grandpa?"

"Yes."

Jake looked at the officer. He was watching Jake, but he didn't offer any advice.

Jake had never done a death knock to a six-year-old.

"He can't come back, Olly," Jake said.

She began to cry.

"May I see the letter?" Jake said, seeing it was addressed to him.

It was a simple note.

This is my last will and testament. Should I die I would like all my possessions and the house sold with the proceeds placed in trust for Olly Dwyer, until she turns 21.

As she has no living relatives I would like her to reside with Detective Miller. Should he be unable to have her, a suitable foster home approved by Detective Miller should be found.

"Olly, would you like to come and live with me?"

Still crying, she nodded.

Jake didn't need to ask Hayley; she would never say no to an abandoned child. Jake had no doubt she would love her as her own.

Both of them would.

Chapter 49

In-between December 2016

I watched from the in-between, but only for a few days.

The last time I saw Jake was at my funeral. He gave the eulogy and performed much better than I would have done had our roles been reversed.

It was tough on him.

In the time between the events of the tunnel and my funeral, Jake applied for adoption papers and was accepted to adopt Olly.

His family had grown. He now had two beautiful daughters to care for.

Paige took me by the hand.

"We can go now," she said.

"What happens to the others, like Gemma? When do they come?"

"You have freed them. When they are ready, they will cross. They are not ready yet."

We turned and walked into the light.

A sadistic killer.
Two rookie cops
The hunt is on!
But who is hunting who?

HUNTED

Jasper Wolf

THE WAITING ROOM

JASPER WOLF

THREE MISSING CHILDREN
IS JUST THE BEGINNING.